IT'S OUR GAME

IT'S OUR GAME

CELEBRATING 100 YEARS OF HOCKEY CANADA

MICHAEL McKINLEY

VIKING

VIKING
an imprint of Penguin Canada Books Inc., a Penguin Random House Company

Published by the Penguin Group
Penguin Canada Books Inc., 90 Eglinton Avenue East, Suite 700,
Toronto, Ontario, Canada M4P 2Y3

Penguin Group (USA) LLC, 375 Hudson Street, New York, New York 10014, U.S.A.
Penguin Books Ltd, 80 Strand, London WC2R 0RL, England
Penguin Ireland, 25 St Stephen's Green, Dublin 2, Ireland (a division of Penguin Books Ltd)
Penguin Group (Australia), 707 Collins Street, Melbourne, Victoria 3008, Australia (a division of
    Pearson Australia Group Pty Ltd)
Penguin Books India Pvt Ltd, 11 Community Centre, Panchsheel Park, New Delhi – 110 017, India
Penguin Group (NZ), 67 Apollo Drive, Rosedale, Auckland 0632, New Zealand (a division of
    Pearson New Zealand Ltd)
Penguin Books (South Africa) (Pty) Ltd, 24 Sturdee Avenue, Rosebank, Johannesburg 2196,
    South Africa

Penguin Books Ltd, Registered Offices: 80 Strand, London WC2R 0RL, England

First published 2014

1 2 3 4 5 6 7 8 9 10 (CR)

Interior design: Lisa Eng-Lodge

Manufactured in the U.S.A.

LIBRARY AND ARCHIVES CANADA CATALOGUING IN PUBLICATION
McKinley, Michael (Michael B.), author
        It's our game / Michael McKinley.
Includes index.
ISBN 978-0-670-06817-3 (bound)
        1. Hockey—Canada—History. 2. Hockey—Canada—History—
Pictorial works. I. Title.
GV848.4.C3M3347 2014   796.9620971   C2014-902073-2

eBook ISBN 978-0-14-319309-8

Visit the Penguin Canada website at **www.penguin.ca**

Special and corporate bulk purchase rates available; please see **www.penguin.ca/corporatesales**
or call 1-800-810-3104.

In memory of my mother, Betty, and my Uncle Bernard

CONTENTS

FOREWORD

by Wayne Gretzky

Anyone who's played a team sport knows there's something about the bond between teammates that inspires you.

As soon as you pull on a sweater, whatever the sport, you're playing as much for the guys or girls wearing the same colours as you are for yourself. I have played on some pretty good hockey teams over the years, and I can tell you that it was always that sense that you were playing for the other guys on the bench that brought out the best in us. In other words, it's not *just* a game when others are depending on you. When others are counting on you, everything seems to matter more.

And that's what a team is—everyone depending on each other.

When you pull a Team Canada sweater over your head, it's not just the guys in the room that you don't want to let down. And it's not just those guys who give you inspiration. It's a whole country.

I've worn the maple leaf a few times now. The first time I was only sixteen. I can't tell you what an honour it was, at that age, to play for my country, and that never changed. It was always a thrill to do whatever I could for Canada because there was always a sense that you were part of something much bigger than just a team. You were part of an entire history.

That's why when I was executive director of the men's team at the Salt Lake Olympics, I brought pennants from previous Olympic championships into the dressing room for the guys to see. I also brought in a team photo of the Edmonton Mercurys, which you'll read about in this book. The Mercurys were the last Canadian team to bring back gold in fifty years, and that 2002 edition of Team Canada was on a mission to make sure the birthplace of hockey didn't have to wait any longer to get back to the top of the podium. Playing for teammates inspires you, but playing for an entire tradition inspires you even more.

Wayne Gretzky and Mario Lemieux celebrate after Lemieux's winning goal at the Canada Cup against the Soviet Union in 1987.

That may sound like a lot of pressure, and I suppose in a sense it is. But that's the kind of pressure athletes love. Remember, for hockey players, the ice is where they feel most comfortable. Too much pressure can be a burden, of course. It can make something that should be easy feel impossible. But on the other hand, if you handle it right, it can make something you've never been able to do before feel like the simplest thing in the world. Pressure can make you better.

If you're a hockey player, you want the puck. You want to be in position to make the big play—the overtime goal or the breathtaking save that steals a game. Those are the kind of heroics that get recorded in a book like this. They are what you dream about when you're playing road hockey with your friends or doing drills at an early-morning practice. Pressure can inspire you to make that big play.

But even more important, it can inspire you to make the *small* play. The little thing the fans may not always notice. Taking a hit to make sure the puck is moving in the right direction. Ignoring a slash when you'd love to give one right back. Taking away a passing lane. Tying up a guy's stick just long enough that he can't make a play. These small plays are what make the difference.

It's worth mentioning them here, because otherwise they might be overlooked in a book like this. There is no way to capture all the small sacrifices behind the success of Canadian hockey teams over the past hundred years. There are just too many of them to record. And yet, without them, the glorious goals would never have been scored. We need to remember that those unforgettable moments were built on a foundation of small sacrifices.

There is something about wearing the maple leaf that inspires you to dig deep and do those small things. And I can tell you, when a Canadian team plays like that, they're all but unbeatable.

I'm not saying that Canada should win every game they play. There are always great teams from other countries. I have suited up against teams that have given Team Canada everything we could handle, sometimes more. Let's not forget that in 1972, in the most memorable series ever played, even after eight games, it came down to the dying moments for a victor to emerge.

The message there was not that Canada dominates in hockey. It was that it took everything we had to win.

The thing is, it's giving everything we have that Canadians are so good at.

I'm already on record saying that Game 2 of the 1987 Canada Cup final series against the USSR was the best game I ever played. By far. It wasn't just me. That may have been the best game the players on both teams played. It was the fastest, most fluid, exciting game I've ever been part of, and I know I never played better than I did that night. Was that because the Soviets' game-winning overtime goal in Game 1 had gone in off my skate? I knew I'd let people down, so maybe I was making up for that.

But you don't need to have made a mistake to have something to prove. We *all* wanted to win, and we all dug deep. And though, as I say, it was the best I ever played, I didn't score a goal. But I did give it everything I had.

We won in overtime, setting up a third and deciding game between two evenly matched teams. Make no mistake—the Russians could skate with us. They were strong, they were well coached, and they had individual skills that were out of this world. And they had already beaten us twice in the tournament.

It was a quiet dressing room before Game 3. But there wasn't anyone in the room who didn't think we could win. We all knew the kind of opportunity that was in front of us, and it would have been impossible not to be aware of what this meant to Canada. The energy and the excitement was incredible.

I don't know whether the pressure got to us, whether we were a little flat after the emotion of Game 2—I know I was exhausted—or whether the Soviets just had our number, but we fell behind 3–0 early in that game. Not the start we wanted, but if not for that early stumble, one of the game's most exciting moments might never have happened.

Though we scored a lot of goals in that tournament, being down by three in the championship game against arguably the best team in the world is not a comfortable place to be. We could easily have folded. But I don't think that's something that happens when you're wearing the maple leaf on your sweater.

What happened instead is that our guys went to work. Rick Tocchet, Kevin Dineen, and Brent Sutter just took over the game. They took control of the tough areas of the ice and started grinding down the Russians. It was pure willpower. Nothing dirty, nothing unsportsmanlike, just willpower. They were giving it everything they had. It can't have been fun being a Russian that night. It's never fun to watch a lead slip away. And I would be surprised to hear anyone say it's fun to battle for the puck along the boards in an important game with *anyone* wearing a maple leaf.

By the end of the period, we were back in the game. By the end of the third we were tied 5–5.

We know what happened next. Dale Hawerchuk wins a draw in our end. Mario Lemieux takes the puck up the ice. Larry Murphy goes to the net. I was there too, and I had the puck on my stick as we came into the Soviet zone. But I already knew I wasn't going to shoot. I knew all along that I was going to give it to the guy with the best shot in the game, and that's what I did.

That's how championships are won.

Not by having some of the best players in the world on the ice, though that's a luxury Canada always has. It's by everyone doing his job, everyone doing what's best for the team, and everyone doing the little things to give the team a chance to succeed. Sure, if you have one chance to put away your opponent with 1:26 to play, the guy you want shooting is Mario, probably the best ever in that situation. But if the whole team hadn't been bearing down for the previous two and a half periods, if coach Mike Keenan hadn't shuffled the lines at the end of the game, if Grant Fuhr hadn't shut the door—and to be honest, if there hadn't been 20,000 fans in the building that night cheering for us and a whole country behind us—then even having Mario in the lineup wouldn't have made a difference.

That's true of any hockey team in any game. But I think it's even more true when you're playing for Team Canada. You always want to win, but as I began by saying, you take inspiration from the people around you. When you're wearing the maple leaf that means the guys surrounding you are the best in the country. You're even inspired by the guys who *aren't* on the team. You know that a spot on the roster is an honour when players like future Hall of Famers Steve Yzerman, Scott Stevens, and Patrick Roy don't make the team.

And, of course, you're inspired by the feeling that the whole country is behind you. That makes you better; it's as simple as that. When you think of all the things that had to happen for Mario to be in position to score that goal, you have to include the kind of support we got from the fans, who gave us all a bit more jump when we needed it.

I've always had immense respect for coaches and other staff. Players may not realize how much goes on behind the scenes to give them a chance to succeed, but I can say that being part of Team Canada at the 2002 Olympics really opened my eyes. You don't win without doing the small things right on the ice, and it's just the same off the ice. Attention to detail is absolutely crucial to winning a championship, whether it's coaching, scouting, training, managing equipment and travel, or just saying the right thing at the right time.

And really, that's part of why it feels so great to win. As I said, it always feels good to win for your teammates. It feels even better to win for every teammate you've ever had, for every minor-league coach, for your parents, and for everyone else who has given so much for our game. All that is what Hockey Canada means to me. It's not just star players scoring big goals—it's a whole team giving everything they have, on and off the ice.

As you'll read in the pages ahead, when Team Canada does that, there's a reason they bring home more than their fair share of gold. There are teams out there that give us a run for our money, and I know what it feels like to lose. There are never any guarantees, and to be honest, big games wouldn't be any fun if there were. Though I doubt any coach wants to hear this, coming from behind in a big game, as we did in 1987 and our women did in Sochi, may even feel better than dominating from start to finish.

So Canada should cherish its rivalries, borrow from its opponents, learn from its defeats—and savour its victories. I am proud that our victories outnumber our defeats. I believe that it's our culture of giving everything we have to the game we love that puts us in a position to succeed the way we do, and I believe we have Hockey Canada to thank for nurturing not only this country's talent, but our culture of excellence.

INTRODUCTION

by Bob Nicholson

You don't last for a hundred years unless you're doing something right. Looking back at Hockey Canada's history, it would be hard not to conclude that this organization is something special. As someone who was its president for sixteen years, I can confirm that. Hockey Canada really is something special, something much bigger than the sum of its parts.

I suppose that shouldn't be surprising when the parts are our great sport of hockey and our great country of Canada. Together, what you get is something truly amazing.

But then, readers don't need me to tell them that. Canadians know their hockey history. They know about the exhilaration of our most glorious victories. And they remember the disappointment of some of our bitterest losses—and we've had our share of those. You will read about those triumphs and defeats in the pages that follow.

These events have an important place in our culture because hockey *matters* to us. There's no doubt about that. Not when businesses across the country all but shut down to see our women take on the Americans at Sochi. Not when cities rewrote their bylaws to help Canadians celebrate the showdown of the men's team against Sweden a few days later. Hockey matters to us, and that is especially obvious when we're playing on the biggest stage, and even more true when we're winning.

I wonder sometimes, though, whether these dramatic triumphs sometimes *hide* from us what is so special about Hockey Canada. We often talk about the fact that Canadian teams always show up expecting to win. And that's true. But so do our opponents. We often hear about how defeat is unacceptable for Canadians. And that's true too. But I can assure you, our opponents don't like it any better. Playing to win, and hating to lose— these don't set us apart. These are things we have in common with every team we play against.

I would say that what makes Hockey Canada special is *not* what is

Hockey Canada president and CEO Bob Nicholson waves farewell after announcing his retirement at the organization's annual meeting in Calgary, Saturday, May 31, 2014.

different between us and the teams we play around the world. What is important is what the players wearing the maple leaf have in common with the players in every rink across the country, from the little novice wobbling around the ice for the first time to the elite teenaged AAA player honing his or her skills, hungry to make it to the next level. The important thing is they're *all* Hockey Canada players. They're no different.

When Canadians watched Marie-Philip Poulin cap off a brilliant series of passes to win the gold in Sochi, they knew they were seeing something unforgettable. Inspiring hockey, incredible poise, relentless team effort. But they were also watching a handful of the thousands of girls and young women in Hockey Canada. That is, we weren't watching Canada's women play the US. We were watching a small part of a huge group, all of whom should be proud.

The same goes for the men. A lot of attention was paid to the combined salary of our team, as though it was a random collection of millionaires. But those players didn't become part of Hockey Canada when the roster was announced by Steve Yzerman at that first press conference in Toronto. Guys like Sidney Crosby and Jonathan Toews became part of Hockey Canada when they signed up for their first house-league team years before. Their teammates back in tyke, their coaches and volunteers who were there before Shea Weber could even raise the puck, the league officials and sponsors over the years—they're all part of Hockey Canada. Those superstars may be the tip of the iceberg, but we're all part of that iceberg. I think that's why so many of us are so proud when we succeed. We all share in it, because we were all part of it.

Still, as you'll read in the pages ahead, we don't always win. Not even close. And though we always play to win, we all know we're not going to win every game. In fact, it wouldn't even be fun anymore if we did. In the earliest days of our game, we could count on winning just about every international game. The first loss, in 1933, was devastating. But the game was better for it from that point on.

As difficult as it is to imagine now, there was a time when the world had caught up to us so completely that we went through a serious drought. Losing is part of the game. But the thing that every athlete should remember is that losing can make you better. If you think hockey is really all about winning, you're missing out on some of the most valuable lessons it offers.

There is powerful research that shows that kids who play competitive team sports have an advantage in their later careers. It's not hard to see why this might be. Any sport, but especially one as fast and intense as hockey, will teach kids the importance of hard work and the benefits of working together. It will teach them how to take criticism, how to respond to a challenge, how to turn dreams into reality. And hockey is not just any sport. It's the sport that Canadians dream about. So it's no surprise that it brings out the best in our kids.

But I think there's more to it than that. People talk about leadership and how important it is not just in sports but also in life. I'm sure that all of us can think of a particularly impressive leader, whether it's in the dressing room or the boardroom. I'd go further and add that the greatest players you'll read about in the pages that follow are also great leaders. Whether it's what they do or what they say, the legends are the men and women who make a difference.

Let's not make the mistake, though, of assuming that only the stars make a difference. And let's not assume that only the men and women wearing the "C" are the leaders. What every hockey player learns from a very young age is that leadership and responsibility are really the same thing. You sometimes hear a coach say that the dressing room is full of leaders, and that's the way it should be.

I was lucky enough to be in the room in Salt Lake City. Do you think anyone had to tell those guys what to do? No one had to say a word. Their eyes said it all. Each of them could tell at a glance that every other guy in the room would do everything in his power for that team. Leaders make everyone around them better, and I can guarantee that everyone in the room made everyone else better. That's making something bigger than the sum of its parts. And I think that's what hockey means in Canada.

Anyone who has played the sport knows that thrill of inspiration, that extra gear, that last gasp of energy, that once-in-a-lifetime play that becomes easy when the game is on the line. That's the effect of the people around you.

I've never played for Team Canada, but I've seen that kind of leadership in action a thousand times. And I've been lucky enough to benefit from it myself.

When I first joined Hockey Canada in 1990, I was thrilled to be taking an executive position in a sport I loved. But I was as excited by the opportunity to work with Murray Costello as I was to work at Hockey Canada—and it was the best move

I ever made. Murray and I may have disagreed from time to time, but I never left his office with any doubt that the decision he had made was what he believed was best for our players and our game.

Bill Hay is another leader whose vision cut a path for me personally and for the game as a whole. It was largely his work that brought Hockey Canada and the Canadian Amateur Hockey Association together, and I don't think for a minute that the game would be where it is today if he and Murray hadn't brought those two organizations under one roof.

Since then, hockey has grown to a whole new level in Canada. I would identify three key things that helped make that happen. The first was our relationship with Wayne Gretzky. Not only is his career in international play the stuff of legends, but I don't think I have ever worked with someone who wanted so strongly to give back to the game. He inspired all of us.

The second is the way the country has embraced the World Junior Championships. That's Canada's Super Bowl—and it's Canadian not so much because it's our Canadian game. It's because those kids aren't superstars. They're all the kids next door. They're what hockey is all about.

The third is the NHL's participation in the Olympics. Everybody plays to be the best they can be. That's what the dream is all about. Our best players want to line up against the best in the world, and as this book shows, it's been that way for a hundred years. Let's hope it stays that way.

These three things stand out as strong reasons why Hockey Canada has done so well these past years, but they don't explain one key thing: without the hundreds of thousands of volunteers who keep minor hockey going, none of this would happen. None. My hat is off to all of you.

Hockey should be fun. That's why we sign our kids up. Of course it's fun for parents too. What parents don't look into a kid's eyes and see a reflection of the fun they had as kids themselves. The sound of the puck on the boards, the smell of a rink when you first walk in, the laughing and bantering in the dressing room. That doesn't change from generation to generation

Even at the very highest level, guys will say they're going out to have fun. That gives us a clue as to what is fun. Sports are fun when you take them seriously.

Kids don't need to be told that a game is serious. They take everything seriously. For a six-year-old, a house-league championship game is the Stanley Cup Game 7. That means that if we want our kids to have fun, we don't need to push them to take things seriously; we need to give them the opportunity to take things seriously. Not every boy or girl is destined for the Olympic team, and not every kid wants that. Some kids are going to have a ball playing with their neighbourhood friends in a local league, and we need to make sure those kids have that opportunity. Hockey Canada needs to be there to make sure that those kids are able to play the game they love, to the level they are drawn to.

And that means everyone. I have been to a lot of hockey games over the past decade and a half, and been part of some very special moments. But I can't think of anything that beats the look in Jean Labonte's eyes at the Torino Paralympics in 2006. Jean was an assistant captain of the men's sledge hockey team, and he had the country's first gold medal around his neck. When I think of what men and women like Jean have been through in their lives to get to the top of their game, and what it means to them to excel, I couldn't be more proud to have been a part of it.

But nothing lasts forever. I remember just after we'd won the men's gold at Sochi, Steve Yzerman turned to me and said, "Bob, it's been a heck of a ride, but it's time for me to pass the torch." Steve had led the program for two Olympics, and he figured it was time to give someone else a chance. It was at that moment that I began to think about moving on myself. Steve announced his departure that night; I announced mine a month later.

But Steve would be the first to tell you that leadership is not about one executive, any more than it's about the guy or girl on the bench wearing the "C." It's about the whole community. That is what Hockey Canada is all about. From coast to coast to coast, from generation to generation, from the local rink to the Olympic podium, we're all in this together. It was a huge honour for me to have been part of this organization for as long as I was, and that really comes into focus as I look at some of these chapters and see the way so many people had to pull together to get the results the whole country was looking for. In the end, the defeats and the victories recorded in this book are not those of a few players who wore the maple leaf. They are shared by everyone in Canada who loves this game. I hope you enjoy the book as much as I have.

PART 1

CANADA'S GAME

When the first board members met to create the Canadian Amateur Hockey Association in 1914, hockey was in its robust first period, one which looked much different than the game we know today. Teams dressed only seven players—in the most basic of gear, with limited padding, no helmets, and no goalie masks—and the players were all on the ice at the same time, playing a sixty-minute game divided into two thirty-minute periods. There was no forward pass, no touching or kicking the puck, no blue lines or red lines, no slap shots, and the goalie could not fall down to stop the puck. Hockey had only been played indoors in Canada for less than forty years, and Canada, where hockey was invented and continuously perfected, was only forty-seven years old. Indeed, of the six provinces represented at the first meeting of the organization, two had been in Confederation less than a decade.

For the next thirty years, the Canadian Amateur Hockey Association and the country whose national game it helped to govern would see two world wars, an influenza pandemic, and global economic depression. It would also see Canadian hockey grow deeper into the national imagination, and come to dominate the world, at international tournaments and the Olympic Games, where hockey would debut in 1920. By the end of World War II, "Canada" and "hockey excellence" will be synonymous, but the world will also be getting much better at Canada's game. Here is the story of how that came to be.

1914 — 2014

CANADA

THE CREATION OF THE CANADIAN AMATEUR HOCKEY ASSOCIATION

At ten o'clock in the morning of December 4, 1914, Canadian history was made. It was not a military triumph in the cold and bloody trenches of Flanders, where the soldiers soon to be fighting and dying in the colours of the Canadian Expeditionary Force now knew that they would not be home by Christmas. This history was far more genteel but no less significant in the forging of the national identity: next to the country's majestic Parliament buildings in a chandeliered meeting room of the Château Laurier, Ottawa's two-year-old grand hotel, a group of twenty-one hockey executives gathered to change the world.

Of course, on that chilly December morning, the stated purpose of hockey's guardians seemed clerically humble: to create "a governing body for the sport of hockey." *The Toronto Daily Star* added the spin the next day, shouting out in an almost relieved headline, "National Hockey Body Formed at Last," explaining that this new group would have "jurisdiction over the amateur game throughout the whole of Canada."

Indeed, the men at that historic inauguration represented hockey's breadth and complexity in a vast country just past its forty-seventh birthday: from New Westminster, BC, was Reverend Albert E. Vert, a Presbyterian minister and local amateur athletics champion; from Winnipeg, was C.C. Robinson, an executive of the historic Winnipeg

The first minute book of the Canadian Amateur Hockey Association, formed December 4, 1914.

Victorias Hockey Club, winners of the Stanley Cup in the days of horse and carriage; from Montreal, was the US-born entrepreneur Leo Dandurand, future owner of the soon-to-be fabled Canadiens; and fellow Montrealer William Northey, founder of the Canadian Arena Company, and chair of the meeting. In between those worthies were representatives from Alberta, Saskatchewan, and Ontario, with as many from Manitoba—six—as there were from Quebec.

The gathering reflected the breakaway growth of the sport in the Canadian landscape. Just four decades after James Creighton had staged the world's first indoor hockey match in Montreal, the sport was so popular in Canada that it now needed a national governing body.

The amateur game in particular needed regulatory supervision, now that hockey had gone so robustly professional. As Canada settled to the west, hockey went with it, and by the turn of the twentieth century, elite league teams, school teams, company teams, and women's teams could be found across the country. By 1904, the game had such a range of players and popularity that the world's first professional hockey league took off to rich success in the United States. In Canada, the game was still resolutely amateur, resulting in the great hockey event of the late winter of 1905 that saw the Dawson City Nuggets, a Yukon amateur team, travel by bicycle, steamship, and railway across Canada to challenge for the Stanley Cup in Ottawa. The Nuggets captured the imagination of the public, but they got a pasting from the slick Ottawa Silver Seven, who sent them back to stare at the northern lights and contemplate their 32–4 beating over two games.

Hockey became professional in Canada in 1908, which served only to focus the distinction between those players who were paid and those who were not. And so in Ottawa on that December morning in 1914, the men who assembled at the Château Laurier also took a crack at creating an organization to govern both professional and amateur hockey, an idea "promptly opposed by many of the representatives present."

But they won the agreement from Allan Cup trustee William Northey that this trophy would become the chief prize awarded by the new governing body. Montreal banker, steamship-line owner, and Canadian blueblood Sir H. Montagu Allan, C.V.O., had donated the Cup in 1908 to encourage excellence in amateur hockey after the Stanley Cup increasingly became the domain of championship professional teams. And now, the Allan Cup would become the symbol of excellence for Canada's newest sporting body, one which would govern and grow the game for the next century and beyond. After thanking the hotel manager for use of the room, the founders adjourned and went about their business of the day, having just created the Canadian Amateur Hockey Association.

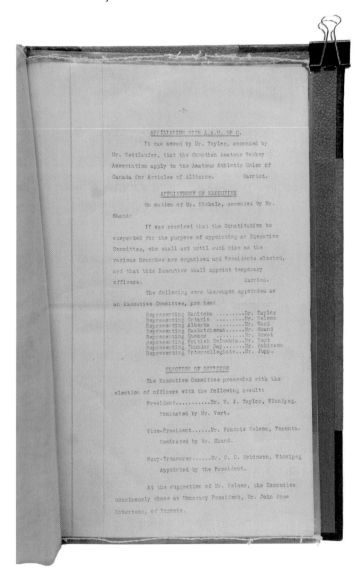

The first CAHA meeting appointed the first executive committee, showing the CAHA's national range with representatives from British Columbia to Quebec.

WORLD WAR I AND SOLDIER HOCKEY TEAMS

When the Canadian Amateur Hockey Association (CAHA) met in Winnipeg for its first annual meeting in December 1915, the war to end all wars had now engulfed the world, expanding to Russia and Poland, Serbia and Greece, to the Middle East, and to Italy. Canadian troops had experienced the horror of chemical attack at the Second Battle of Ypres in April, but they fought back to become the first former colony ever to defeat a European nation in battle, which they did by vanquishing the Germans at St. Julien. It was during this battle that John McCrae wrote his beloved war poem "In Flanders Fields" to mourn the death of his former student, Alexis Helmer, in that battle. The poppies would sprout from the blood of the dead in Flanders Fields for the next three years.

Despite daily reports of the slaughter, Captain James Sutherland, now president of the CAHA, drew upon hockey to inspire players to sign up for war. "With every man doing his bit, Canada will raise an army of brain and brawn from our hockey enthusiasts the likes of which the world has never seen. The whistle has sounded. Let every man play the greatest game of his life."

Fittingly, a team of soldiers entered the hockey arena. The Allan Cup would be a challenge playoff for one more year (then discarded by the CAHA in favour of a playoff system of east versus west champions), and as a result, Winnipeg's 61st Battalion, which had won the Pattison Trophy as champions of the Winnipeg League, won the right to defend the Allan Cup

against teams from Winnipeg, Manitoba; Fort William, Ontario; and Regina, Saskatchewan.

The 61st's captain was Corporal Joe Simpson, a future NHL star who was nicknamed "Bullet" Joe because he was so fast on his skates, and the squad featured other incipient pros, such as two privates, "Spunk" Sparrow and "Crutchy" Morrison. With their battalion number proudly lodged in the middle of a maple leaf on the chest of their sweaters, the 61st lost only one of their five challenge games, and took the 1916 Allan Cup, with Simpson scoring four goals and adding two assists.

Simpson's nickname soon took on a frightening reality, when he was wounded twice in battle at the Somme and Amiens. For his battlefield courage, he won the Military Medal and was promoted to lieutenant. Having survived "the greatest game," Simpson re-entered the world of hockey, where he played professionally from 1921 to 1931, winning a place in the Hockey Hall of Fame in 1962.

The 61st Battalion team of Winnipeg, winners of the 1916 Allan Cup, captained by "Bullet" Joe Simpson (second from the left in middle row).

THE
WOMEN'S GAME

With the men away at war, women's hockey established itself in the Canadian imagination. Women had been playing hockey on outdoor ponds for decades, and Lord Stanley's daughter, the feisty Lady Isobel, used to play hockey at Rideau Hall, the governor general's residence in Ottawa in 1890. In 1896, women's teams first took to the ice at McGill University, while a women's team at Queen's University in Kingston called itself the Love-Me Littles, censured as they were by a local bishop for daring to play the game the whole country was playing.

By the time World War I was entering its second year, the women's game was drawing large crowds desperate for entertaining escape from the grim visage of war. In January 1916, *The Globe* reported from the factory town of Cornwall, Ontario, that "the first ladies' hockey match played here in years took place Saturday night ... before a crowd which taxed the rink to capacity. Some startling plays were pulled off on both sides." The Cornwall Victorias had a genuine star in 26-year-old Albertine Lapensée, a goal-scoring wizard who notched a hat trick in her debut. The team's coach, Cornwall hotelier and promoter Ernie Runions, called Lapensée his "Miracle Maid," though rival teams questioned Lapensée's maidenhood, even pulling off her toque to see if she was really a girl. An investigation of her gender by the *Cornwall Standard* newspaper concluded that she was indeed a female, and so good because she had played the game with her brothers.

The following year, she was even more dazzling. "The speed and stickhandling of Miss Albertine Lapensée was too much for the Ottawa

Women's hockey was popular across the nation at the turn of the twentieth century. The women used their long skirts to tactical advantage when keeping the puck away from opponents.

Alerts, and the Cornwall Ladies' Hockey Club won the match at the Arena last night by the score of 6 to 3," reported the *Ottawa Journal*. "Miss Lapensée notched five of the six goals her team secured, and during every minute of the game was head and shoulders over her opponents and team mates alike."

By 1920, the women's game had its first championship trophy, when Sir Montagu Allan's cousin, Lady Isobel (Allan) Meredith, donated the Lady Meredith Cup for the Quebec Ladies' Hockey Association. In 1922, the Ladies Ontario Hockey Association was formed, yet despite the popularity of the women's game, the Canadian Amateur Hockey Association refused to recognize women as hockey players at a meeting in 1923. It didn't stop women's hockey, which over the next decade would see the rise of one of the greatest hockey teams that Canada has ever produced: the Preston Rivulettes.

The University of Toronto women's hockey team on an outdoor rink next to Trinity College.

THE
MEMORIAL CUP

The University of Toronto Schools team, winners of the first Memorial Cup. Their coach, Frank Carroll, had been the trainer of Allan "Scotty" Davidson's Toronto Blueshirts, winners of the 1914 Stanley Cup.

The end of World War I saw countries around the world mourn the loss of a generation, with Canada especially bloodied. More than 600,000 Canadian men and women—out of a population of eight million—went off to war, with 66,655 Canadians killed, and another 172,950 wounded. Many hockey players who had heeded CAHA president James Sutherland's call to take up arms in the "greatest game" did not return, having lost their lives in the carnage. Two of the dead came from Sutherland's beloved hometown, Kingston, Ontario.

Allan "Scotty" Davidson, a speedy, two-way right winger had played for Sutherland as a member of the Kingston Frontenacs, whom he captained to two Ontario Hockey Association championships in 1910 and 1911. Davidson then moved west to play senior hockey in Calgary, challenging for the Allan Cup, before returning to Ontario to play professionally for the National Hockey Association's Toronto Blueshirts. Davidson was their captain when the Torontos won the Stanley Cup in 1914, and when war broke out, he became the first professional hockey player to enlist, serving as a lance corporal with the 2nd Canadian Infantry Battalion (Eastern Ontario Regiment) when he was killed on June 16, 1915, during a bombing raid on a German trench. He had refused to retreat, and then to surrender, using his last grenade to blow up a German officer, before being shot to death. A later account in a private letter suggests he was, in fact, killed by Canadian artillery fire.

His fellow Kingston Frontenac and regimental member, Captain George Taylor Richardson, who set a record in the Ontario Hockey

Association's 1908 championship by scoring seven goals in a 9–7 win for Kingston, wrote to Sutherland with news of Davidson's death. He declared that his friend "was absolutely fearless in the face of the greatest danger." In February 1916, Richardson was killed, too, shot while leading a trench raid.

The loss of these two Kingston hockey stars hit Sutherland hard. While the war dead were commemorated with various memorials—street names, monuments, and stadia—Sutherland imagined a tribute that would live on in celebration of the game these two men had loved. And so began the Ontario Hockey Association's Memorial Cup.

The first contest for the trophy that has become the pinnacle of Canadian junior hockey was played between the University of Toronto Schools (a "laboratory" high school attached to the university to train teachers and be a place of educational experiments), winners of the George T. Richardson Memorial Trophy as eastern champions, and the Regina Patricias. The Patricias, christened after the daughter of Canada's governor general, the Duke of Connaught, also bore a name redolent of the war. A Canadian infantry regiment was also named after Princess Patricia, and in their storied history became the first Canadian soldiers to reach the battlefield in December 1914.

The Patricias hockey team, as western champions, had won the Abbott Trophy, itself a war memorial. The Abbott Trophy was named in memory of a superlative Regina athlete, Edward "Hickory" Lyman Abbott, who had captained the Regina Victorias to an Allan Cup championship in 1914, before enlisting the next year. Abbott won the Military Cross First Bar for bravery, rose to the rank of captain, and was killed on August 14, 1918, in the Battle of Amiens, during Canada's tide-turning Hundred Days Offensive. Toronto won the first Memorial Cup in a two-game series, outscoring Regina 29–8.

Though the Memorial Cup was intended to commemorate those soldiers who had died in World War I, the trophy was rededicated in 2010 to honour all Canadian soldiers who had been killed in service since 1918, when "the war to end all wars" finished—but only as a prelude to the next war that would ignite the world two decades later.

The Memorial Cup was created to honour the memory of those athletes killed in World War I. In 2010, it was rededicated as the trophy to honour all of Canada's war dead.

THE 1920 OLYMPICS

By the spring of 1920, the world had seen enough of suffering. The Great War of 1914–18 had killed more than sixteen million combatants and civilians, with the Spanish influenza epidemic of 1919 killing another twenty million people. More than anything, people needed something to celebrate, and so they turned away from the cemetery to the arena.

The 1920 Olympic Games took place in war-ravaged Antwerp, Belgium, which had survived a siege by the German Army in August 1914, bombarded with artillery and bombed by Zeppelins until it surrendered two months later. More than a million people fled the city, which the Germans occupied until the end of the war. As punishment for "starting" that war, which killed a generation of athletes, Germany and Austria, as well as Hungary, Turkey, and Bulgaria, were all excluded from the first Olympic Games to take place since 1912.

In January 1920, the International Olympic Committee (IOC) announced that ice hockey, however, would be included, and due to the most unsent-imental of reasons: the owners of the Palais de Glace in Antwerp refused to allow figure skating in their arena unless they got to showcase ice hockey, too. And so it was in, on probation as a demonstration sport.

Given that the Olympic ice hockey competition started in April, the Canadian Amateur Hockey Association decided that Canada's best chance of success was to send the winner of the Allan Cup to represent the country, thus beginning a tradition that would last for the next three

The Winnipeg Falcons won Canada's first Olympic gold medal for hockey in Antwerp in 1920. Captain Frank Frederickson stands to the right of W.A. Hewitt (centre), *Toronto Star* sports editor, Olympic representative, and father of Foster.

decades. More than eight thousand fans paid as much as $25 for a ticket to see the Manitoba champion Winnipeg Falcons play the University of Toronto Varsity Grads for the Allan Cup in March 1920, which the Falcons won in two games, outscoring Toronto 11–5.

More than being Allan Cup champions, the Falcons were a symbol of Canada's new identity, one forged in the battles of the war. Indeed, the Winnipeg Falcons had been a soldier team, playing as the 223rd Scandinavian Battalion, winning a Manitoba senior league title in 1915. Led by the scholarly and civilized centreman Frank Frederickson—who was also a gifted violinist— the Falcons had struggled against the anti-Scandinavian prejudice of the "Canadian" clubs in the Manitoba senior league, even after the squad had returned from fighting in the war. The Falcons, with the exception of one player, Allan Woodman, were all of Icelandic descent, and they saw their chance to compete in the Olympics as an opportunity to claim, once and for all, their true place as real Canadians.

After winning the Allan Cup, there was no time for the Falcons to return to Winnipeg, so they set sail for Europe again, but this time to wear the maple leaf in peace. Or the kind of peace only Canadian hockey could bring to Europe. "All through the tournament we tried to limit ourselves to fourteen or fifteen goals a game against the European teams," Frederickson recalled. "Believe me, it was difficult, but we managed to stay within reasonable bounds."

The Palais de Glace was as far as the Falcons could get from the frozen ponds of their Winnipeg boyhoods, where Frederickson had learned English by playing hockey. With an elegant terrace where patrons could eat and drink while they watched the hockey matches, and an orchestra that played all day long, the Palais was also a smaller rink than the Canadians were used to playing on, just 168 feet by 58 feet, instead of 200 feet by 85 feet.

It didn't matter. In the course of three games, the Canadians had defeated their opponents, Czechoslovakia, the United States, and Sweden, by a combined score of 29–1. The one goal they did allow was to the Swedes—partly because the Canadians thought they were their best competition, and perhaps as a little bit of revenge on those back home who disliked Scandinavians.

The Belgians and other European fans adored the élan of the Canadians, fast and skilled in their mustard sweaters showing a red maple leaf emblazoned with "CANADA" in white dominating the black bar that circled the chest. Fans would crowd their dressing room before matches with such zeal that the Falcons had to be escorted to and from the rink by Belgian soldiers, fearing for their safety should the mob try to crush the Canadians in worshipful embrace.

Canada's first Olympic hockey sweater, worn by the triumphant Winnipeg Falcons in 1920.

In addition to establishing the Canadian mastery of the game, they also established the rules of play. W.A. Hewitt, sports journalist, hockey executive of both the Ontario Hockey Association and the Canadian Amateur Hockey Association, as well as the father of Foster, was the team manager, and convinced the Olympic committee to use the ice hockey rules that Canada had perfected. As proof of their gratitude, the IOC asked Hewitt to referee the first Olympic ice hockey match, when Sweden defeated Belgium 8–0 on April 23.

Five years later, the International Olympic Committee decided that the winter games would be "official" only from 1924 onward, so the Winnipeg Falcons' gold medal became an asterisk on paper. It was much more than that to the nation and the game that it gave the world, for the Falcons' masterful hockey triumph in a world still wounded by war became the first great beacon of excellence to all Canadian Olympic hockey teams in the years to come.

THE 1924 OLYMPICS

The Toronto Granites represented Canada at the 1924 Winter Olympics, outscoring the opposition 110–3 in the shadow of Mont Blanc, in Chamonix, France.

The 1924 Olympic Games became the first official "winter" Olympics, and unlike the 1920 games, which saw ice hockey played in April, the 1924 edition was actually held in winter, at the foot of majestic Mont Blanc in Chamonix, France, from January 25 to February 5. The Toronto Granites, another team made up of war veterans, had won the Allan Cup the two years previously, and were selected to wear the maple leaf once more into battle.

Before sailing for Europe, the Granites played exhibition games at home, leaving no doubt in the minds of those hockey-savvy Montrealers who saw them play on January 8 as to the quality of Canada's team. "Furnishing one of the most finished exhibitions of hockey witnessed in Montreal in a long time," gushed a reporter, "Canada's Olympic hockey team easily disposed of the local All-Star team at Mount Royal Arena tonight, winning by 5–2."

The Granites would continue their dominance of the ice, once it froze, as a four-day thaw had made the outdoor Olympic rink "a slushy swamp, dotted with large pools of water." On January 25, the ice was good enough to allow four speed skaters, including Canada's Charles Gorman, to bring 5,000 spectators to their feet with impromptu racing, before the athletes of seventeen nations entered the rink after marching from the city hall, their banners and emblems aloft. "The band of the 97th Alpine 'Blue Devils' played 'O Canada,' 'God Save the King,' the 'Star Spangled Banner,' and the national anthems of other competing nations. The athletes were given an ovation by the crowd, Canada, France, the United States, and Belgium receiving the most enthusiastic welcome from the crowd."

Despite the warm weather, the Canadians won their three preliminary games by a total score of 88–0. Their first real challenge came in a medal-round game against Great Britain, which featured four Canadian players, who managed two goals to Canada's nineteen.

Left winger Harry Watson filed dispatches for *The Toronto Telegram* to entertain the people at home, a first-person stroke of genius based on the miserliness of *The Telegram*, which wouldn't pay to send a reporter to cover the Granites' exploits. Watson, nicknamed "Moose," had been a pilot in the war, becoming an ace with six kills. He was an ace on the ice as well, scoring thirty-six goals in five games as Canada outscored the opposition 110–3, despite the variable ice conditions, and side boards only a foot high.

Watson also earned a bloody nose from the Americans for his suggestion that Canada would defeat the USA 10 or 12 to nothing in the gold-medal game. He was proven wrong when, on a cold day with hard, fast ice, the Canadians managed only a 6–1 victory for gold, with Watson notching a hat trick. He was so good that the NHL would woo him with riches and fame, but he never succumbed, opting to end his hockey career with an Olympic gold medal and turning to business.

The Granites followed their Olympic tour de force with a trip to Paris, where they agreed to play an exhibition match against Great Britain on a 120-foot circular rink, where, like the Palais de Glace in Antwerp, spectators could enjoy the game from the comforts of a balcony, with waiter service. The Canadians had enjoyed their own Parisian wining and dining and trips to the Folies Bergère, and they took it easy against the British. As centre Hooley Smith recalled, the only way the players could get a breather was to shoot the puck out of play "up among the champagne drinkers at the tables surrounding the rink. It was messy but effective."

They were also received by one Edward Windsor, the Prince of Wales in London, who praised their skills despite the fact he had never seen a hockey game, though he promised to do so on his next trip to Canada. The power of Canada's hockey prowess had reached the man who would briefly be king (abdicating after a reign of 326 days in 1936). Much more important, it had reached the hearts of Canadians from coast to coast who knew that Olympic gold in the sport that mattered most, again belonged to Canada.

The 1924 Canadian Olympic gold medal winners in hockey. Harry Watson, (front row, second from left) was a World War I flying ace, goal-scoring wizard, and Olympic diarist for *The Toronto Telegram*.

THE 1928 OLYMPICS

Though it was only a decade since the Great War had shuddered to a bloody close, the world in 1928 was riding a champagne high to the tune of the Jazz Age and seemingly infinite credit at the bank. Canada, fresh off its sixtieth birthday, had grown to a proud and muscular young country of ten million people, and looked forward to the 1928 Olympic Winter Games in St. Moritz, Switzerland, as another stage on which to display its supremacy at the game that it gave to the world.

Once again, the Canadian Amateur Hockey Association chose an Allan Cup winner to represent the country. In a gesture that seems as distant as the 1928 games, a team of graduates from the University of Toronto (called the Varsity Grads), who had defeated Fort William in Vancouver to win the Allan Cup in March–April 1927, were chosen to represent Canada.

The Grads generated some bad press early on, when two players, goalie Joe Sullivan and scoring wizard Hugh Plaxton, did an end-run around coach Conn Smythe to get their brothers on the team instead of Wes Kirkpatrick and Dick Richards, the college players whom Smythe wanted. Some players supported Smythe; others threatened a boycott if the nepotism was denied. In the end, the two college players were jettisoned and the Sullivan–Plaxton faction won the day. Furious, the scrappy Smythe declared, "If Wes and Dickie don't go, I don't go!" They didn't, and so Conn Smythe stayed home, occupying himself in spring 1927 by inventing the Toronto Maple Leafs. CAHA executive and Ontario sportsman W.A. Hewitt once again took over as team manager.

The University of Toronto Varsity Grads endured nepotism and slushy ice to win the 1928 Olympic gold medal in hockey in St. Moritz, Switzerland.

The CAHA's rules had been adopted by the International Olympic Committee in February, though the IOC wouldn't go so far as to allow the defending team to advance the puck inside their own blue line by kicking it, nor would they allow the goalie to drop to his knees to defend his goal. The boards, however, were now five feet high instead of just one foot, though the Olympic ice rink would once again be outdoors.

It was a problem. "Avalanches of soft snow tumbled down from the mountains and ice skating rinks resembled swimming pools under a warm sun and balmy breezes," reported *The Globe*, on February 17, 1928. "'We came here to play hockey, not water-polo'" said P.J. Mulqueen, chairman of the Canadian Olympic Committee. Canada's first match against Sweden had to be rescheduled to 8:00 A.M. the following day, "when the sun is neither high nor warm."

To the Canadians, it could have been pitch-dark. The country was now so highly regarded that the IOC exempted them from the preliminary round robin, played by ten other countries in three divisions, from which would emerge three Davids to take on Canada's Goliath. Since the United States had failed to muster a team, Canada faced Sweden, Great Britain, and Switzerland, outscoring the trio 38–0 to win their third consecutive (and second official) Olympic hockey gold medal. Bert Plaxton and Frank Sullivan, added on at the expense of the two college players forced out due to the power play by Hugh Plaxton and Joe Sullivan, scored four of those goals. By way of redemption, Hugh Plaxton scored twelve goals, and Joe Sullivan posted two shutouts in the two games that he played in goal.

After the games, the Varsity Grads did a victory tour of Europe, playing matches in Vienna, Berlin, Paris, and London, before setting sail on the RMS *Celtic*, one of the White Star Line's "Big Four" passenger liners. The *Celtic* had survived hitting a mine and being torpedoed in World War I, and it would also survive passage with a crew of robust Canadians, boisterous after their Olympic triumph.

The celebration continued when the Varsity Grads rolled into Toronto's Union Station at 5:40 P.M. sharp on March 20, 1928. Cheering crowds lined the street from Union to the city hall, and tickertape from brokerage houses fluttered with coloured streamers hanging from lampposts, as the team made its way along with mounted police and hollering U of T undergraduates, who did the "Varsity snake"—a Jazz Age version of the conga—through the throng.

While the 1924 Canadian Olympic gold medal winners had produced a crop of pro hockey stars, the Varsity Grads, as expected, produced pillars of society, with goalie Joe Sullivan going on to become an otolaryngologist as well as a senator and Hugh Plaxton a federal Member of Parliament. There was also another infamously eminent Canadian in that triumphal mix: the team's cunning assistant manager, who managed to finagle himself into the limelight as Canada's flag-bearer when the athletes marched into the outdoor stadium to begin the games. Harold Ballard would go on to become an eccentric and polarizing hockey figure as majority owner of the Toronto Maple Leafs, and his presence in 1928 prefigured turbulent hockey years to come—and come they would, sooner than anyone realized.

The 1928 Canadian Olympic hockey team marches in the games' opening ceremony, led by flag-bearer Harold Ballard, soon to make his distinct mark on Canadian hockey.

CANADA'S FIRST INTERNATIONAL HOCKEY GOLD

The Toronto Canadas represented the country at the first International Ice Hockey Federation tournament in 1930.

In February 1930, Canada made hockey history when it sent a team to play in the first International Ice Hockey Federation (IIHF) world championship that was not part of the Olympic Games. The *Ligue Internationale de Hockey sur Glace* (LHG) was founded in Paris in 1908 to promote Canada's game in Europe, and their first international tournament took place two years later in the Swiss mountain resort town of Les Avants.

Canada showed up at that contest in the form of the Oxford Canadians, a sextet from Oxford University made up of Rhodes scholars. The Oxonians were the first Canadian team to sport the maple leaf on their sweaters, and their reputation preceded them: the British, a team made up of Canadians playing for the Princes Ice Hockey Club in London, refused to play them. The Canadians instead engaged and defeated Switzerland 8–1, Germany 4–0, and Belgium 6–0, though the team wasn't considered officially part of the tournament. As a result, though Canada posted the best tournament record in terms of wins, as well as goals for and against, and despite Britain's refusal to play the Canadians, Britain won the gold medal.

For the 1930 contest, which was shared among Chamonix, France, and Vienna and Berlin, Canada didn't send an Allan Cup winner, or even a regional powerhouse. Instead, the Toronto Canadas had won both the Toronto and the York Mercantile Leagues as the Toronto CCMs, representing the hockey gear manufacturer. CCM wanted to promote its product internationally, and thought that sending its championship team

on a tour of Europe would be the perfect way to do so. The CAHA agreed and named the Toronto CCMs as Canada's team for the world championship, as they were already going to be in the neighbourhood, and with the Depression in its first year, money was tight. If you could pay for a European tour, chances were good that you could play one.

Even so, Canada's hockey reputation determined the standings before the opening faceoff. While the other ten nations battled each other for a berth in the final, Canada was already there, by virtue of being Canada. So the Toronto Canadas played exhibition games while they waited to see who they would meet for the title, managing to earn the distinction of becoming the first Canadian team to lose a game to a European squad when they were shut out 1–0 by Austria's national team in Vienna on an outdoor rink in a heavy downpour.

The warm, wet weather saw the final game played inside, on artificial ice in Berlin's Sportpalast, an arena that could hold 14,000 people and was the city's largest—a fact exploited a few years hence by Joseph Goebbels when he made his rabble-rousing speeches to Nazi supporters. On the night that Canada faced Germany for the championship, 8,000 people showed up to watch the game, including the British ambassador Sir Horace Rumbold, and Germany's ex–crown-prince Wilhelm, who had abdicated during the German Revolution of 1918 and who had returned home as a private hockey-loving citizen.

The game opened at a fast pace, before Canada started taking the body to Germany. Even so, the Germans scored first to the delight of the partisan crowd. German joy was brief, as Canada answered quickly, and then took over the match. Afterward, the two teams dined together, and the Toronto Canadas flew off to England the next day to continue their barnstorming tour before returning to a triumphant Union Station welcome in Toronto on February 25, having won thirty-two of their thirty-three games. "As exponents of the winter pastime, their play must have undoubtedly had great missionary value wherever they were seen in action," wrote *The Globe*'s sports editor, Mike Rodden, on a wink, "and the teams that played against them, it may be assumed, picked up valuable pointers."

The 1930 Toronto Canadas pose in Berlin's Sportpalast, soon to be the sight of Nazi rallies. The Canadas defeated Germany to win the tournament.

One of those teams learning from the Canadian missionaries was the squad from Japan—in truth a team of Manchurian medical students—who lost their only game against Poland, 5–0, but received an enthusiastic welcome partly due to being far outside the northern European and North American hockey ambit. Yet it was in Vancouver where Japanese businessmen had first seen hockey on artificial ice, and they liked what they saw. Canada's game had now spread to Asia. But as the country would soon see, the world was starting to get better at Canada's game.

CANADA REPEATS AT THE WORLD CHAMPIONSHIP

The Great Depression once again dictated who would represent Canada at the IIHF world championship in Poland in February 1931. Six members of the University of Manitoba Grads had played on the team's 1928 Allan Cup winner, and so they formed the backbone of the crew who went on Canada's latest hockey tour of Europe.

Canada opened the tournament with a 9–0 rout of France, but things tightened up quickly. In the final round of the fourteen games played, Canada's 8–0 defeat of Austria stood out, for in all other matches—including those played by Canada—the result never saw a goal differential rise above three. Indeed, Canada's match against Sweden ended in a 0–0 tie, marking the first time that Canada had not won an international game in official competition.

The Canadians were fast and skilled, but the Swedes and the other European teams had finally learned that what they lacked in speed and hockey talent, they could make up for in defensive play. As a result, most of the final-round matches in the tournament, save for the title match that Canada played against the United States, were defensive chess matches. The final, which Canada won 2–0 against the US entry from Boston, was, despite the low score, an exhibition of "fine aggressive play with both teams attacking at every opportunity." The report also noted that some "lumps were handed out"—as one might expect between Canada and the United States. The Americans were catching up to Canada fast, and would be gunning for Canada's title soon—on Olympic home ice.

The University of Manitoba Varsity Grads, who had won the 1928 Allan Cup, defended the nation's 1930 IIHF title the following year in Poland.

THE 1932
WINTER OLYMPICS

By the time the 1932 Winter Olympics welcomed the athletes from seventeen countries to Lake Placid, New York, in February 1932, the Great Depression had hit the world hard. Unemployment had topped 23 percent, and the idea of playing games as the world seemingly spiralled into the abyss was both an escape and a barrier. The first true Winter Olympics in 1928 had seen twenty-five nations come to St. Moritz, but to the world's hockey-playing nations in 1932, it was too expensive an escape. As a result, only four teams competed for the ice hockey gold: host USA, along with Germany, Poland, and Canada.

The Winnipeg Hockey Club, winners of the 1931 Allan Cup, led Canada to its fourth consecutive Olympic gold medal in hockey in 1932, at Lake Placid, New York.

The CAHA decided to send as Canada's representative the 1931 Allan Cup champion Winnipeg Hockey Club, a speedy and skilled team that suffered from a depression of their own: they didn't put a lot of pucks in the net. Known, with a mixture of affection and derision, as "The Scoreless Wonders," the Winnipegs sufficiently alarmed the CAHA that they insisted the team bolster its ranks with two other Manitoba goal scorers, Norm Malloy and Walter Monson, both forwards with the Selkirk Fishermen.

Even that didn't mollify fears. "Olympic Hockey Players Fail to Score against Local O.H.A Seniors," grumbled one headline, just five days before Canada's first Olympic match, after the Winnipeg team, who were strong defensively, went down 1–0 to the Toronto National Sea Fleas. "Scoreless Wonders of the West Lived Up to Reputation," sniffed another newspaper.

The Canadians had a chance to redeem themselves for their lack of scoring once they were at the Olympics, at least as far as getting chances went, since the Americans gave them nine games in eleven days. The schedule had been created in the belief that eight countries would be vying for hockey gold, and when only four showed up, the organizers just doubled

up the round-robin portion of the tournament. The team that had the most points at the end of the tournament—two for a win, one for a tie—would win gold.

The Americans didn't want to refund money to people who had bought tickets in these tough economic times, and so they turned two games into exhibition matches against McGill University and a team from the Lake Placid Athletic Club. The Winnipeg crew beat the US team, and lost 2–1 to McGill. The late, great Canadian sportswriter Jim Coleman, a Winnipeg boy and McGill student, said, "The outlook [for Canada] was rather gruesome."

For a country used to winning hockey games even before its team took to the ice, the Lake Placid Olympic Games could be said to mark the beginning of Canadian hockey angst, the feeling that while it's indeed our game, some disaster could befall us when playing it at the highest level—a disaster often of our own making.

The hockey venue at Lake Placid contributed to the concern. Despite the fact that the US Olympic Committee was rightly proud of their state-of-the-art $300,000 indoor arena, which had excellent ice and could seat 4,000 spectators, most of the hockey games were played on the outdoor rink so figure skating could take place inside.

The outdoor rink was encircled by a speed-skating oval, and races took place around the perimeter while hockey games were underway in the centre. The real problem, though, was the bright winter sun. That, and the fact that the Canadians' first game was against their burgeoning rivals, the USA.

The Canadians were angry that the US team had played an exhibition game against the Boston Bruins and had taken a healthy cut of the gate receipts, a mercenary act in direct and fatal disobedience of the Olympic code of amateurism. Canadian Olympic Committee boss Patrick Mulqueen said the Americans had "professionalized" themselves, but the Americans countered disingenuously that taking money in Boston was the only way they could afford to go to the games—three hundred miles away in Lake Placid.

The Canadians decided to answer that insult on the ice, and for the first fifteen-minute period, they fired blanks. So did the USA, but then the Americans scored two minutes into the second period with an unassisted goal. The Yanks then played stingy defence, blocking Canadian rushes and heaving the puck down the ice. It looked as if the Winnipegs were going to repeat their result against the Toronto National Sea Fleas in Toronto, the game that generated such sneering headlines, and lose their first Olympic game by a score of 1–0.

Canada's "Hack" Simpson, a rangy 6'3" defenceman whom Coach Jack Hughes had turned into a forward, came to the rescue with just less than two minutes left in the game, scoring the first of his six Olympic goals. Canada took over the game in the first five-minute overtime, but couldn't score. Neither could the USA. When Canada's Vic Lindquist scored an unassisted goal at 2:14 of the second overtime period, Canada collectively exhaled, having averted a "near catastrophe."

The Winnipegs had no trouble scoring against Germany, with the Selkirk Fishermen add-ons tallying: Walter Monson scored two goals and Norm Malloy got another in Canada's 4–1 win. Their confidence building, the Canadians then thrashed Poland 9–0, beat Germany again 5–0, and humiliated poor Poland 10–0. Monson potted another five goals in that stretch, with Simpson adding four, and the smooth left winger Romeo Rivers notching four as well.

It was Simpson and Rivers who would save the day for Canada in the end. The last hockey match of the 1932 Winter Olympics pitted the Canadians against the USA. The US scored first and early, barely two minutes into the game, but Hack Simpson tied it up with a solo rush. In the second period, the USA took the lead—and they were about to take the game as the third period wound down.

Simpson was on a seemingly leisurely skate with the puck for Canada when Coach Hughes jabbed his star forward's sense of urgency, reminding the player that there was less than a minute left. "That's lots of time," Simpson replied, then passed the puck to Romeo Rivers, who tied the game for Canada with forty seconds to play. Three ten-minute periods of overtime failed to break the deadlock, and IOC officials called the game a tie. The one point gained by Canada in the draw was enough to top the standings, two points ahead of the USA. And so Canada won its fourth consecutive Olympic gold medal.

It had been a very close call. "The United States never before made such a potent threat to gain the world's hockey supremacy Canada has so jealously guarded as her own," declared a post-game report. It would be a warning whose meaning Canada's hockey trust would soon learn painfully.

THE 1933
WORLD
CHAMPIONSHIP

The year 1933 was a bad one for the world. The Great Depression swooned into its nadir, Adolf Hitler became chancellor of Germany, and Canada finally lost an international hockey game—one that would further rattle the confidence of the nation when it came to "our game."

The omens were there from the beginning. The Toronto National Sea Fleas had won the 1932 Allan Cup as senior hockey champions of Canada under the coaching of the superlatively talented, and resolutely amateur, Harry Watson, who had lit up the 1924 Olympics with thirty-six goals in five games. Watson had even suited up for the Sea Fleas when one of the players couldn't make a road trip, but by the end of the 1932 season, he decided to retire from the game.

Enter the team's business manager, the brash and bullying Harold Ballard. The man who would one day torment the hockey world as owner of both the Toronto Maple Leafs and their shrine, Maple Leaf Gardens, had come to hockey via powerboat racing. The National Sea Fleas were named after the small outboard hydroplanes that Ballard raced for the National Yacht Club.

He had won the Toronto–Oakville marathon regatta in 1929, and finished second in the 133-mile Albany–New York City marathon in 1930. He had also nearly drowned, like a fellow racer in his boat, after being hurled from their speeding Sea Flea into the hypothermic chill of Lake Ontario.

The Toronto National Sea Fleas, skippered by the eccentric Harold Ballard (front row, sixth from left), earned the distinction of losing for Canada for the first time in international play at the 1933 IIHF tournament in Prague.

That same year, the National Yacht Club decided to sponsor a team in the Ontario Hockey Association, and despite the optics—and because of their deep pockets—the Yacht Club decided to send the Sea Fleas on a European tour in the middle of the Depression, with Ballard behind the bench. For the CAHA, this Allan Cup–winning team was also the perfect choice to represent Canada at the IIHF world championship in Prague—even if the squad had failed to make the playoffs in the 1932/33 OHA season.

Some Sea Fleas had already voluntarily walked the plank after witnessing Ballard's volatile coaching, but the Canadians arrived in Europe with winning ways, defeating Britain twice and beating the Paris Blue Devils 4–0 in Paris, with the Canadians of Oxford University playing them to a 1–1 tie. Once in Prague, the Sea Fleas, in their red sweaters, fuelled on Czech beer and belligerence, sliced through the opposition, defeating Germany, Austria, Hungary, and Czechoslovakia with a combined score of 16–1.

And then, on February 26, they met the USA, represented by the Boston Olympic Club (also called the Massachusetts Rangers) in the gold-medal match. Over the course of three fifteen-minute periods, the two teams battled it out. "Each scored a goal in the opening period and for the next two sessions of regular time they fought each other to a standstill," reported *The Toronto Daily Star*. "Close defensive work and sparkling performances by the rival net guardians were the main reasons why goals were hard to get. Time and again the forward lines swept in to the opposing rearguards but were foiled repeatedly."

Canada's goalie, Ron Geddes, and the USA's Gerry Crosby (who would later open his internationally celebrated goalie store in Madison Square Garden) held the line until six minutes into the first overtime period. American defenceman John Garrison, who had lost gold to Canada at the 1932 Winter Olympics, made a solo rush that he capped by putting the puck past Geddes. Even though overtime was not of the sudden-death ilk, the Canadians were done. The United States had won its first international title, and Canada, for the first time, had lost one.

Lou Marsh, a superlative athlete and referee who was also a National Yacht Club sailor, vented from his pulpit as sports editor of the *Daily Star*. "And as for the Boston team—it was not even from the club which won the US amateur title last year. It was just a team which went on a Cook's tour around Europe. And that is exactly what the Sea Fleas were doing over there—on a sight-seeing tour, with hockey as an excuse."

Marsh's greater ire, however, was reserved for the CAHA, and would also be prophetic. "It serves us right for being so soft as to allow the control of Canada's national winter sport to slip into the hands of a European group," he fumed. Canada would soon see just how powerful the European group running international hockey was to become, and how the world—having seen it done—was now aiming for Canada's golden hockey crown.

THE
STATE OF
THE CAHA

Fourteen-year-old Howie
Morenz (front row, first
from left), began his
career with the 1916–17
Mitchell, Ontario, juve-
niles as a goalie. Wisdom
soon prevailed, and
Morenz unleashed his
speed and skill as a
forward en route to his
Hall of Fame career as
the most glorious of
Les Glorieux—the
Montreal Canadiens.

In April 1933, the Canadian Amateur Hockey Association held its
sixteenth annual general meeting perfumed by Pacific breezes at the
Hotel Vancouver. The CAHA was now two decades old, and while the
Depression would claim three NHL teams in that turbulent decade
(the Pittsburgh Pirates/Philadelphia Quakers, Ottawa Senators, and
Montreal Maroons), the CAHA was holding steady.

Registrations had fallen slightly from the year before, from 17,772
to 17,646, but that was still a robust increase from a decade earlier, when
6,855 players were registered in its ranks. The CAHA also had $14,546.59
in the bank, according to its treasurer W.A. Hewitt, which at the time
was enough to buy a mansion in Vancouver.

The CAHA made two significant rule changes at that meeting. For
the first time, the forward pass would now be allowed in all three zones
in amateur hockey. Previously, teams couldn't use the forward pass in
the attacking zone. Players could also advance the puck by kicking it in
the attacking zone. And amateurs who wanted to try out for professional
teams would not lose their amateur status until they actually made those
pro teams.

One of the issues occupying the CAHA was making sure players were
actually competing in their correct age group. The regulatory body didn't
want to prevent boys who did not have a birth certificate from registering
to play hockey, and W.A. Hewitt ventured that baptismal records

(reflecting the values of the age) were acceptable and indeed a better record, as they more accurately reflected the age of the player.

The meeting was told the parable of one Howarth Morenz, who was born in Mitchell, Ontario, where he played junior hockey. However, by the time his registration wound up at the provincial buildings in Toronto, he had been listed as "female." When Morenz became a junior star, hockey officials suspected him of playing under his younger sister's birth certificate. Everyone at that meeting would have had a hearty laugh at the expense of the provincial records, for Howie Morenz was, at the time, the Art Ross Trophy–, Hart Trophy–, and Stanley Cup–winning dazzler of the Montreal Canadiens.

Revealing the cutthroat level of junior hockey, the CAHA's past president J.W. Hamilton warned the members about players who had multiple birth certificates. "There was a case of another boy who was born three different times, and this fellow was presented with a gold watch as one of a championship team."

The solution was to use baptismal certificates as backup evidence if a boy had obtained a birth certificate after he reached 15 years of age—itself a very Christian thing to do. But for Canada's international hockey life, the issue of birth certificates would soon become a battleground, for a wily Irish travel agent would use birthright to take on Canada for Olympic gold.

Howie Morenz was the most dazzling of the "The Flying Frenchmen," so much so that his hockey talent persuaded "Tex" Rickard to put ice in Madison Square Garden so that Morenz and the Canadiens could play there.

ORDER RESTORED

On February 11, 1934, Canada reclaimed world championship hockey gold when the Saskatoon Quakers, western finalists in the 1933 Allan Cup, travelled to Milan and won all four IIHF matches. However, the Quakers had to win in overtime against both Switzerland and the USA to take back the title for Canada. And in the dark shape of the world to come, Nazi Germany finished in third place.

After outscoring their opponents 36–2 during their European barnstorm, the Quakers returned to Saskatoon to profound gratitude. "WELCOME HOME QUAKERS!" shouted a banner headline in the Saskatoon *Star Phoenix* on a page dedicated to the team's triumph. "You have Vindicated Our Confidence and Brought Renown to Your City." Thousands of people gathered in front of Saskatoon's train station to celebrate the return to Canada's rightful place in the international hockey cosmos.

The following year, in 1935, the Winnipeg Monarchs represented Canada at the world championship in Davos, Switzerland, where a record number of fifteen countries had entered the competition. The Monarchs had won the Manitoba Senior League in 1934, and boasted three members of the 1932 Olympic gold-medal team—Vic Lindquist, Roy Henkel, and Romeo Rivers, who scored the dying-seconds tying goal to give Canada the Olympic title in 1932.

This time, the Canadians didn't get any free pass to the final based on past glories, and the Monarchs had to play in all rounds. The Canadians responded to this affront by winning every match in every round they played, blowing out Latvia 14–0, Italy 9–0, and easily handling Great Britain 6–0.

The Saskatoon Quakers reclaimed Canada's international hockey supremacy by winning the 1934 IIFH world championship in Milan.

The other teams proved tougher, especially Czechoslovakia. The Czechs were being advised by Canadian Matej "Mike" Buckna, the son of Slovak immigrants who learned his hockey as a Trail Smoke Eater. Buckna would go on to lead Czechoslovakia to international glory, but for the time being, the Canadian hockey that he was teaching the Czechs was tough to play against, and Canada squeezed out two 2–1 wins against the Czechs before moving on to play the host Swiss for the championship on January 27.

The Swiss team was suffering from a flu epidemic, and their players, swathed in blankets, had to be driven to the 5,000-seat arena in horse-drawn sleighs. Speedy Canadian forwards Albert Lemay and his brother Tony scored two of Canada's goals, with Romeo Rivers notching another and Vic Lindquist assisting on two. Canada won its eighth international hockey title, but had been given fair warning that the upcoming 1936 Olympic Winter Games were going to be a challenge. Mike Buckna's work with the Czechs had given the Canucks a hint as to just where their greatest challenge might come from, but the reality of Canada's next big hockey battle would be one that no one could have predicted.

The Saskatoon Quakers, dressed like the 1934 world champions that they were.

THE 1936 OLYMPIC
WINTER GAMES

The 1936 Winter Olympics held in the twin towns of Garmisch-Partenkirchen, Germany, was notable for many things: the Nazi swastika flying over the athletes, many of whom would soon be at war with it; the "sport" of military patrol, a precursor to the biathlon, introduced as a demonstration sport on Hitler's orders; and the beginning of an Olympic interlude in Canadian hockey supremacy, whose catalyst was an Irish travel agent who never saw an angle that he couldn't play to his advantage against the Canadians.

"A cocky little Irish conniver," as scribe Jim Coleman pegged him in one of the more generous characterizations, John Francis "Bunny" Ahearne had first seen ice hockey in North London, watching some exiled Canadians chase pucks on a rink in Golders Green. A County Wexford boy, Ahearne had moved to London after World War I—where, it is said, he tried to serve in the British Army as a 16-year-old. Once in Blighty, Ahearne started his own business, and through his Blue Ribbon Travel Agency soon saw a profitable way to combine his touring business with this exciting and violent colonial sport. And he saw power, working his way from handling the European travel arrangements for Canadian and US barnstorming hockey teams to becoming the general secretary of the British Ice Hockey Association (BIHA) in 1933.

Ahearne also, Coleman believed, had a "mole" inside the registry office of the Canadian Amateur Hockey Association. Somehow, Ahearne managed to get his hands on the records of all players who had been born in the United Kingdom and who grew up and learned their hockey

The Port Arthur Bearcats, 1935 Allan Cup finalists, were tapped to represent Canada at the Nazi Olympics in 1936. The Canadians lost the gold to another team of Canadians representing Great Britain.

in Canada. When the 1936 Olympic Winter Games rolled around in January of that year, Ahearne had assembled his British team, which saw nine of the thirteen players having grown up in Canada, with one, Gordon "Don" Dailley, having even been born there.

Ahearne had dangled the prospect of $50 a week to Canadian players with British connections to come play in the English League. In the midst of an economic depression that gave no sign of letting up (it would take war with the German Olympic hosts to end it), the pay to play hockey seemed like a wild dream. Canadian lads whose parents had hauled them across the Atlantic as children now moved themselves back to play the game that Canada had taught them.

Their English League play also made the British players professionals, but the CAHA had its sights aimed at the two Canadians who had done something even worse: Jimmy Foster and Alex Archer had gone to Britain without its consent. CAHA president E.A. Gilroy filed a protest with the IOC the night before the games opened to prevent Foster, a two-time Allan Cup–champion goalie, and Archer, a two-time Manitoba All-Star right winger, from wearing the Union Jack.

The Canadians were playing on a strict and narrow interpretation of amateur, as the idea of *needing* consent from the CAHA to go to Europe to play professionally seemed to undermine the very argument they were making to prevent Foster and Archer from playing for Britain. Nevertheless, the CAHA's position was that the duo were suspended by the CAHA, and as per agreement with member nations of the IIHF, they couldn't play for anyone else.

Canada had money problems to worry about on its own team. The CAHA's usual strategy was to send the Allan Cup winner to the Olympics to represent Canada, but the 1935 champions, the Halifax Wolverines, had lost five of their best players and their coach to better-paying hockey gigs. So the CAHA picked the Port Arthur Bearcats, 1935 Allan Cup finalists, to go instead, bolstering the Bearcats with four players from Halifax, and two from the Montreal Royals, who had lost to Halifax in the semi-finals and were peeved that they hadn't been chosen to go to Germany. When the Halifax ringers demanded payment for economic loss caused by their Olympic venture, they were booted off the team and replaced with four "pure" amateurs.

A crowd of 80,000 people, including SS standard-bearers (taking a break from running Germany's concentration camps) and führer Adolf Hitler, watched 1,500 athletes from twenty-eight nations march through a blizzard into the ski stadium. Led onward by 2,000 Hitler Youth, the athletes passed the reviewing stand, and most—including Canada, and the only Jewish athlete in the Games, Germany's hockey star Rudi Ball—returned the "Heil Hitler" salute that the führer himself extended from the reviewing stand, with France and Austria especially enthusiastic in the gesture. The United States refused to return the salute that would soon terrify the world, but instead marched past the reviewing stand "eyes right." The US Olympic Committee president Avery Brundage remarked that he had seen "no evidence of any discrimination against Jewish athletes or Jewish citizens," although the world was well aware that the Nuremberg Laws for the Protection of German Blood and German Honour had already been enacted, and would soon "legally" open full-scale persecution of Germany's Jews and other non-Aryans.

The Canadians withdrew their protest against the two Canucks playing for Britain just before the hockey tournament began, a move that might be seen as more cynical than generous, based on the belief that the British certainly couldn't win the gold medal. It was a gesture they would soon regret.

The Olympic hockey contest divided the fifteen teams into four divisions playing three rounds: at the end of each round, the top two teams would move on to the next. Canada made easy work of its first round, outscoring Poland, Latvia, and Austria 24–3, and managing to thrash the Poles 8–1 on an outdoor rink on Lake Riessersee in the middle of a blizzard. The Poles' lone goal came when Canadian goalie Frank "Dinty" Moore knocked the puck into his own net while trying to clear it during a goalmouth scramble.

The Canadians won all their other matches in the competition, except for one: their second-round game against Bunny Ahearne's team of Canadian-taught hockey players representing Great Britain. The front-page news report from Germany began in shock: "Canada's amateur hockey authority, unchallenged since the Icelandic Falcons of Winnipeg won the first Olympic championship 16 years ago, was stripped from the Dominion at the Olympic Winter Games tonight by England—and Jimmy Foster of Winnipeg."

With Jimmy Foster—whom the CAHA originally had managed to get suspended—in goal for Britain, the UK players followed their Canadian coach Percy Nicklin's strategy perfectly: score first, which they did just twenty seconds in, then hold off the white-sweatered Canadians with the proud red maple leaf on the chest, and let Foster work his magic between the pipes. The Canadians tied the game near the end of the first period, then Foster shut them out, as former Hershey B'ar Edgar Brenchley, who learned his hockey as a boy in Niagara Falls, scored the winner for Britain with just over a minute left in the game.

Canada's first Olympic loss was made even worse when team officials learned that this second-round match against Britain would count in the final round. The usually dominant Canucks would not get another chance for revenge against the British-Canadians, and just as bad, the Canadian players had no idea this was so when they skated out to play against Britain. Despite vigorous Canadian and German protests to the IOC, Bunny Ahearne had managed to persuade even the United States to side with him and won the day. The format stood, and so Britain, by virtue of having beaten Canada in the semi-final round, won the 1936 Olympic hockey gold medal, with Canada finishing in the silver position.

The Canadians promised to avenge their loss at the next Winter Olympics in Sapporo, Japan, in 1940, but when war broke out between Japan and China in 1937, Japan gave the games back to the IOC. After trying and failing to place them in Switzerland, the IOC gave the 1940 Games back to Germany. That plan was destroyed, and so, too, was the chance of Olympic play, when Germany invaded Poland in 1939. The world would have to wait until 1948 to see another global competition in the name of sport. And Canada would have to contend with the shrewd anti-Canuck politics of Bunny Ahearne for the next thirty years.

Top:
John Francis "Bunny" Ahearne, manager of Great Britain's ice hockey team and future president of the IIHF, diagrams seeding for a world cup—and, in the eyes of Canada's hockey trust, Canada's downfall.

Bottom:
This dramatic shot from a late-afternoon game hints at the shadow cast by the threat of another world war.

REVENGE
IN 1937

Despite the CAHA's notion to create some sort of national hockey team, an idea that had been getting more serious attention in hockey rinks and boardrooms alike since Canada's loss to Britain at the 1936 Olympic Winter Games, the CAHA decided to stick with the tried and mostly true, and send the 1936 Allan Cup winners to represent Canada at the 1937 world championship. The fact that the IIHF's tournament was taking place on Bunny Ahearne's home ice in London made Canadian desire for revenge even sweeter, for it was Ahearne and his squad of British-Canadians who swindled the Canadians out of a gold medal in 1936.

So, the Kimberley Dynamiters travelled from the snowy Kootenay Mountains of British Columbia to the foggy dank of London in February to take back the world title for Canada. The Dynamiters had beaten the Sudbury Falcons 2–0 and 4–3 in a two-game, total-goals series to win the Canadian senior hockey championship, the first time that a team from BC had captured the Allan Cup.

When Kimberley, a small town in the Kootenay Rockies, was established in 1896, it was named after a South African diamond mine. For the next century, mining defined Kimberley, with the massive Sullivan mine exploiting one of the world's largest zinc and lead deposits and becoming the town's major employer—of miners and of hockey players, who were often one and the same.

The company that operated the mine, the Consolidated Mining and Smelting Company of Canada, which became known as Cominco in 1966,

The Kimberly Dynamiters travelled from the Kootenay Mountains into the heart of "Bunny" Ahearne's lair to win the 1937 world championship by defeating Great Britain and Switzerland in London.

wanted badly to beat its corporate rival from Trail, BC, where the Smoke Eaters ruled senior hockey in the West Kootenay League. So they spent money to recruit players who could earn more playing for Kimberley and working for Cominco than they would in the NHL.

But still, these players were considered amateurs. And off they went to Europe to compete against other national players who played for European clubs for money but were considered amateur, too. The Kimberley Dynamiters, led by captain Harry "Smiler" Brown, forward James "Puffy" Kemp, and goalie Ken Campbell, dapper in his tweed cap, put on a clinic in Europe, having survived a tough tour across Canada before the world championship with a record of 11–3. Once in England, the Dynamiters thrilled the crowds in Wembley and Harringay arenas, winning eight games by outscoring the opposition 60–4. Their revenge came on the night of February 26, when they faced Great Britain, a team stocked with many Canadian-schooled players who had beaten Canada at the 1936 Olympics.

George "Red" Goble scored for Kimberley in the first period, breaking Jimmy Foster's incredible eight-game shutout streak. Ralph Redding scored twice to put the Canadians up 3–0, but winning on the scoreboard wasn't enough for a Canadian crew that still seethed at the country's "loss" of the Olympic gold medal to Britain in 1936. Fights broke out in the first period between Red Goble and Britain's Winnipeg-born Don Dailley, and again in the third between Kimberley defenceman Bill Burnett and Niagara Falls' Englishman Edgar Brenchley.

The crowd, upset at seeing their Canadians being beaten by Kimberley's Canadians, got ugly, and "littered the ice with newspapers, orange peel, tin cans and any other missiles within reach. Order was finally restored when the band played the National Anthem."

Canada still had one more game to win to take the gold, and on Saturday, February 27, 10,000 fans, all pulling for the Swiss, crammed into the Harringay Arena. Canada's Puffy Kemp opened the scoring in the second period, but the Swiss tied it before the frame was finished. The third period decided nothing, so the teams entered overtime. If the Swiss won, then Canada and Britain would be tied for top spot. Red Goble was having none of that, and popped the puck past Swiss goalie Albert Hirz before three minutes had elapsed in the extra period. The Kimberley Dynamiters had reclaimed Canada's hockey superiority from a bunch of Canadian mercenaries.

Indeed, the IIHF was considering a motion at its 1937 annual general meeting put forward by the Swiss to declare all Canadians playing in Britain to be professionals. Some British rink managers were all for the idea, as it would free them from the control of the British Ice Hockey Association and Bunny Ahearne. They felt the BIHA "had not kept pace with the development [of the] game," which meant keeping the pace of money into their coffers a slow one.

The IIHF would compromise in the end, allowing professionals and amateurs to play in the same leagues, with amateurs only being allowed to play for their countries at the Olympics and world championships. Paul Loicq, president of the IIHF, reminded the world of whose game it really was. Canadian players, he said, were necessary in Europe, however they came to be there, for "teaching purposes." The Europeans were getting better at hockey, but they were still learning from Canada.

THE
PRESTON
RIVULETTES

It was a game of summer that began the country's greatest winter dynasty—amateur or otherwise. In the difficult autumn of 1930, 17-year-old Hilda Ranscombe and her younger sister Nellie were standouts on a local women's softball team in Preston, a small industrial town in southern Ontario. When the season wrapped up, the girls wanted to keep their team together, so they decided to play hockey, a game at which Hilda shone on Preston's frozen ponds as a little girl. And so the Preston Rivulettes were born, their name a feminized version of the term for a small river. They were, in fact, a hockey tsunami.

With Hilda Ranscombe playing like the Wayne Gretzky of her day, along with the talents of her sister Nellie in net, and the offensive gifts of the Schmuck sisters, Marm and Helen, the Rivulettes were unstoppable. From 1930 to 1940, the Rivulettes owned the Bobbie Rosenfeld Trophy as champions of Ontario and won the Elmer Doust Cup six times as champions of Eastern Canada. In 1933, Roberte de Neuflize Ponsonby, better known as Lady Bessborough, wife of Canada's governor general, donated a trophy to honour the best women's hockey team in the country. The Rivulettes won that trophy six times, drawing thousands of fans to their matches.

Throughout their decade of hockey triumph, the Rivulettes and other women's hockey teams were hard pressed for money to pay for travel and equipment, and the Depression made maintaining their excellence even

The Preston Rivulettes, Canada's most successful hockey team ever. Hilda Ranscombe (front row, first on left) led the team to six Dominion championships.

Bobbie Rosenfeld and the Rise of Women's Hockey

Women's hockey teams flourished across the country in the 1920s, picking up on the liberating spirit that infused the world after the carnage of World War I. No longer did women have to wear skirts that reached almost to the blades of their skates in the name of modesty. McGill University's "Debs" wore short culottes that were both stylish and much easier to play in, even if you couldn't hide the puck beneath them as the long swirling skirts had allowed in days of yore. There was not only style but also substance. The University of Saskatchewan team's Genevra "Ginger" Catherwood and her sister Ethel were formidable athletes. Ethel would win a 1928 Olympic gold medal in high jump, and on a two-game hockey road trip to Manitoba in 1921, Ginger scored twenty-one goals.

Ontario women's hockey was dominated by Ottawa's Alerts, champions of Eastern Canada. In March 1922, they met a Toronto women's team, led by Fanny "Bobbie" Rosenfeld, who would go on to dazzle with the city's Patterson Pats (and win Olympic gold and silver medals in track and field in 1928, as well as the honour of being named Canada's female athlete of the first half-century, 1900–1950). After the Pats won a playoff game in the 1927 Ontario Ladies Hockey championship, *The Toronto Star* was confident that Bobbie Rosenfeld and her teammate Casey McLean "could earn a place on any OHA [men's] junior team." It was not to be. The CAHA refused to allow women "officially" into the ranks until 1982, even though they were very much already there. So Bobbie Rosenfeld helped form the Ladies Ontario Hockey Association in 1922, serving as president of the organization from 1934 to 1939.

more of a challenge. The team members all held down jobs in local factories and funded their own success—and its celebration. When they beat the Montreal (women's) Maroons in 1936, the Rivulettes had to pony up $5 a player so that the host Maroons could pay for their victory party. Two years later, the Rivulettes' coach, Herb Fack, had to mortgage his house so the team could pay for the Canadian women's championship in Prince Edward Island—which they won.

The Rivulettes were about to take a page from men's senior hockey and embark on a European tour when another world war got in the way. With the war's fuel rationing and travel restrictions, the players decided to hang up their skates in 1941. They were feted at a banquet where it all began, in Preston, at the Preston Springs Hotel. Each of the Rivulettes was given a red silk jacket with a crest as a memento of their triumph as a team, and one of hockey's greatest dynasties was done because of the war. This time it would take decades before Canada again saw women's hockey played brilliantly on a grand stage.

The Preston Rivulettes do a star turn atop the team bus in Edmonton.

THE 1938 WORLD CHAMPIONSHIP

In 1938, the International Ice Hockey Federation celebrated its thirtieth birthday. When it began in 1908, Belgium, France, Great Britain, and Switzerland signed the document giving birth to the IIHF, with Bohemia (later Czechoslovakia) joining later that same year. Thirty years later, it had grown to twenty-two member nations, and the game that Canada gave to the world was now healthy in Europe, even if Europe was descending into madness. England now boasted 21 artificial ice arenas, and Germany had 14; Czechoslovakia had 361 club teams, the most in Europe, with Sweden next at 116, and Poland third with 92.

So, since Czechoslovakia had the most club teams, it was fitting that the world championship returned to Prague, where in 1933 the Toronto National Sea Fleas were coached to a silver medal by Harold Ballard in his final brief and volatile coaching stint. This time, the Canadian Amateur Hockey Association authorized Sudbury's Max Silverman to create the closest thing yet to a national team: Silverman, who knew hockey talent as president and general manager of the 1932 Memorial Cup–winning Sudbury Cub Wolves, was given permission to trawl the rinks of Ontario and create a Sudbury Wolves team that could not lose.

In the first of three rounds, the "Canadians who play as Sudbury Wolves" didn't lose, but they didn't trounce the first-round competition as they once had done; they beat Sweden 3–2, and both Austria and the host country 3–0. In the second round, they fared even worse, defeating

Max Silverman (background portrait) used his well-travelled hockey knowledge to create the 1938 Sudbury Wolves, the closest Canada had yet come to developing a national team.

Nazi Germany 3–2 in overtime, and failing to solve anything in a 1–1 overtime tie with Hungary.

The Canadians beat the Germans 1–0 in the semi-final, then met their old nemesis, Great Britain, still stocked with Canadian–taught Olympic gold medal winners, in the final. More than 11,000 people watched as Copper Cliff defenceman Johnny Godfrey carried the puck up the length of the rink, to dish off a pass to Red Chipman of Kirkland Lake, who scored Canada's first goal five minutes into the game. Pat McReavy, a Copper Cliff forward, made a "brilliant solo dash" two minutes later to score Canada's second goal, but former Port Arthur forward Gerry Davey answered for Britain straight off the next faceoff. Johnny Godfrey scored again for Canada before the first period was out, and that was it: Canada's Sudbury Wolves 3, Canada's Great Britain team 1.

The following year, the Trail Smoke Eaters, winners of the 1938 Allan Cup, travelled to Basel, Switzerland, to try to win Canada's eleventh world hockey title, with Finland and Yugoslavia making their world championship debuts. The Smoke Eaters chose to wear their club uniforms and not the maple leaf, intriguing the Europeans with their orange and black sweaters showing stacks belching out smoke above Trail's smelter, the image that gave them their name.

The Smokies won eight straight in the tournament, outscoring the opposition 42–1 en route to shutting out the USA 4–0 in the gold-medal match. The Smoke Eaters' toughest test came in the second round against the Czechs, who were led by their player-coach Mike Buckna, himself a former Trail Smoke Eater. The Canadians salvaged a 2–1 victory with two goals in the third period, but notice had been served by the only team to score on Canada. The Canadians would not see them again until after the coming war, but when they did, they would be battling them for Olympic gold.

The 1938 Sudbury
Wolves in London,
England, where they
won the 1938 IIHF
championship.

HOCKEY GOES TO WAR AGAIN

Another world war bled the planet from 1939 to 1945, but this time hockey played it safer, not trumpeting calls to glory—and doom— by equating war with a hockey game. As a result, NHL hockey players wound up playing next to amateur players—the very scenario that helped to create the CAHA. Imagine playing amateur hockey, and having one of the NHL's top lines join your team—as a unit. That's what happened when the Ottawa RCAF Flyers, who played in the Ottawa City Senior League, received a shot into the wild blue yonder when the Boston Bruins' "Kraut Line" of Bobby Bauer, Woody Dumart, and Milt Schmidt signed up, helping Ottawa to win its first and only Allan Cup in 1942.

The New York Rangers' coach Frank Boucher helped to create a Canadian Army hockey team, the Ottawa Commandos, which included Neil and Mac Colville, and Alex Shibicky, all members of the 1940 Stanley Cup–winning Rangers squad, as well as their goalie, "Sugar" Jim Henry. Rich with NHL talent, the Commandos took the Allan Cup in 1943. Montreal Canadiens defenceman Ken Reardon played for the Commandos, and his NHL coach, Dick Irvin, split shifts for both the Habs and the soldiers.

In Calgary, former Hart Trophy winner Tom "Cowboy" Anderson led his Currie Barracks team, along with Frank McCool in goal, who would go on to star in the NHL with Toronto. Maple Leaf Nick Metz and Chicago Black Hawk Bill Carse played for the Victoria Army squad and

won the BC Senior Championship. Since the soldier teams were classified as "senior hockey," their presence in the ranks made pure profits for rinks and their owners. In 1943, the senior league soldier games more than doubled the 112,693 tickets sold in Maple Leaf Gardens in 1942. As in the previous war, hockey helped the nation forget about its woes, even if the players were wearing the colours of war.

Toronto Maple Leafs goalie Walter "Turk" Broda had won the Vezina Trophy in 1941 as the NHL's top goalie, then backstopped the Leafs to win the 1942 Stanley Cup after being down three games to none in the final. He spent two and a half years playing goal for the Canadian Army team during World War II.

Top:
The Boston Bruins scoring duo of Milt Schmidt (left) and Woody Dumart (right) continued their high-flying hockey ways with the RCAF team during World War II.

Bottom:
Montreal Canadiens defenceman Ken Reardon won the 1943 Allan Cup as a member of the Ottawa Commandos.

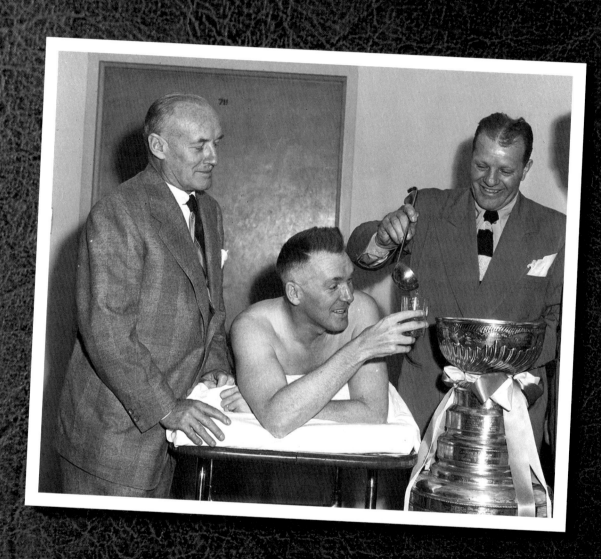

THE STATE
OF THE GAME
IN 1945

I n August 1945, a week after the United States dropped the atomic bomb
on Hiroshima and the end of the world's latest plunge into madness
was in sight (though the Cold War would soon heat up), the Canadian
Amateur Hockey Association met at Toronto's Royal York Hotel to discuss
the state of the national game. The executives were aware that Canada
would be called upon, as custodians of the game, to keep hockey in good
international health. Too good, as it would turn out for Canadians.

The CAHA had realized $250 from broadcasting the 1945 Memorial
Cup between Toronto's St. Michael's Majors and the Moose Jaw Canucks,
despite difficulties with broadcasting "chains." Only a few regions were
able to receive the broadcasts, called out by none other than *Hockey Night
in Canada*'s voice, Foster Hewitt, who was paid $125 for his services and
was appointed the CAHA's radio representative for the following season.

The main focus of business was Europe, and the CAHA's secretary
G.S. Dudley reported that he was in touch with the British Ice Hockey
Association who did not expect to be able to carry on operations in the
forthcoming season but would be able to get a league in order for the
following year. The Scottish Ice Hockey Federation was in better shape,
planning to operate six of its ten rinks in the 1946 season, "and would
require a considerable number of players from Canada."

As far as the amateur game went at home, registration had gone up in
a little over a year since D-Day in June 1944, with 28,091 players signed up

Maple Leafs boss
Major Conn Smythe
(left) and goalie
"Turk" Broda (right)
visit Sgt. Tom Hudie,
wounded in World
War II.

under the auspices of the CAHA. Registrar W.A. Hewitt was pleased. "Altogether it is a very satisfactory showing under existing conditions and indicates much encouragement for the future when Peace reigns again."

Of course, the CAHA had no way of knowing on that summer day in 1945 that Canada's long reign as undisputed hockey champion of the world was soon to encounter not so much an end as an interregnum. The pupil was about to school the teacher.

The voice of hockey in Canada for half a century, Foster Hewitt.

PART 2

CANADA AGAINST THE WORLD

World War II was over, and a spirit of peaceful coexistence was finding its way into the Canadian hockey world. On June 30, 1947, the CAHA, the NHL, and the Amateur Hockey Association of the United States came to an agreement that would set the international hockey stage for the next decade. The new accord stated that no amateur player under age 18 could become a pro unless his amateur team agreed—this rule protected amateur clubs but not the professional ambitions of their players. As well, no player under 16 could be offered a pro contract, which kept the NHL from poaching. The CAHA would win a bounty from this agreement: the NHL teams would now have to pay $2,000 to the respective amateur association for each one of its players who turned pro. The agreement would last ten years, and even though players were far from being free agents, with their professional opportunities still controlled by the NHL, it was an important stage in the evolution of players' rights. Evolving, too, was the way the Canadian Amateur Hockey Association, which began at the beginning of one world war, looked toward the future at the end of another. Canada's regional championship teams would do the country proud for a while, but then the world would show the Canadians it had learned our game, with the Soviets rising up to become the dominant international foe. Canada responded with a national team, full of high ideals and noble aims, but it was not enough. Even the Team Canada victory in 1972—after a good shock from the Soviets—wasn't the definitive triumph needed to give Canadian hockey a stable, successful future. Indeed, Canada yearned for more: we wanted to reclaim our place at the pinnacle of the game that we shared with the world.

THE
ST. MORITZ
WINTER GAMES

The 1948 Olympic Winter Games were the first to be held since 1936, when Adolf Hitler had given the Nazi salute to athletes parading before him in the stadium at Garmisch-Partenkirchen. The world had changed in ways unimaginable to even the darkest souls who had competed in those games, and after five years of global war, and many more years of the genocidal horrors perpetrated by the Nazis, the world was once more ready to come together in a spirit of sporting peace.

At least, the athletes were. While the NHL and the Canadian and American amateur hockey associations had come to agreement on the difference between amateur and professional in 1947, the International Olympic Committee redrew the rules on amateurism that same year and made a much tougher and starker distinction. As a result of the new IOC order, Canada could not send the 1947 Allan Cup champions, the Montreal Royals, to the Olympics. The Royals were much too "professional" with future Hall of Famer and 1947/48 Montreal Canadiens defenceman Doug Harvey on the team.

Part of the fracas was a legacy of Canada's 1936 Olympic silver medal. The CAHA—and the country—felt Canada had been bamboozled out of a chance for gold. Their second-round results, and lone defeat in that round to the Canadians playing for Great Britain, had suddenly counted in the final round, depriving them of a chance for gold. In protest, Canada organized the Independent Ice Hockey Association (IIHA) in 1940 with

The 1948 Olympic champions, the RCAF Flyers.

an aim to replace the IIHF. At the CAHA's annual meeting in August 1945, the British proposed that Canada's independent initiative should rule the day, which they'd happily administer in Europe—partly, no doubt, out of long-standing animosity toward the Europeans who ran the IIHF.

The world war had interrupted the hockey war, and so there were no world championships at which to test this challenge from 1939 until the 1947 world championship—which Canada boycotted, to drive home their point. The IIHF was well aware that without Canadian participation in the world championships, the value of their "brand" lost its lustre on many levels. So they smoothed things over by coming to the CAHA's meeting in 1947 and agreeing to alternate the presidency between Europe and North America. And that was the end of the IIHA.

It was not the end of the war, though, for now Canada's fight with the International Olympic Committee's purist (and hypocritical) definition of *amateur* led to another boycott. The CAHA decided not to send any team to the 1948 Olympics, partly in disagreement with the IOC, and partly because national pride demanded excellence—especially after the scheming Bunny Ahearne had finagled the Canadians out of a shot at the gold in Canada's previous Olympic outing. The CAHA didn't think it was possible to find a team "amateur" enough that was also good enough to beat the world and put Canada in its rightful place atop the gold podium.

Dr. Alexander "Sandy" Watson, the senior medical officer at Royal Canadian Air Force headquarters, had an idea. Watson had managed the 1942 RCAF Flyers to an Allan Cup win, and he convinced the CAHA that he could do it again. Not everyone, though, was a believer. The 1942 team was stocked with NHL players doing their military service on the ice. And the CAHA had not decided to send a team to compete in the 1948 Olympics until October 1947—less than four months before the games began. An *Ottawa Citizen* editorial grumbled, "The folly of sending a hurriedly organized RCAF hockey team to the Olympic Games should have been obvious from the beginning. Unscrambling this muddle is of national interest far beyond the limits of organized sports circles."

The fact that the national team was occupying editorial writers in the nation's capital was due to the RCAF Flyers being on the wrong end of a 7–0 result the night before thanks to McGill University's Redmen. The Flyers' coach, Frank Boucher, who had also coached the 1942 squad and was now taking time off as general manager of the New York Rangers, had to make a decision.

Boucher had been a Mountie before he caught on in the NHL as one of the original New York Rangers in 1926, where he would win the Stanley Cup three times and the Lady Byng Trophy seven times—until the NHL finally gave him the trophy to keep and the league made another. Gentlemanly, to be sure, but the cop and the competitor in him demanded justice, and that meant a gold medal for the country. So he cut players and brought in reinforcements, adding George Mara and Wally Halder, two players who had tried out for the Rangers, and tinkering with the team until he had what he thought was the best squad he could muster. Then nature weighed in when Boucher's starting goalie, Dick Ball, was sidelined with a lung infection, so 22-year-old Murray Dowey of the Toronto Mercantile Hockey League was quickly drafted into the Flyers, arriving in New York by train just in time to set sail for Europe with the team on January 8.

Though the war had been over for two and a half years, the Canadians now found themselves in the crossfire of one of the strangest Olympic wars yet, this one between the US Olympic Committee and the IOC. At issue was an internal battle between the US Amateur Athletic Union (AAU) and the US Amateur Hockey Association (AHA). The IOC supported the AHA, because the IIHF supported them. The US Olympic committee did not, because the AHA paid its players. The AAU representative was their team of choice. The US Olympic committee voted to withdraw the entire US Olympic contingent from the 1948 Winter Games in St. Moritz if the AHA professionals were allowed to play hockey. In the amateur ideal of the day, the Americans were boycotting themselves to prove a point.

The AHA team had already arrived in St. Moritz, and just before the hockey tournament was to begin, the IOC threatened to make hockey a "demonstration" sport, just as it had been in 1920, when the games returned to life after the first global war. Finally, an astonishing compromise was reached on February 7. The US team—the AHA squad—would play in the tournament but not have its games counted in the official results. Every team who played against them, though, would have their games count.

This was good news for the Flyers, who had thrashed the USA 12–3 on February 5, because the following day, the Czechs fought the Canadians to a 0–0 tie. It was a sign of things to come, but for now, the Canadians knew that they had to win their two remaining games if they hoped to win gold. The Flyers dispatched Austria 12–0 on February 7, and the following day played Switzerland in a game they had to win, unless the Czechs, who had an identical record to Canada's (6–0–1), lost their game to the USA's unofficial team.

As they had done for their previous seven games, the RCAF Flyers took to outdoor ice, which had been plagued by hot sun or heavy snow on alternate days throughout the tournament. On the day the Flyers met the Swiss, the ice was a slushy mess. "They wouldn't let school kids play on ice like that [in Canada]," said Flyers captain George Mara, one of Boucher's late additions, who scored seventeen goals for Canada.

With the Canadians up 1–0 after an early goal by Wally Halder, Canada's leading scorer with twenty-one goals, the referee asked Mara if the Canadians wanted to continue. "I told him we didn't," said Mara, double-checking with Coach Boucher, who agreed. "I knew we could beat the Swiss on good ice, but I thought they might fluke through on that ice."

The referee took Mara and the Swiss captain to see the IOC president Sigfrid Edstrom at rinkside, who ordered them to play to a finish. It was easier said than done, as the two referees, the rules, and the Swiss fans did their best to get in Canada's way. The fans threw snowballs at the Flyers, while the rules decreed that bodychecks were allowed only on the checking team's side of the red line, checking near the boards drew an automatic penalty, and hip checks were forbidden. The Canadians felt the referees also made up some rules as they went along. "We played eight men, the Swiss players and the referees—and still beat 'em," said the Flyers' trainer, Corporal George McCaul.

The Canadians emerged from the slushy farce with a 3–0 win, and their last-minute goalie, Murray Dowey, notched his fifth shutout of the games. But the Czechs had won their game, too, beating the phantom Americans 4–3. The Canadians and the Czechs had identical records—and their one tie had been in a game against each other. Now the winner of the gold medal came down to a question of math. IIHF rules said that the team with the higher goal average would prevail: Canada's 69 goals "for" divided by 5 "against" gave them a quotient of 13.8; the Czechs' 80 goals "for" divided by 18 "against" gave them a goals quotient of 4.3.

Despite the doubts of many who thought the Flyers weren't good enough to represent Canada, and even the IOC itself, they had won the country's fifth Olympic hockey gold medal in six tries. But as they left the Olympic Games, there was doubt that Canada would get a chance to repeat its hockey triumph the next time. "May Exclude Hockey from Olympics in 1952" said the headline from St. Moritz. The Games were done, but the question of what an amateur was, exactly, was now threatening to remove hockey from the Winter Games for good.

The RCAF Flyers in action at St. Moritz, 1948.

THE HOCKEY HANDBOOK

"Hockey Is Now a Science" proclaimed a March 1951 review of Lloyd Percival's *The Hockey Handbook*, one which respectfully suggested that to call the $5, 320-page volume a "handbook" was deceptive. No, Percival's manual was nothing less than "the first printed attempt to teach hockey as a contest of trained skills."

Percival was, at the time of publication, the 38-year-old host of CBC Radio's *Sports College on the Air*. He had competed in the Canadian junior tennis finals, won the Golden Gloves as a boxer, and he'd been a stellar cricketer, who, at age 23 in 1936, had taken a Canadian cricket team to England and shocked the British by defeating the Marylebone club in English cricket's shrine, Lord's. He had also been a championship-winning coach of track and field as well as hockey, but it was *The Hockey Handbook* that was truly revolutionary, with its emphasis not just on skill and fitness, but on strategy, how to play each position, and how to score on any goalie. Illustrated with clear and simple diagrams and charts, the book, said the reviewer, would have already been read by "top coaches … just in case there might be some small point they might have overlooked."

The Montreal Canadiens' head coach Dick Irvin summed up much of the Canadian hockey establishment's response to Percival: the book, Irvin said, is "the product of a three year-old mind." Not all in the hockey brain trust agreed, for Detroit's Jack Adams—hardly a hockey anarchist—asked Percival to evaluate the physical condition of his players.

The Hockey Handbook revolutionized the way hockey was thought about and how it was taught—though Canada was slow to join that revolution.

For Coaches · Players · Spectators

THE HOCKEY HANDBOOK

by LLOYD PERCIVAL

Percival further provoked Irvin by suggesting that Gordie Howe, with his superior strength and physical endurance, was better than Maurice "The Rocket" Richard. Indeed, Howe would go on to smash all of Richard's seemingly unbreakable records over his twenty-six NHL seasons (Richard played eighteen seasons).

Junior hockey was also a battleground for Percival's theories. Eric Nestorenko, a budding NHL star who played for the Toronto Marlboroughs, was giving manager Stafford Smythe and coach Reg Hamilton alarm by his devotion to Percival, and by his game-day diet of grapes, yogurt, apples, and raisins. Hamilton went so far as to write Percival, begging him to cease his Svengali-like hold on Nestorenko, and he received a five-page reply in refusal from *The Hockey Handbook*'s author. On trains to road games, with "the rest of the team in the diner munching on $3 steaks," Eric Nestorenko could be found "pulling grapes from a giant paper bag resting on the floor, while the Marlboroughs management glowers from the other end of the car."

While many of Canada's top coaches might have sneered at Percival and his methods, the Soviet Union's hockey commissariat was very interested in what he had to say. History was about to show that Percival knew what he was talking about.

Lloyd Percival was the multi-sport genius behind *The Hockey Handbook* and, like so many other Canadian prophets, ahead of his time.

Lloyd Percival

LLOYD PERCIVAL

THE
HOCKEY
HANDBOOK

THE COPP CLARK CO. LIMITED • TORONTO

THE EDMONTON MERCURYS

Despite the dire predictions for the end of Olympic ice hockey after the squabble-filled 1948 games, the sun rose in the east on eight hockey-playing countries who turned up to compete for hockey gold at Oslo in 1952. Canada had several teams clamouring to go to Norway: the Winnipeg Buffalos, the St. Francis Xavier University X-Men, the Trail Smoke Eaters, the Noranda Copper Kings, the Cornwall Falcons, the Smiths Falls Rideaus, and the Edmonton Waterloo Mercurys. The fact that the Mercurys had also won the 1950 world championship in London made the decision to send them in quest of Canada's sixth Olympic gold in hockey easier. So did the fact that the Mercurys were named after an Edmonton Ford dealership owned by Jim Christianson, who bankrolled the Mercurys—and the CAHA—with $100,000 for the European tour that landed them in the 1952 Olympic Winter Games.

It wasn't all open roads to the games. First, goalie Ralph Hansch, an Edmonton firefighter, had to get permission from his boss, Edmonton mayor William Hawrelak, to leave the firehouse for a spell. He did. He would also have to get permission from the IOC to wear his traditional number, 0, which they didn't want to give, but couldn't refuse, as there was no IOC rule against it (until Hansch asked, so there is now). Then Dave Miller's status as an amateur was questioned by the Czechs, since he had played semi-professional hockey in Streatham, England. The Mercurys also played a punishing exhibition schedule, a seven-week odyssey of thirty games in Scotland, England, France, Germany, Italy, Switzerland, Sweden, Belgium, the Netherlands, and Norway. They dazzled the Europeans with their speed and skill, and dominated their European

The Edmonton Mercurys, named after a car and not the Roman god with winged sandals, were still fleet enough to win the gold medal at the 1952 Olympic Games in Oslo.

opponents, who were supposed to acclimatize the Canadians to the European game.

In Oslo, the team bus skidded off the road and into a ditch, only slightly injuring players Miller, Tom Pollock, and George Abel. Which was good news, all things considered, as the Mercs had an exhibition game that night against Norway, which they won 7–2. Bad news was that their benefactor, Jim Christianson, had fallen ill in Norway; he would die of pneumonia upon his return to Canada shortly after the games ended.

The team's final exhibition game was scheduled for the night before the Olympics opened. The exhausted Mercurys tried to dodge their match against the USA, but all 10,000 seats in the arena had been sold. The Mercurys played on, and beat the US 3–2, with the winning goal coming from Dave Miller, who had finally been reprieved as an "amateur" just an hour before game time.

Three of the four Olympic arenas were outdoors. The games had been saved just before opening day with a blast of winter that chased away the balmy temperatures. Even so, to avoid playing dice with bad weather, which a playoff system and three outdoor rinks would create, the nine countries competing for hockey gold played a round-robin tournament. A win earned two points; a draw received one.

The Mercurys tried to get their February 15 game against West Germany postponed due to the death of King George VI, whose state funeral was that day. The English king's death, on February 6, was enough to have colonial arch-patriot Conn Smythe call off that day's Leafs–Rangers game in Toronto, but the IOC said play on, though they did allow the Canadians to wear black arm bands on their red sweaters with blue trim and a white maple leaf crest.

Dave Miller scored five goals, Bill Gibson scored four, and playing manager Frank Sullivan notched three as the Mercurys pounded the Germans 15–1. They played their next game against Finland, who thought using four defencemen, a forward and a goalie might halt the Canadian attack. "The Canadians played it free and easy, roaming about the Finns' net and not bothering too much at times about the opposition. As a result, the Finns scored their three goals on only seven shots." The Canadians scored thirteen.

After shutting out Poland 11–0 in a blizzard, the Mercurys faced their toughest challenge of the tournament: the Czechs. The Czechs had won the world championships in 1949, but on March 11, 1950, just before that team was about to board the plane to London to defend its title, the Stalinist "security" police arrested them en masse, on trumped-up charges of treason and attempting to defect. They were sentenced to prison terms ranging from three months to fifteen years, a term imposed on their superb goalie, the 1948 Olympic silver medal winner Bohumil Modry. He died in 1963 from the ravages of his time in prison, and a great Czech hockey team was destroyed by the harsh Soviet authorities.

The 1952 Winter Olympics marked the return of the Czechs to the ice hockey stage, and their now "Communist-approved" team wanted to make even more of a statement by beating the Canadians. The Mercurys responded by punishing them with such physical play that Canada took seventeen penalties in their 4–1 win. Bodychecking, as seen in the NHL, was not officially allowed in the Winter Games until 1968, and the Europeans saw the Canadians as a horde of ruffians, defiling their pure and elegant style of hockey with brute thuggery. The crowds and the media booed them in person and print, calling them, and the USA, "rowdies" and "gangsters."

The IIHF responded by suggesting that both the USA and the Edmonton Mercurys adjust their game to a more Euro-friendly style, and the Canadians responded, taking just one penalty in their 11–2 pasting of Switzerland. They next beat the Swedes 3–2, despite outshooting them 39–6, and faced the USA in the gold-medal game.

Canada needed a tie to win the gold on points. Despite Canada taking a lead with two late-first-period goals, the Americans fought back with two of their own midway through the second period. Canada's Don Gauf put them up 3–2 with a goal late in the second period, but the USA responded with the tying goal late in the third. The result stood, with Canada taking its sixth Olympic hockey gold and the USA its fourth silver. As a sign of things to come, TASS, the Soviet news agency, reported that the hockey tournament had been fixed to prevent communist Czechoslovakia from winning silver (the Czechs wound up taking home the bronze). Soon, the Russians would be winning hockey medals of their own, but for now, the Edmonton Mercurys enjoyed their victory. The Mercs' Olympic ice hockey gold would be Canada's last—for the next fifty years.

CANADA
MEETS THE
NEW HOCKEY
ORDER

While the USA and Russia raced to test the hydrogen bomb in their pursuit of mutually assured destruction, there was a cold war heating up on the ice, as Canada met Russia for the first time at hockey in the 1954 world championship. It was a meeting that would launch Canada's hockey crisis for the next two decades.

The Soviets had started their hockey program just eight years earlier, building on their history of bandy—a game played with a ball on ice, by eleven players on each side, and over a larger surface that dictates speed and precision passing. The decadent capitalist West, however, played hockey. The Soviets wanted to create a hockey program designed not just to compete but to win, and so expand the Communist brand and polish its lustre.

In 1948, three years after the end of The Great Patriotic War—as World War II was known in the USSR, where 27 million citizens had been killed—the Soviet Union held a hockey clinic in Moscow. The teachers were the now-colonized Czechs, who themselves had been taught by Mike Buckna, the son of Slovak immigrants to Trail, BC, where Buckna had played for the Smoke Eaters. Under his tutelage, the Czechs won the 1946 and 1947 world championships, and the Soviets, now their political masters, wanted to know how to play the game.

Soviet player-coach Anatoli Tarasov had learned much already from Canada's hockey philosopher-scientist Lloyd Percival's *The Hockey Handbook*. Now he and his fellow hockey pioneers Arkady Chernyshev, Vsevolod Bobrov, and Anatoli Seglin wanted to see theory in practice. Over the next six years, the Soviets—who got their first artificial ice rink in the early 1950s—trained in the middle of winter nights on natural ice, and on tennis courts in summer, puzzling passersby who wondered what these sweaty soldiers were doing chasing after a rubber ring in the dirt. By 1954, they finally felt they were ready to show the world what they had learned.

Back in Canada, the CAHA decided to send into a fierce battle (worse than anyone yet realized was coming) another team sponsored by a car dealership, this time one in suburban Toronto. The East York Lyndhursts were a Senior B squad who had made it to the Ontario final, and lost. Indeed, they were more than a little short on championship hardware—having won first place in the East York League only once, in the 1952/53 season. They did, however, have one thing that Senior A teams did not or could not risk losing by jaunting off to Europe: a surplus of money from the sales of Nash cars to pay their own way to the championships in Stockholm, Sweden. Despite a growing concern from the grassroots to the boardrooms of the CAHA over the need to find a better way to create a national team, and despite warnings from Europe that the Canadians couldn't pursue their current strategy and win forever, the Lyndhursts were tapped to wear the maple leaf for Canada in '54.

Even so, at a time when the NHL had just six teams, there were many Canadian hockey players who would have been good enough to play professionally had there been room in the NHL. So they played hockey at a semi-pro level, and as long as hockey wasn't their main source of income, these players were considered "amateur."

The East York Lyndhursts, despite their Senior B status, had some talented players. Moe Galland, 23, could score goals, and he played professional baseball with the Brooklyn Dodgers organization in the off-season. In between hockey and baseball, he worked as a deliverer for Eaton's.

The team's second-highest scorer, John Petro, also 23, drove a truck for his father's construction business. Doug "Benny" Chapman, a big and bruising 23-year-old defenceman, worked for Avro Aircraft, and team captain Tommy Campbell, 29, had actually played a season of minor-pro hockey with the Pittsburgh Hornets.

But their pedigree was a source of mockery to the Europeans. "MISTAKE OF THE YEAR?" was the banner headline to Bob Giddens's column in England's *Ice Hockey World* magazine. Rudolf "Putte" Kock, the boss of a Swedish club team that had lost three games to the Russians, finger-wagged that "the time has passed when Canada could send a scrub team to Europe, confident that it would be good enough to win."

And so it seemed when the Lyndhursts played an exhibition match against a team of (Canadian) all-stars from the English League in Paris, before 15,000 people, a crowd the size of which the Lyndhursts had seen only on *Hockey Night in Canada* (if they knew someone with a television). The only consolation to the firepower of the opposition and the disdain of the crowd was that the Lyndhursts were served glasses of beer when they were sitting in the penalty box. Hopefully, the suds helped nurse the pain of losing 11–2.

Or maybe those suds acted as hair of the dog for the collective hangover the Lyndhursts suffered the day before when they landed after a week at sea, a voyage on which most of them had been seasick. By the time their world championship schedule began on February 27, they had found their game. The Lyndhursts went on a streak of crazy eights, beating Switzerland 8–1, Norway 8–0, Sweden 8–0, and West Germany 8–1. Then, to win Moe Galland a place in the record books, they beat Finland 20–1. Galland had seven goals in the game, which elevated him to third place for goal scoring in Canada's international history (so far).

The Lyndhursts also failed to shed the reputation that Canadian teams were thugs. Bodychecking was allowed only on the defensive side of the blue line, and even then, Canada could easily get penalized just based on reputation. In the 8–0 victory against Sweden, Canada's six-foot-tall Benny Chapman lunged for the puck at the same time as a Swede who was six inches taller. The Swede got his elbow up and broke Chapman's jaw in two places, which ended the Canadian's tournament. It also got Chapman a penalty for charging.

The Lyndhursts had a tougher time against the Czechs, whom they played on slushy ice in the rain, needing two goals in the third period to defeat them 5–2. A Canadian Press story out of Stockholm trumpeted that the win meant "Canada ... virtually clinched the 1954 World Hockey Championship when Sweden later held the strong Russian team to a 1–1 tie." The USSR–Sweden game had taken place in even worse weather than Canada's match against the Czechs. Even so, if Canada could tie—or beat—the Russians, they would win the gold.

The Russians, with their shabby gear, their oddly shaped sticks, and their funny helmets, made the Canadians look slow, sloppy, and unimaginative on March 7, 1954. In fact, the Lyndhursts were tense and flat, hearing the echo of all the propaganda as they took to the ice, which, in the rain, became slush, and then, when the slush froze, became a terrible surface on which to play catch-up. But that's what faced them after going down 4–0 to the USSR in the first period. Canada's Moe Galland scored in the second, but the Russians scored three more. Canada won the third period, but Bill Shill's one goal was not enough. The Canadians stood on their blue line as the rain teemed down to watch the hoisting of the hammer and sickle as the Soviet anthem hymned the golden triumph. And here on this day was the reality of Canada's shocking new rival.

"Reds Give Us Lesson in Game We Invented," mourned a *Toronto Star* headline the day after. "No one but the CAHA can be held responsible for Canada's defeat," said the *London Free Press*. "Perhaps the defeat of Canada by the Russians is the best thing that could have happened," said the *Winnipeg Free Press*, hoping the jolt to the CAHA would compel it to send "nothing but the best" the next time.

Conn Smythe, boss of the Toronto Maple Leafs, had a solution for next time. The Leafs sent a telegram to the Soviet ambassador in Ottawa asking for permission to take his team to the USSR "to regain Canada's hockey prestige." Amid all the bashing of the CAHA after the Lyndhursts' loss to a very good hockey team, one item stood out on the front page of the *Toronto Daily Star* the day after the debacle. Canada's federal government vowed it would never fund a team to compete for Canada on the international hockey stage. "The government has never gone into the sports business and doesn't believe in using sport for international propaganda," informed sources told the *Star*. And yet the presence of the maple leaf on the sweaters of the team that represented the country internationally meant the government was, by proxy, already in the business of propaganda. The people certainly thought so. And within the decade, the government would catch up to the people as Canada would have a national hockey team, designed to reclaim the nation's hockey prestige.

Moe Galland scoring one of his seven goals against Finland. Still, the Canadian scoring machine was all but shut down by the mighty Soviets.

THE
REVENGE
OF THE VEES

Canada's chance to avenge the national indignity of losing its place atop the world hockey pedestal to the Soviets came a year later in West Germany, when thirteen other nations—a record since the end of World War II—came to see if they, too, could knock Canada further down into the muddy slush of mediocrity. After the Senior B East York Lyndhursts' failure to win gold in 1954 had become a symbol of all that was wrong with Canada's international hockey strategy, the CAHA now seemed to be helping the enemies of the state. They decided to send a hockey dragon slayer from a tourist town in the Okanagan Valley of British Columbia, population 14,000, whose team was named after the local peach crop. But from peaches comes jam, which the Penticton Vees had in large supply.

The Vees, named after the peach varieties Valiant, Vedette, and Veteran, had roared back from being down three games to nothing against Max Silverman's Sudbury Wolves in the 1954 Allan Cup—and even more harrowing, down 5–2 with less than eight minutes to go in Game 4—to win the series. So, in 1955, and following the tradition and reality that in any given year, any team could represent Canada, the Penticton Vees were chosen by the CAHA to reclaim Canadian honour at the world championship in West Germany.

After the Lyndhursts' perceived national disgrace, everyone in the country had an opinion on just how misguided the CAHA decision was

Team Canada stalwart Grant Warwick won the Calder Trophy in 1942 as the NHL's rookie of the year, notching 33 points in 44 regular season games as a right winger for the New York Rangers.

to send a bunch of rubes from beyond the Rockies to defend national honour against the Soviet threat. Montreal Canadiens coach Dick Irvin, echoing Conn Smythe (and many Canadians), said, "Let each NHL team put in two players, and Penticton can fill in the holes."

The Vees did not see themselves as having any holes. They had become a symbol of civic spirit in the beach town nestled between Lake Skaha and Lake Okanagan, especially after their epic Allan Cup comeback. The team was led by the dynamic, mercurial, fun-loving Warwick brothers of Regina. Grant Warwick had won the Calder Trophy with the New York Rangers in the 1941/42 season and had nearly ten NHL seasons under his belt; Bill had never stuck in the NHL but was a goal-making minor leaguer; and Dick, the youngest, was a 130-pound wizard at centre.

At the Vees' first practice in Berlin—a city whose pleasures no amount of time in the beer halls of Penticton could ever prepare them for—Bill Warwick and defenceman George McAvoy managed to get into a fight. The fact that the Soviets had dethroned the Canadians the year before meant that the world's hockey scribes and eminences had shown up to witness the rematch, and those now watching the Vees' practice were shocked. They knew the Canadians were barbarians when it came to playing European teams, but people hadn't realized that they were so savage they didn't even show mercy to their own.

Judgment was confirmed when a Canadian player told a curious European reporter that the Vees' practices were much more dangerous than their games—and that he had twenty-three teeth lost in practice to prove it. Despite blowing off family steam at practices, the Vees played as a team, albeit a rough and merciless one: they thumped the Americans 12–1, the Finns 12–0, the Swiss 11–1, and the Poles 8–0. But the Czechs and Swedes were getting better, and the Canadians were in tough to win their games against them, 5–3 and 3–0.

The Vees had become Canada's latest hope for glory, but to the Europeans and others, they were not peaches but pirates. A *Time* magazine stringer filed a piece called, "Canadians Abroad: Jarring Note," reporting, among other outrages, that one of the Vees had blown his nose in a table napkin at a swank hotel. It turned out that the player had the flu, was ambushed by a sneeze, and so, not wanting to share the misery with his teammates, improvised with the closest thing on hand that resembled a handkerchief. When the same *Time* reporter tried to interview Grant Warwick while the player was eating his breakfast, Warwick—who'd warned the reporter about disrupting the most important meal of the day—threw the man headfirst down two flights of stairs.

The stage for the rematch had been set with high drama, as the Canadians and the Soviets entered the gold-medal final with identical records: they were both undefeated. Foster Hewitt, representing his own radio station CKFH as well as the CBC, came to chronicle the gold-medal game, as did print and radio and journalists from twenty countries. Since TV was now a reality for much of the Western world, TV crews filmed the game to transmit it later to the hockey-watching masses. It was estimated that hundreds of millions of people would see the titanic struggle between Us and Them.

The first period saw the kind of hockey everyone expected: fast and skilled and looking to be a tight, close match. But at 4:25 of the first, Canada's Mike Shabaga deked the Soviet goalie out of position and tapped the puck in the net. The overwhelmingly pro-Canadian crowd—including 1,500 Canadian soldiers stationed in West Germany—went wild, chanting, "Go Vees Go!" And so they went, adding another four goals while Vees goalie Ivan McLelland held off the Soviets, even while the team was playing the final two minutes down two men.

"I finally realized the score was 5–0 and I wanted to keep it that way," McLelland said afterward. "It looks pretty impressive in the records." McLelland had notched his fourth shutout in eight games, and he became the first Canadian goalie to shut out the USSR in international play.

The Vees' victory washed over Canada in a tide of pride and relief. "This was a good one for democracy," said team president Clem Bird, reflecting the widespread belief that the "mechanical" communists couldn't think for themselves when they fell behind. The *Globe and Mail*'s editorial writers saw it as a good win for Canadian hockey, and a challenge to the country: "The Vees accomplishment should remind us that the national game really is national. Central Canada is too much regarded, and too much regards itself, as hockey's centre. The fact that a BC team beat the Russians this year (plus the fact that a Toronto team, East York Lyndhursts, lost to them last year) should encourage some changed thinking on this subject. At the same time it should stimulate hockey enthusiasm in smaller cities and towns from coast to coast. If Penticton, with just 10,000 people, can win world laurels, [then] why can't they?"

Once again, Canada was back on top of the hockey world and had struck a blow against communism. But the Soviets would fight back. It would become a huge hockey duel that would play out for the next seventeen years.

The Penticton Vees, who took their name from types of peaches growing in their lush Okanagan Valley, won the 1955 world championship by defeating the Soviets to restore Canadian hockey pride.

A BOY
NAMED
ABIGAIL

"Ab" Hoffman easily passed as a particularly talented hockey-loving 9-year-old boy.

As Canadian society sprawled into the suburbs in the mid-1950s, television went with it, becoming central to family recreation. *Hockey Night in Canada* gave more people access to live games than ever before, but while the men's game thrived, the women's game suffered. As if to punctuate the misery for girls who didn't want to imitate Canada's gold-medal figure skater Barbara Ann Scott but instead yearned to play hockey, CCM, the company that outfitted players since the turn of the twentieth century, stopped making hockey skates for girls. One 9-year-old girl in St. Catharines, Ontario—who didn't even have television in her house—wanted to play hockey and did something about it. She became a boy.

That wasn't the plan when Samuel Hoffman took his daughter Abigail to the registration meeting for the Little Toronto Hockey League to see if there were any teams for girls—and they found themselves surrounded by four hundred boys. "While I was inquiring about a girls' team, [Abby] wandered off into the crowd and handed in her birth certificate without telling me," he said. "A few days later I received a call from the league saying Abby could play."

And could she play. "We switched her from forward to defence because she was such a good backchecker," said the St. Catharines Tee Pees' coach Bill Brock. "I taught her how to bodycheck and take a man out on the boards."

With short hair, and dressing in her gear before games, then going straight home after, "Ab" Hoffman had a sensational season. Indeed, had she not been so good, she would not have been detected. She was discovered after being named to the all-star team and league officials had to look at her birth certificate again.

This time, they were a little sharper of eye, although Abigail's mother, Dorothy Medhurst, thought that some coaches might have been keeping silent to keep her daughter on the ice. Especially Bob Bowden, whose son played on a team with Abby's brother Muni, and the brother had told his pal about Abby's adventures on the ice as a boy. "Several times Mr. Bowden would come over and say, 'That boy of yours is quite a hockey player' and wink and smile when he said 'boy.' But he never gave the show away."

Ab Hoffman's coaches did their best to keep her on the team, much to the relief of her teammates. Russell Turnbull, a centre on her team said, "I was sure fooled ... but we sure want Ab to stay with the team."

Ab Hoffman was there when the Tee Pees joined three hundred other players later that month at the THL's first annual hockey jamboree. Frank Selke, general manager of the Montreal Canadiens, presented her with a team jacket, and Hoffman's teammates gave her a trophy to commemorate her season.

But that was it for Abby Hoffman's time on the ice with the boys, despite her parents taking a lawsuit to the Supreme Court of Ontario. As Abby didn't want to play hockey with girls, she turned her attention to other sports, eventually winning gold, silver, and bronze medals running the 800 metres at the Pan-American and Commonwealth Games.

Nevertheless, her achievement in a boys' league saw girls getting their chance to play in fledgling leagues of their own. It would take some time before another girl with Abigail Hoffman's ambition could play the game at the highest level on the ice with her own gender, but she had broken the barrier. Women had been playing hockey in Canada since the game was invented. It took a girl disguised as a boy to remind the country of that.

**That's No Lady--
Just a Defense Man**

TORONTO, March 8 (P)—Red-faced Toronto Hockey League officials admitted today that a 9-year-old girl had played in a boys' league for the past three months.

Abigail (Ab) Hoffman, a tough little defenseman for the St. Catharines Teepees in the little THL "A" Series, was discovered to be a girl when she was picked to play in a league All-Star game at the Scarboro Arena March 31.

In order to play in the game, the players had to produce their birth certificates, and that's when flabbergasted officials found out the Teepees' top defense star was a girl.

Her father, Samuel Hoffman, said he didn't reveal Ab was a girl because "she liked playing and hockey is a good healthy sport."

"Hockey is really not a very rough game for 8-year-olds, because they have enough to worry about just holding the stick and staying up on their skates," Hoffman said.

Abigail played more than a dozen games with the Teepees and helped put them in second place in their league. Her father added that she was never interested in dolls and played with hockey sticks from the time she could stand on her feet.

Abigail Hoffman was so good on defence playing for a boys team that she was named a league all-star.

THE
WHITBY
DUNLOPS

The Penticton Vees' world championship marked the beginning of a brief, but nonetheless painful, drought for Canada on the international hockey stage. The 1956 Winter Olympics in Cortina, Italy, saw Canada's entry, the Kitchener-Waterloo Dutchmen, finish in a stunning third place, after losing 4–1 to the USA and 2–0 to the Soviets.

Canada had boycotted the 1957 world championship in Moscow in response to the Soviet invasion of Hungary in 1956, so after two years without winning an international championship, the nation was feeling deprived of the gold to which it had grown accustomed to winning. Once again, the CAHA decided that the honour of the maple leaf would rest on an Allan Cup winner, this time from Whitby, Ontario, and once again it was a team with relatively deep pockets to afford the journey in 1958.

The Whitby Dunlops were sponsored by the Dunlop Rubber Company, and coached by Wren Blair, a former milkman who had proved himself to be one of the shrewdest minds in hockey by scouting and eventually signing a kid named Bobby Orr. (He would go on to coach Orr in Boston.) Because Wren Blair—despite his name—had a fear of flying, the Dunlops travelled to Europe by ship across the rough Atlantic Ocean in winter, a six-day torment that revealed that the team had sea legs only on frozen water.

The Dunlops were finally freed of their heaving misery when they reached England, but followed up seasickness by embarking on

The Whitby Dunlops defeated the Soviets to win the 1958 IIHF world championship. Here, they are pictured winning the Allan Cup. Dunlops' defenceman Harry Sinden would take the lessons learned into the 1972 Summit Series as Team Canada's coach.

a fourteen-game exhibition tour. Once the IIHF championship began, the Dunlops crushed the opposition, outscoring their opponents 78–4 (including a 24–0 embarrassment of Finland) to take six wins and no losses into the final against the Soviets. The USSR had five wins, and one tie—having played to a 4–4 draw against Czechoslovakia, a team that Canada had handled easily, winning 6–0.

The Dunlops were captained by another future Bruins great in Harry Sinden, who was having his first exposure to international play against the Soviets (something which would serve him well as head coach of Team Canada in the epic 1972 Summit Series). The tension before the game in Oslo's outdoor Jordal Amfi rink, where Norway's King Olav V had shown up to watch the battle, was as "clear and sharp as the chill of the Norwegian winter breeze." Or as dangerously frigid as the Cold War. Only a few months earlier, Soviet leader Nikita Khrushchev had boasted of Russian missile superiority and challenged the United States to a "shootout" to prove it. The US Strategic Air Command was already on 24-hour alert in case of a surprise Soviet nuclear attack, and the general feeling was that the world was teetering on the edge of doom. The geopolitical climate only intensified pre-game jitters for the Dunlops, with some of the younger team members being so nervous "that they broke down and cried in the dressing room, just before the start of the game, caught up in the grip of tremendous tension."

Tension reigned back in Canada as well. Would the Dunlops, who had not yet played a tough game in the tournament, be ready to take on a Soviet squad that now bore the reputation of Soviet teams for the next generation: disciplined, skilled, opportunistic, and resilient? The Dunlops had played the Moscow Selects in Maple Leaf Gardens late in 1957 and beaten them 7–2. Their player-coach was Sid Smith, who won three Stanley Cups with the Toronto Maple Leafs, the Lady Byng Trophy twice, and had been an NHL All-Star left winger three times. Leading scorer Connie Broden had won the Cup the season before, with the Montreal Canadiens. They knew what pressure was.

Foster Hewitt had called Smith's Cup-winning games, and once again he brought his game voice across the Atlantic to the gold-medal match, broadcasting the Dunlops' triumph to a huge audience back home.

But with only five minutes left to play, the triumph was very much in doubt, with the score tied 2–2. Harry Sinden had hit the post in the first—with forward Jack McKenzie, a schoolteacher in civilian life, heatedly arguing, to no avail, that the puck had crossed the line—but after the Soviets went up 1–0, Canada's record-setting centre Bob Attersley tied the game, then Connie Broden put the Canadians ahead in the third. Konstantin Loktev tied it for the USSR and gave "renewed hope to the Russians who by this time were sagging from the relentless power of the Canucks."

Coach Wren Blair needed his star players to do more. Trading on the knowledge that Bob Attersley was a devout conservative who was planning a political career, Blair tried to squeeze a little more out of Attersley by playing on the "capitalism versus communism" theme of the game. Given his play so far, Blair barked, he doubted the sincerity of Attersley's conservative political convictions. An infuriated Attersley hopped over the boards—only to watch the Soviet forward Veniamin Alexandrov break in and deke the Dunlops goalie Roy Edwards to the ice. But he rang the puck off the crossbar. Attersley scooped up the puck, and raced down the ice to score the winning goal. He then set up the insurance goal less than thirty seconds later.

Despite the aura of Cold War politics around the match, the post-game awards ceremony was full of ecumenical respect, with Harry Sinden winning a roar of approval from the crowd when he reached down from the champion's pedestal to embrace the Soviet captain Nikolai Sologubov. "For this moment they were not Russians and Canadians. They were superb hockey players who had tested each other severely and not found each other wanting ... Canada had won the game, but no one had been disgraced."

Even so, Soviet coach Anatoli Tarasov clearly had his sights set on the future, and on the tilting of the ice. "We have progressed to the stage where we can challenge Canada with a chance to win." Later that summer, Wren Blair would warn the CAHA that unless they applied a more comprehensive strategy to the national team, the Soviets would be having more than just a chance to win. Soon, the country would see how true that was.

THE KELOWNA PACKERS GO BEHIND THE IRON CURTAIN

Kelowna Packers line up on the ice in Russia in 1958 with the stands full of fans.

In November 1958, another plucky team from the Okanagan Valley of British Columbia made hockey history, when the Canadian Amateur Hockey Association sent the Kelowna Packers through the Iron Curtain to become the very first Canadian hockey team to play inside the Soviet Union.

The Packers were Okanagan Senior Hockey League champs and had fought the Belleville McFarlands to the seventh game of the Allan Cup final, despite Kelowna being without five of their best players. When the CAHA chose the valiant losers to once again represent Canada against the perfidious Soviets, the Cassandras of Ontario were loud in their despair. "All Canada [knows] we aren't sending our best team," said Whitby Dunlops coach Wren Blair. Foster Hewitt, the voice of the hockey nation, dismissed the Packers' chances of winning a game in Russia as "fearful."

The Soviet Union itself was a scary place. Upon landing in Moscow, the Kelowna team's plane was filled with soldiers. Soviet law could "reclaim" any offspring of Russian nationals, regardless of their current citizenship, a "law" which was news to the Packers. Players Greg Jablonski and Russ Kowalchuk—of Ukrainian parentage, who spoke good Russian—had their Canadian passports confiscated, and played the entire series fearing they would never see Canada again.

The Canadian embassy told the Packers their hotel rooms were bugged; they were tailed by KGB agents; and they couldn't fraternize with the locals. Canada had boycotted the 1957 world championship in Moscow after the brutal Soviet invasion of Hungary in November 1956, but the locals were glad that the Canadians were back: the five-game series had been sold out for weeks.

The first two games were played at the brand new 15,000-seat Lenin Sports Palace, while the last three were played in a 60,000-seat soccer stadium—outdoors. Soviet coach Anatoli Tarasov, already a devoted student of Lloyd Percival's *The Hockey Handbook*, was keen to learn from the Packers' boss Jack O'Reilly, and the duo kept their interpreters talking hockey. The Soviets even filmed the Canadian practices, and players suspected that the Soviets had higher ambitions than beating a senior hockey team from the far west of North America.

The Packers opened the tour against the Central Sports Club army team, and in a fast-paced game lost 4–3 to the smaller, speedier Soviets. The second game against the Soviet Wings was a 1–1 battle, featuring a standout performance from the Packers' goalie Dave Gatherum, despite almost being knocked unconscious by a puck to the head. "Gatherum was the star of the game and the favourite of the crowd, as he came up with one spectacular save after another," reported the Canadian Press.

Moscow Dynamo tied the Canadians 2–2 in Game 3 with the help of some familiar "reinforcements": Soviet players whom the Packers had already seen in the first two games. Game 4 saw the Packers take on the "Youths of the Soviet" team, which had some ringers on the wrong side of 30. Even so, the Russians were fit and fast, but played their game "as if it was all designed on a blackboard," forward Mike Durban recalled. "But when we knocked one of their guys down, the whole thing fell apart."

Goalie Dave Gatherum once again saved the day. "The fans shouted themselves hoarse during the final minutes as the Russians threw attack after attack at the Packers. Gatherum turned in some spectacular saves to hold on to the win."

Now, with their 4–3 victory, two ties and one loss, the Packers had the same record as the Soviet teams did. Their fifth and final game against the Moscow Selects, the best team in the Soviet Union, would decide the championship. The Packers saved their best for last and nearly shut out the Soviets, until the Selects managed their only goal with less than four minutes left in the game to make the final score 5–1 for the Packers.

"The crowd was all for the Packers when the final buzzer sounded," reported *The Globe and Mail.* "They cheered and applauded wildly. The Canadians tossed their sticks to the fans."

Packers coach Jack O'Reilly, who had lambasted the CAHA for lack of player support before setting out on the historic voyage, was more than forgiving in victory. "Old Canada's still the land of the hockey players," he said.

Anatoli Tarasov agreed, expressing a wish that Canada would make the USSR a regular hockey destination. "It will be well if our games with the Canadians become traditional" he said. "We shall always be happy to receive the Canadians, the great masters of ice hockey, here in Moscow."

The Canadians would be back, though having forgotten the lesson the Packers learned: the Soviets could play hockey at the highest level. And they wouldn't be satisfied until they had beaten Canada at its own game.

28

THE BELLEVILLE McFARLANDS' GOLDEN GOALS

The Belleville McFarlands had won their chance to represent Canada at the 1959 World Hockey Championship by pulling off a miraculous comeback in the 1958 Allan Cup final against the Kelowna Packers. After taking the first game of the seven-game series, the McFarlands lost the next three, before rallying to win three straight.

The team's unusual name came from the nature of small-town, small-money senior hockey at the time. When wealthy Belleville construction boss Harvey McFarland gave the team $3,000, he also gave them his name. He would give them more cash as they went forth to defend the hockey honour of the nation, but first the team needed something more basic: players.

One of the truths of senior amateur hockey at the time—an especially contentious one at the Olympic Games—was that players were paid, and many of them had already enjoyed professional careers. While the Soviet "amateurs" were employed by the military, and spent their working days training for and playing hockey, the senior Canadian players held down jobs, despite earning a few bucks playing hockey. Even NHL stars like Toronto's Tim Horton worked in the off-season; he drove a gravel truck for Leafs owner Conn Smythe's gravel business.

The Belleville McFarlands, named after a construction company, were bolstered by ex-NHL talent and coached by fired Maple Leafs bench boss Billy Reay. Even so, they only won the 1959 IIHF world championship on goal differential.

Before the McFarlands set off to the world championship in Czechoslovakia, Billy Reay, the fired coach of the Toronto Maple Leafs whom Harvey McFarland had hired to help manage the club, set about "strengthening" the team. As a result, the McFarlands travelled to Europe with a lineup featuring many NHL veterans, as well as minor pros. Player-coach Ike Hildebrand, a right winger, had played with the Chicago Black Hawks; goalie Gordie Bell had played for the Maple Leafs; defenceman Jean Lamirande had played for the New York Rangers and Montreal Canadiens; centre Barton Bradley had played a game with the Boston Bruins; and bruising D-man Al Dewsbury had nine NHL seasons on his resumé, two with Detroit and seven with Chicago. Most of the rest of the team had played minor- or semi-pro, with a couple of amateurs: George Gosselin, a winger added to the squad, and Red Berenson, a future NHLer who was then a junior at the University of Michigan.

Once again, the Canadians' physical play collided with European reality. During a 3–1 exhibition victory against the Finns, Al Dewsbury punched the referee (which many a Canadian player has wanted to do in Europe) and was tossed from the game. George Gosselin got into a fight with officials in the penalty box, which turned into a melee when other McFarlands joined in. "'GO HOME CANADA' FINNS TELL MACS" was a headline in the *Toronto Star*. When they beat the Finns again 6–0 in Czechoslovakia, the crowd threw ice balls at the Canadians.

Enter J.F. "Bunny" Ahearne, president of the IIHF. Ahearne, considered an enemy of the state by Canadian hockey players and management, saw that developing the game internationally meant giving teams other than Canada—and now the USSR—a smidgen of hope. While this translated to persecution of those wearing the maple leaf, Ahearne was unapologetic about his strategy, and as a result, the 1959 world championship saw the twelve competing nations divided into three groups for round-robin play, spread over three Czech cities.

Canada knocked off Poland 9–0 in Bratislava, then the Swiss 23–0, and then the host Czechs 7–2. The score, however, flattered the Canadians, as they had outshot the Czechs only 37–31. It had not been the romp that it seemed on paper.

The McFarlands, with the maple leaf on the front of their sweaters and the construction magnate's name on the back, knocked off the Finns and then met the Soviets before 15,000 fans—and it was the same Soviet team that had played the Whitby Dunlops the year before. The Soviets had a national team, but the Canadians were still rolling the hockey dice. Even so, after the McFarlands, with tight defence and friendly goalposts, beat the Soviets 3–1, it seemed as though they would finish the tournament undefeated, having previously beaten the opponent they would meet last, the Czechs.

The McFarlands had been on the road for two months, and had played some tough hockey. The Czechs were playing at home, and they took a 2–0 lead; the Canadians never caught up, taking penalties and losing 5–3 after the Czechs scored an empty-net goal with Gordie Bell on the bench.

"The Czechs played as if they had invented the game, which everyone knows was invented by the Russians," wrote George Bain in *The Globe and Mail*, tongue planted firmly in cheek, "and the Canadians played with more desperation than inspiration. They had a bad day."

It was still good enough to win Canada the world championship on goal totals, but two of the McFarlands, the student Red Berenson and the veteran Al Dewsbury, didn't stick around to sing "O Canada" at the trophy ceremony, instead skating to the team's dressing room close to tears. It was symbolic of both the old order, and the new, for Canadians expected to win games, not goal totals. Despite being world champions for the eighteenth time, there were those in Canada who knew the country had to respond to the new world hockey order or face an unthinkable period of hearing other nations' national anthems at the end of tournaments.

THE 1960
OLYMPICS

In May 1959, as a result of the Belleville McFarlands' loss to the Czechs in the final game of the world championship, the Canadian Amateur Hockey Association was galvanized into rethinking its strategy for the upcoming 1960 Olympic Winter Games in Squaw Valley, California.

The problem with the Olympic Games was that the Canadian teams could not use former pros in their lineups. The CAHA's solution to this was to rule that any Canadian team representing the country internationally could draft fifteen additional players from across the country, to be cut down to ten before the team set out for the world championship or the Olympics. While this meant that teams tapped for international play didn't have to scramble to bolster their lineups at the last minute, it wasn't quite a national team. But it was a step toward forming one.

When the 1959 Allan Cup champion Whitby Dunlops said thanks but no thanks to an invitation to pay the bulk of their own way to play hockey in Squaw Valley, the Kitchener-Waterloo Dutchmen became Canada's contestant for the country's seventh Olympic hockey gold medal, having managed only a bronze medal while attempting the same at the 1956 Winter Games in Cortina, Italy.

Along the way, the Dutchies would encounter the man who would become the face of Canada's national hockey program. But when the Dutchies met Father David Bauer, he was not only the brother of their coach, Bobby, but also the coach at St. Michael's College in Toronto. He told them he'd loan them his player Dave Keon for only three prep games,

In 1947, Bobby Bauer joined the Kitchener-Waterloo Dutchmen, a senior Ontario Hockey Association team, after his stellar NHL career. He went on to coach the team when they wore the national colours.

plus two weeks for the Olympic Games. Wren Blair, managing players for Canada, didn't think it was fair to give Keon, no matter how good he was, special treatment, so instead the Dutchies wrangled Bobby Rousseau from the Montreal Canadiens' farm team.

The Kitchener-Waterloo team also tapped the Toronto Maple Leafs, getting $2,000 from Conn Smythe for expenses, another $1,000 from Montreal, and raising another $12,000 selling raffle tickets for a car. The spirit of seat-of-the-pants planning carried over to Squaw Valley, where the spartan living conditions were more suited to a penal colony; the indoor ice was hijacked by figure skating; the outdoor ice was melting due to warm California weather; and the schedule was punitive: eight games in ten days.

Even Bunny Ahearne was aghast, as befitting an IIHF president, who wanted to achieve a balance of excellence in the world of international hockey but didn't think you could do it playing "on that slush." After intense meetings with the IOC, the schedule was changed, the bulk of games moved indoors, and Canada thrashed the Swedes 5–2 in their opening match, literally, breaking ribs by boarding one player, fighting with others, and cutting the goalie on a deflected puck. The Swedes protested the Canadians' rough play to the IOC, and, in the oft-maligned Ahearne's defence, he came to Canada's aid: "It was a matter of judgment by the referees, and you cannot change an official's call on a play. Too much has been made of the incident already."

The Dutchies then beat Japan 19–1, Germany 12–0, the Czechs 4–0, and then they met the USA. The first period saw the States outshoot Canada 15–8, with the US goalie Jack McCartan making two point-blank stops on the Canadians. The USA scored a power-play goal midway through the first, and the Dutchies poured it on in the second, firing twenty shots at McCartan. None of them went in the net, but the US scored another goal on six shots. Canada finally broke the US shutout with less than seven minutes left on a goal by Jim Connelly.

"I thought that was it," said US coach Jack Riley. "Sometimes when a team has been playing as hard as the Canadians, a goal will suddenly relax them and they'll pour in more."

But they did not. The United States had defeated Canada. The country's gold-medal hope was not lost but dependent on the Czechs beating the USA and the Canadians defeating the Soviets. The Czechs made a game of it, scoring eight seconds into the match, and taking a 4–3 lead into the third period. During the intermission, Scott Young, reporting for *The Globe and Mail*, left the press box to see what was happening below decks. He wound up in the US dressing room, astonished to see the American players taking hits from an oxygen tank, all the while being exhorted to win by Nikolai Sologubov, the Soviet captain. The Soviets knew that if the US could beat the Czechs, and they could beat Canada, then the silver medal could be theirs.

The US came out flying in the third and scored six goals, to vanquish the astonished Czechs 9–4. But the Soviets could not beat the Kitchener-Waterloo Dutchmen, who were up 4–0 in the second before they took a pause, let the Soviets back in the game with three goals, and then scored another four to beat the Soviets 8–5. The USA took gold in what has become known as the Forgotten Miracle, Canada took silver, and the USSR won bronze.

Even so, the response back in Canada to the Kitchener-Waterloo silver medal was cruel. Kingston alderman George Webb sent a telegram to coach Bobby Bauer that said, "From the birthplace of hockey I'm going to call for an official day of mourning, and ask that our flag be hung at half mast. Congratulations for nothing."

A few weeks later, Wren Blair chaired a panel on what Canada could do to improve its international hockey chances, and it was another of Bobby Bauer's brothers, Ray, who shone a light into the near future. "The Russians didn't have to raffle cars to raise the money to come [to the Olympics].... This should be a national thing, not something loaded just onto one small city." Very soon it would be. But not yet.

THE TRAIL SMOKE EATERS OF 1961 AND THE END OF AN ERA

Canada was looking to reclaim gold at the world championship in Switzerland in 1961 and once again the CAHA had to scramble to find a team to represent the country, as the Allan Cup champion Chatham Maroons had declined to disrupt their season by accepting the invitation to play a Christmas tournament in Moscow. So the team they beat, the Trail Smoke Eaters, said yes, and once again took up the torch for Canada.

The Smokies had success at the world championships before, also in Switzerland, winning the gold in 1939 before 19,000 fans in Zurich. But the fact they were going again at all was due to a hockey strategy endorsing the belief that a team playing together all season could beat tuned-up national teams composed of their country's best players. That, and national pride.

"The whole financial aspect for that trip was so damned bad that anybody in their right mind wouldn't have touched it with a 10-foot pole," recalled team manager Ugo DeBiasio. "But we were so anxious to go, we just ignored that factor."

Eight of the Smoke Eaters had begun their hockey careers together as peewees, and that sense of kinship compelled them to take out personal loans to top up the money kicked in by the town's major employer, the Consolidated Mining and Smelting Company of Canada, which would

The Trail Smoke Eaters' brand of hockey—skilled, speedy, and smart—became the model that the USSR used to develop its own program of excellence.

pay the players' families a weekly stipend while they were on the road, and by the CAHA, which would cover road expenses. The Smoke Eaters, in between staging raffles, wrote to all six NHL teams asking for help, but only the Montreal Canadiens, and their owners, the Molson family, replied. The brewery kicked in $1,000, and the hockey team supplied some equipment. Once again, Canada's international hockey representatives for the country's national sport were begging and borrowing for the honour of representing their country.

The Smoke Eaters went on an eighteen-game, five-week barnstorming road tour of Europe, which ended with a win in Cortina, Italy. Their Family von Trapp–like dash to the bus after the game was over, leaving fuming Italian officials with no Canadians to give gifts to because the Smokies were trying to set a land-speed record to catch the 4:00 A.M. train from Innsbruck to Switzerland, in order to have a 24-hour rest before their first world championship game.

They arrived at the championship with the Canadian reputation for butchery preceding them, after thrashing the Swedes en route, and the IIHF referees had all been warned to keep an eye on the boys from Trail. With goalie Seth Martin showing the all-star form that would see him inducted into the IIHF Hall of Fame, the Smoke Eaters rose above the machinations of the referees to beat the Swedes 6–1, the West Germans 9–1, the Americans 7–4, the East Germans 5–2, and the Finns 12–1.

It was the Czechs who gave them trouble, and with no small irony. The Czechs had become such fine hockey players because they had been taught "Canadian hockey" by Mike Buckna, a Trail Smoke Eater who returned to the land of his Slovak parents for a visit and wound up coaching the national team. The Trail Smoke Eaters were playing a Czech Smoke Eaters team, but once the Czechs got the 1–0 lead at the end of the first period, they played kitty-bar-the-door defence, lining up at their own blue line and fending off the Canadian attack. When they forced a turnover, they would break out.

It was on one of their breaks that Canada's Jackie McLeod, a former New York Ranger and the top point scorer in the tournament, broke up the play and passed the puck to Hugh McIntyre, known to all in Trail as "Pinoke" due to his 143-pound self, and a nose worthy of Pinocchio. Pinoke broke into the clear, and fired a shot under the arm of the Czech goalie.

The Czechs were happy to play for a tie, as it would mean that they and Canada had identical records, but the Czechs had a better goals-for-and-against record, and they were sure the Soviets would beat or tie the Canadians in three days' time. They nearly won the game when a Czech player lobbed the puck toward the Canadian goal, and it took one of those mad pinball bounces, pinging off both of Seth Martin's skates and the goalpost before bouncing out of danger. The game ended in a 1–1 tie, and now Canada had to beat the Soviets. They didn't know yet how many goals they needed, so they resolved to score as many as they could.

The Soviets came out hard, testing Martin in wave after wave, while his teammates did something that would soon become all too familiar to Canadian hockey fans when it came to meeting the Russian onslaught: they took penalties under the pressure. Finally, at nine minutes into the game, Jackie McLeod passed to defenceman Harry Smith, who found himself in the clear, ten feet in front of the Soviet net, and he "whipped [the puck] past the startled Russian goalie Vladimir Tchinov." Once Canada had scored, they relaxed, then McLeod added another goal, and then Canada scored again to take a 3–0 lead.

In the first minute of the third period, the Soviet goalie robbed Canadian Hal Jones close in, but Jackie McLeod scooped up the rebound and popped it in the net. The Soviets finally put one past Seth Martin midway through the third, and the Canadians worried that their goal differential might not be good enough to claim the gold. So rather than sit on their lead, they attacked, and with two minutes to play, Norm Lenardon stole the puck off Soviet captain Sologubov in the Soviet end, lost it, got it back, and while falling to the ice shot it over the shoulder of Tchinov to make it 5–1.

For the rest of the game, the Canadians owned the puck, and they played the last thirty seconds of the game in the Soviet end, while back in Canada's goal, the heroic Seth Martin swung his goal stick over his head like he was a helicopter about to take off. He was soon swigging from a bottle of rye that a jubilant Canadian soldier, one of the many in the crowd of 12,500, had hopped over the boards to give him.

The Smokies' coach, Bobby Kromm, threw his red Hudson's Bay team jacket into the air, and whooped in relief. Kromm had been player-coach until he benched himself to concentrate on the medal round. He had worked the team so hard and mercilessly that his neck veins bulged as he harangued them on their failures, and he had alienated some in his pursuit of this moment. "I felt as if the Royal York Hotel had been lifted off my shoulders," he said, now that Canada had won its nineteenth world title, even if on goal differential.

The next day, the hungover Smokies went to Paris to decompress for a day, and then they went onward to the Canadian Army base at Soest, West Germany, for one more match. The exhausted Smokies played an exhibition game against a Canadian Army team in a packed arena, but when they learned that children living on the base couldn't get into the game, they played another one the next morning, just for the kids. Then they made the long journey back to Trail, blissfully unaware of their bittersweet place in hockey history: the last Canadian amateur team to win a world championship.

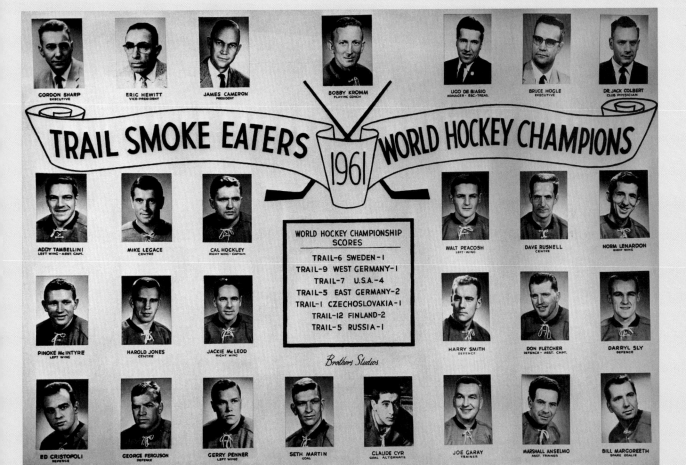

Led by the heroics of goalie Seth Martin, the Trail Smoke Eaters defeated the Soviets to win the 1961 world championship—the last Canadian amateur team to win that title.

THE HOCKEY HALL OF FAME IS BORN

On August 26, 1961, Canada launched a new museum, one celebrating an exuberant and vital national culture that was not yet a century old, but had captured the imagination of Canadians and of the world. The Hockey Hall of Fame opened its glass doors in a white stuccoed building perched on Toronto's Canadian National Exhibition grounds, a building whose $500,000 cost was paid for by the six NHL teams. Prime Minister John Diefenbaker promised another $5 million in annual grants to Canadian amateur athletics when he declared the Hall of Fame open, and thousands of CNE visitors gathered to view Canada's newest monument to itself.

Of course, this being hockey and Canada, there had first been a fight. In January 1961, reports surfaced that the Canadian Amateur Hockey Association was preparing to seek a court injunction to prevent Kingston, Ontario, from building a Hockey Hall of Fame, and to divulge what had happened to the $40,000 that various groups, including the CAHA and the NHL, had contributed to the Kingston venture.

In 1943, largely due to the efforts of James T. Sutherland, a Kingston hockey man who, among other things, was the prime mover behind the Memorial Cup, the CAHA and the NHL decided to create a Hockey Hall of Fame in Kingston, which Sutherland and others had worked to promote as hockey's birthplace. Baseball had created its Hall of Fame in Cooperstown, New York, in 1939, and hockey had more than enough outstanding players, coaches, and builders to do the same.

On August 26, 1961, Canada celebrated its national sport with a proper museum when the Hockey Hall of Fame opened in Toronto.

In 1945, the first class of members were inducted, with Sir Montagu Allan and Lord Stanley among the honoured. Two years later, Sutherland was inducted, but still there was no actual Hall for the honoured members. In 1955, Sutherland died without realizing his vision of a hockey pantheon, and in 1958, NHL president Clarence Campbell cancelled the Kingston plan and relocated the project to Toronto, though Kingston would open an International Hockey Hall of Fame in 1965.

Toronto Maple Leafs founder Conn Smythe took command, and wrangled land out of the City of Toronto and money out of his fellow NHL owners to begin—and supervise—construction on the shrine to Canadian and American hockey luminaries.

At the opening ceremony, also attended by the US ambassador, Prime Minister Diefenbaker said, "There is nothing greater than hockey to bring about national unity and a closer relationship between the United States and Canada," a noble sentiment that was even truer when Canada was winning.

The CAHA would be responsible for all the exhibits related to amateur hockey, as well as for trophies under CAHA jurisdiction, and international competition—making an organization less than fifty years old a steward of a national museum no less important to the culture of Canada than the National Gallery in Ottawa.

In the spirit of belonging to the nation, the Hall of Fame was open every day of the year from 2:00 to 4:00 P.M., and assured the public that "at no time will admission be charged." Hours were extended on special occasions, such as Grey Cup Day from 10:00 A.M. to 5:00 P.M., so that people could celebrate the country's two great sporting cultures in tandem.

Toronto Maple Leafs founder, Conn Smythe (first on left), listens to Canadian Prime Minister John Diefenbaker open Canada's newest national museum, the Hockey Hall of Fame.

THE DIVINE VISION OF DAVID BAUER

The March 1962 World Hockey Championship in Colorado was notable for several firsts. It was the first time the IIHF had staged its annual tournament outside of Europe. That provided reason for the Soviets, and their Communist colony Czechoslovakia, to stay home as retaliation for the Canadian and US boycott of the 1957 tournament in Moscow. The Australian team won its first-ever international hockey match by defeating Denmark 6–2. And Canada, represented as was often the case by the previous year's Allan Cup winners, saw easy pickings without the USSR and the Czechs there to make things difficult. But when the Galt Terriers lost 4–2 to the Swedes for the first time in world and Olympic hockey history—and finished with a silver—the shock waves finally landed back home.

Indeed, it was as if the Canadian Amateur Hockey Association had experienced a religious awakening, and no small reason for that was because of Father David Bauer. As one of eleven children, the 10-year-old David Bauer saw his older brother Bobby winning the 1934 Memorial Cup with the Majors of St. Michael's College School in Toronto, and then starring as right wing of the Kraut Line for the Boston Bruins in the 1930s and '40s. It was David, though, who lit up the ice even more than his Hall of Famer brother Bobby, turning down an offer at age 16 from the Boston

Father David Bauer coached the St. Michael's Majors to the 1961 Memorial Cup title. It was Bauer's third Memorial Cup, the previous two wins having come as a player.

Bruins farm team so that he, too, could go to St. Mike's and get an education, as strongly advised by his father, Sir Edgar Bauer, an automotive supplies manufacturer, and Knight Commander of St. Sylvester, thanks to Pope Pius XII, for his services to Rome.

Young David also played hockey at St. Mike's, becoming team captain in 1942, and leading them into the Memorial Cup playoffs the following season. Despite the talented winger's seven goals and five assists in twelve games, the Oshawa Generals prevailed. However, Bauer had so impressed the Generals that they selected him—and his teammates and future NHLers Ted Lindsay and Gus Mortson—to join their club on loan for its Memorial Cup final against Trail. Bauer scored four goals and added five assists over the seven-game series, and won his first Memorial Cup.

He would win his second as a member of St. Mike's in 1945, but he played only one game for the Majors that season, instead doing his military service as a hockey player. And then, instead of taking up a professional career of fame and fortune that certainly would have been his, Bauer decided to become a Catholic priest. And it was as a priest that he would win his third Memorial Cup in 1961 as coach of the St. Michael's Majors team for which he had once starred.

In June 1962, Gordon Juckes, now the secretary-manager of the Canadian Amateur Hockey Association, and its president, Art Potter, were about to fly to a meeting in Montreal when they received a phone call from Father Bauer, asking to meet them en route in Toronto. He had an idea.

Juckes, who would become a powerful force for good in Canadian hockey, had been a major in the Canadian Army during World War II, and had returned to Melville, Saskatchewan, after the war, where he became involved in intermediate hockey, and published a weekly newspaper. He had written a report for the CAHA after Canada's 1960 Olympic hockey travails, arguing that the country needed more coherence and continuity in its international hockey representatives. He knew who David Bauer was, and so did Art Potter. They would listen to whatever he had to say.

When the duo met Bauer in an airport hotel, he told them he was about to take up a teaching post at St. Mark's College, at the University of British Columbia. He wanted to know what the CAHA executives thought about creating a national team of scholar-athletes, playing together at UBC in preparation for the 1964 Olympics.

"One way or another," recalled Juckes, "we'd all wished somehow we could attract some of the best juniors to stay amateur and let us build up an Olympic team over a whole season, instead of trying to put it together at the last minute as we'd been doing in the past."

Juckes and Potter invited Father Bauer to come to the CAHA meeting in Montreal and make his pitch. Father Bauer told the delegates about his vision, and tapped them for some cash: he'd need money for room, board, and tuition, as he'd be going after the same crop of talented juniors that the NHL was wooing with $12,000 salaries. Using the same kind of persuasion he had used on Juckes and Potter—part priest, part athlete, part unyielding visionary—Bauer left the meeting victorious. And Canada now had the beginning of its first-ever national hockey team.

CANADA'S NATIONAL HOCKEY TEAM

Eight of them lived on the UBC campus in double-bunked rooms in a two-storey house as the term began in September 1963—with the rest camping in a glass-fronted cabin next door. And they all shared a single bathroom and the cooking sorcery of the ox-strong, 70-plus Ma Byers, but Canada finally had a national hockey team.

"We got along amazingly well," recalled centre Roger Bourbonnais, who had won the Memorial Cup with the Edmonton Oil Kings (and teammates Pat Quinn and Glenn Sather). "The fact that we were all in it together did a lot for team spirit, too—everybody was equal, at the bathroom door, the kitchen table with Mrs. Byers, or anywhere else."

Father Bauer, missionary hockey priest, had used his pedigree as a hockey coach and his powers as both orator and confessor to recruit twenty-two of the country's finest hockey prospects to his experiment on the Pacific Coast, the site of another visionary hockey experiment a half century earlier, when the Patrick Brothers built an artificial ice palace in Vancouver and started their own league.

In the morning, Father Bauer's nationals would attend class. In the late afternoon, they'd practise. The team was built for speed and skill, to compete with the European teams that Bauer had been studying for the better part of a decade. Even so, the Canadian players had to be untaught before they could learn. "The first few weeks of practice were really weeks just for conditioning and breaking down each boy from his previous system of play," recalled national team centre Brian Conacher, son of

Father David Bauer had a missionary-like vision to create Canada's first national hockey team, and thanks to his talent and persistence, he took the inaugural team to the 1964 Olympic Winter Games.

hockey legend Lionel, Canada's male athlete of the first half of the twentieth century. This deconstruction was done "so that Bauer could then rebuild each player into a key link in his team."

And from October to December, they'd play—as the UBC Thunderbirds—two or three games a week, leaving Thursday night or Friday morning, and not returning to campus until early the following week. The schedule meant players had to be ultra-disciplined to maintain their course load, and the team's travel bill over the vast spaces between town and wilderness in Western Canada meant they always needed more money.

After losing to a senior league hockey club in Regina, Father Bauer's crew were suspicious of an old guy, a cigarette dangling from his lips and guarded by a pack of tough-looking kids, who showed up in their dressing room. To the team's collective surprise, Father Bauer reverently introduced the grizzled smoker as Monsignor Athol Murray, the fabled hockey priest who founded the Hounds of Notre Dame in Wilcox, Saskatchewan. "So you're the Canadian bastards who are going to represent us in the Olympics," growled Pere Murray, unimpressed. "I hope you do better than you did tonight." Then he handed them a cheque for $1,000, a collection taken up by him and his Hounds.

The nationals—still identified as the Thunderbirds—played thirty-three exhibition games across the country in preparation for the 1964 Winter Games, trying to establish their bona fides as Canada's Olympic team. In Sudbury, in a game against the Czech national team they discovered that the fans in the arena—heavily Czech—were cheering more for the foreigners than for the Canadians. And as the nationals played the cleanest hockey many of them had ever known, to uphold Father Bauer's credo, "thou shalt not take penalties," the Czechs showed them their skills at spearing, slashing, spitting, and swearing. The nationals won the game 4–0, and at a banquet in their honour afterward, their host, a pillar of Sudbury's substantial Czechoslovakian-Canadian community, wished them all well, but hoped the Czechs would win gold.

The team found it a relief to escape Canada. After losing a couple of exhibition games in the USSR, the players arrived in Innsbruck, Austria, to test Father Bauer's hockey theory at the Olympic Games in Innsbruck, Austria. They easily dispatched the Swiss, 8–0, with the Trail Smoke Eaters' hero Seth Martin sharing the shutout with Ken Broderick. They beat the West Germans 4–2, the Finns 6–2, and managed a six-goal run in the second period to stage an 8–6 comeback win over the USA.

It was their game against Sweden, however, that saw a turn in Canada's hockey profile. For decades, the Canadians had been viewed as invading barbarians, whose physical play was interpreted by the Europeans as unabashed thuggery. During the Canadians' 3–1 victory, the Swedish forward Carl Oberg broke his stick late in the game, and out of frustration, hurled a piece of it toward the Canadian bench. The stick struck Father Bauer on the face and cut him. His outraged players wanted to leap over the boards and pummel Oberg into a Swedish meatball, but Bauer, bleeding, grabbed their sweaters and reminded them of their higher mission. Peace reigned, and when Oberg apologized to Bauer, he accepted and invited the Swede to sit with him and watch the USSR–Czechoslovakia game the next night. Oberg accepted, and the gesture won applause from the Swedish team and from around the world.

It was the only bit of grace left for the Canadians in the 1964 Olympics, as far as the IOC was concerned. Canada was leading the Czechs 1–0 in the third period when a rushing Czech player crashed into goaltender Seth Martin's leg. Martin was hurt, but he played a few minutes more and held the Czechs off the scoresheet. With seven minutes left, Martin was too sore to continue, so Ken Broderick came in to close out the game. The Czechs, desperate, and smelling new blood, attacked, scoring three goals in three minutes to win 3–1.

IIHF president Bunny Ahearne ruled that if Canada defeated its last opponent, the USSR, Canada would win gold, as both teams would then have identical 6–1 records. The nationals played brilliant hockey against the USSR for two periods, but then the thing that Father Bauer had tried to drill out of them crept back in, and when Brian Conacher took a retaliatory penalty, the Soviets scored on the momentum of their just-finished power play to tie the game 2–2.

Father David Bauer was blessed with both natural hockey talent and an ability to teach.

Bauer, in his Roman collar and maple-leaf-crested black priest's blazer, pulled Ken Broderick and started Seth Martin in goal for the third period. The Canadians had exhausted their arsenal in the first two periods, and while Martin performed his heroics in net, he couldn't stop them all. The USSR won the game 3–2.

The Canadians, based on their understanding of goal differential, were proud to have won bronze. The differential results would be counted from the top four teams only, and that meant the Swedes would take silver, the Soviets gold. During the Sweden–Czechoslovakia game on February 8, the IOC, led by Ahearne, decided that the goal differential for all games would now count.

No one told the Canadians, so when they showed up that night to stand on the podium and accept Olympic bronze in their inaugural outing as the national team, they were shocked to learn that they had been dropped to fourth, and the Czechs had taken bronze. Father Bauer was given a gold medal for good sportsmanship for restraining his team after the Swedish stick-throwing incident. As Gordon Juckes would later put it, "Father Dave was the only one who got a medal, and that was because he got hit on the head by a Swede."

It was a swindle that rankles Canadian team members to this day. Early in 2005, the International Ice Hockey Federation attempted to pass a motion that would have awarded Canada the bronze medal—but only for the world championship result—and then decided, no, they wouldn't change the results after all, as it set too dangerous a precedent. Canada appealed.

"We will do everything we can in Hockey Canada's power to get this medal for the players," Hockey Canada president Bob Nicholson said at the time, but in September 2005, the IIHF rejected Hockey Canada's appeal.

From 1964 to 1968, Father David Bauer led Canada's national team to two Olympic Games and four world championships.

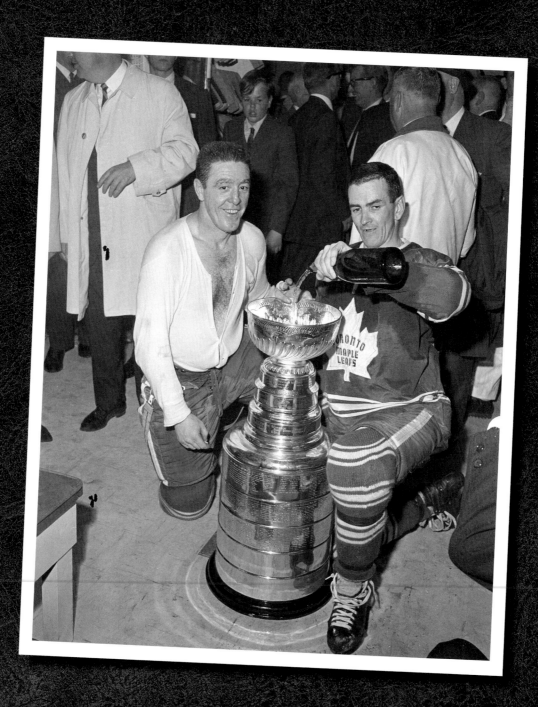

HOCKEY
IN CANADA'S
100TH BIRTHDAY

It was Canada's centennial year in 1967, and across the nation, people were creating centennial projects to give a gift to the country on its hundredth birthday. Montreal was hosting Expo 67, the exciting world's fair celebrating Man and His World, and everything seemed possible for the muscular—and still young—country, except perhaps an all-Canadian Stanley Cup final, such as the one just played between Montreal and the victorious Toronto Maple Leafs. The NHL was about to double in size from six to twelve teams, with all the new NHL clubs operating south of the Canada–US border. So when the Canadian Amateur Hockey Association held its annual meeting in Saskatoon in May, it decided to give a gift to itself: the organization needed to consolidate its vision of amateur hockey in Canada, and to begin by consolidating itself. For the first time in its history, the CAHA would have a national office, to be based in Winnipeg, which would help to focus the country's collective efforts to restore Canada's international hockey prestige.

The CAHA also streamlined the 1936 agreement between itself and the NHL—two groups who have often been in uneasy coexistence. Now, NHL clubs' professional sponsorship of amateur teams would be eliminated and no longer would NHL teams own the rights to amateurs playing under their auspices. An amateur draft would replace the NHL's junior draft, and professional tryouts and option forms were eliminated. The age of player power had dawned, and the CAHA rolled with the times

Corks popped across Canada in 1967 as the country celebrated its birthday, and the Toronto Maple Leafs celebrated a Stanley Cup victory. Here, Marcel Pronovost (left) and Dave Keon (right) toast the Toronto Maple Leafs Stanley Cup win over the Montreal Canadiens, May 2, 1967.

to try to protect those who played their game. And, by extension, to protect its own power.

There had been challenges to that power. The president of the Quebec Amateur Hockey Association said that some groups, under the influence of separatists, had broken away from his CAHA affiliate, protesting that both were English organizations that had no business setting rules for French groups.

The maverick Canadian Major Junior Hockey League was welcomed back into the fold after agreeing to drop its legal action against the CAHA for suspending it, though the CAHA did pass a motion to assert that the CAHA itself was the law and last resort for all amateur hockey, and that any member who launched legal action against it would be cut from the herd.

That got the attention of Alan Eagleson, then a rising player on the hockey stage. Eagleson, who would emerge that June as the executive director of the newly formed NHL Players' Association (NHLPA), pointed out that the CAHA received money from the federal government and could not place itself above the law, a concept that would eventually come to undo him at the pinnacle of his power. The CAHA had received $40,000 from the National Advisory Council on Fitness and Sport to be used for five coaching clinics in the summer of 1967, open to 13,895 member teams and their 230,000 players.

And while the CAHA was moving to Winnipeg, Father Bauer's national team was already there, having relocated to the University of Manitoba after the travel expenses of their UBC headquarters proved to be too costly. In January, the country hosted the Centennial Tournament, and on January 6, the Feast of the Epiphany for Father Bauer and other Christians, the Canadians smote the Soviets 5–4 in a nationally televised game, and went on to win the tournament with a perfect 3–0 record, having also defeated the Czechs and the USA. Perhaps now the true epiphany would come: international gold for Father Bauer's hockey mission.

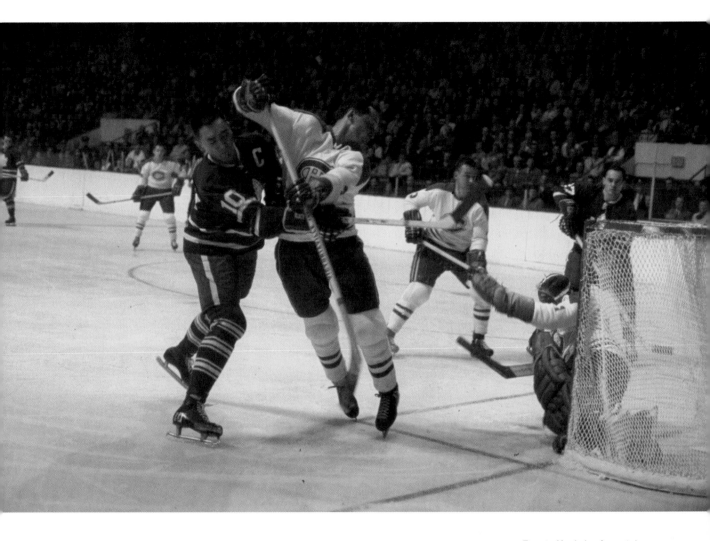

Toronto Maple Leafs captain
George Armstrong (left)
collides with Montreal's
Jacques Laperrière (right).

THE BIRTH OF HOCKEY CANADA

In June 1968, Pierre Trudeau, the wealthy playboy law professor who had risen from serving as justice minister under Lester Pearson to become Canada's prime minister in April after winning the Liberal leadership contest, was campaigning in British Columbia for a federal election that he had called. Though Trudeau had grown up in Montreal during some of the Canadiens' most glorious days of *Les Glorieux*, hockey was not one of his sporting passions. Nevertheless, he had followed the disappointing fortunes of Father Bauer's national team, and he certainly had his finger on the restless pulse of the nation. "Hockey is considered our national sport," he said in a campaign speech on June 3 at Selkirk College, in Castlegar, "and yet, in the world championships, we have not been able, as amateurs, to perform as well as we know we can." Trudeau promised that if he was given a new mandate, he would create a task force on sport and give it the power to change Canada's amateur sporting culture in the pursuit of excellence.

Trudeau's use of the word "amateurs" caught the attention of everyone, especially the executives of the Canadian Amateur Hockey Association. It was no secret that Canadians wanted the country's best to play the world's best, and that meant a total rethink of Canada's hockey strategy. Indeed, since Father Bauer's team of scholar-athletes had been representing Canada at the world championships and Olympics since 1964, Canada had failed to win a single gold medal. The USSR had won five golds, and the Czechs and the Swedes had shared the silver position. Canada had won three bronze (and had been hornswoggled out of another bronze medal in 1964 by Bunny Ahearne).

Charles Hay, a Canadian industrialist with a love of hockey and a son, Bill, who was an NHL star, was a driving force in the founding of Hockey Canada.

On December 10, 1968, Canadian industrialists Charles Hay, Max Bell, and Ian Sinclair attended a meeting in Ottawa that was just as significant as the one fifty-four years earlier that created the Canadian Amateur Hockey Association. Hay, who had played goal for the Saskatchewan Huskies and led them to the 1921 Allan Cup final, was a successful oil industry executive with a lifelong devotion to hockey, and he was about to retire as chair of Gulf Canada. His son Bill had won a Stanley Cup with the Chicago Black Hawks, and Hay, as one of the top hockey minds and supporters in the country, was called to this meeting to help create the next chapter in Canada's national sport. Max Bell had played two seasons of senior hockey for the Kimberley Dynamiters while unsuccessfully prospecting for gold in the Kootenays in the 1930s. By 1965, he owned a media empire, thoroughbred horses, and was the single largest shareholder in Canadian Pacific Railway. Ian Sinclair, the third member of the industrial establishment, would become president and CEO of that same railway in 1969, and chair of its board three years later.

The presence of this high-powered trio—in addition to representatives from the CAHA, NHL Players' Association, and Canada's two NHL teams—was a clear signal that the federal government, while trumpeting the virtues of amateurism, was bringing in the professionals to handle the best way to create another revolutionary organization to bring Canada back to the top of the global hockey heap. It would be called Hockey Canada, with a mandate to manage "the national hockey teams of Canada" and to develop the sport across the nation to restore Canada's hockey supremacy, with Max Bell serving as Hockey Canada's first president.

The formation of Hockey Canada created an unexpected and not always welcome partnership with the CAHA, an organization that saw much of what it had built now suddenly under the auspices of a new body that had powerful ties to the NHL, and this would soon come to haunt. But still, Hockey Canada's mandate was to do even more of what the CAHA had done: train players and coaches, and research the sport to do even more. And yet, if this new hockey plan were to work, the two groups would have to pull together in the direction that everyone knew was necessary: finding a way to get Canada's best players on the same ice as the Russians, to see who truly was best at our game.

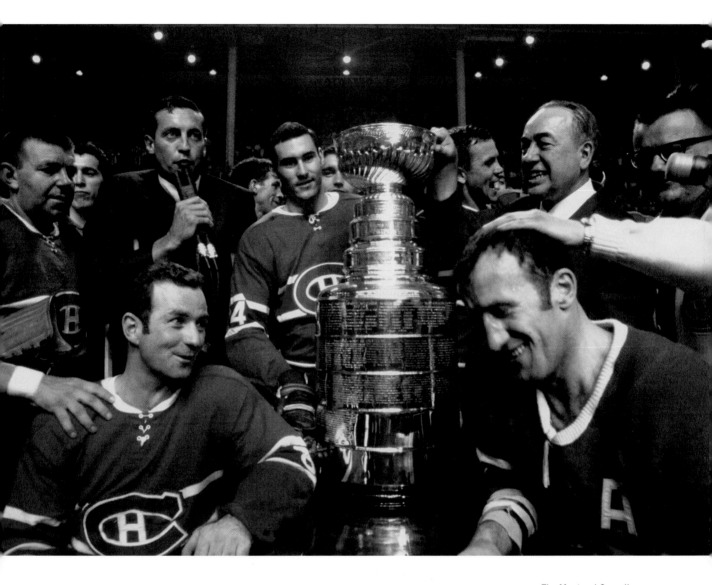

The Montreal Canadiens
won their fifteenth
Stanley Cup at the
Montreal Forum on
May 11, 1968, prompting
fellow Montrealer and
Canadian prime minister
Pierre Trudeau to make
the point that Canada
now needed to beat the
world at "our game."

THE END
OF THE
NATIONAL TEAM

Within three months of Hockey Canada's formation, Father Bauer's national team travelled to the world championship in Sweden in March 1969, secure in the knowledge that it now had money and the support of the federal government in its quest to re-establish Canada's hockey supremacy.

Father Bauer was that rare being: an idealist who also had a strong streak of realism running through his veins. Before the tournament began, he said, "If the Russians don't win, you'd have to call for an investigation." His team's coach, Jackie McLeod, who had lit up the world championship with the Trail Smoke Eaters in 1961, elaborated: "We played Russian teams seventeen times in Canada this year and won three. Their national team has beaten us eleven straight. You begin to get the message after a while."

The tournament was originally scheduled to take place in Czechoslovakia, but after the Soviets had invaded the country the previous spring, the Czechs were in no mood. So the Canadians would play their Pool A games in Stockholm. Of their ten games, the Canucks won only four—beating the USA and the Finns twice. In their first three games against hockey powers now considered superior to Canada, the USSR, Sweden, and Czechoslovakia outscored Canada 18–3. It was Canada's worst international hockey showing in its history.

In a 7–1 loss to the Soviets, Canada's worst since the Soviets drubbed

Cornell University graduate Ken Dryden debuts as a rookie goalie for Father David Bauer's national team in 1969.

Junior Hockey Hits Open Ice

In 1969, Canada's young hockey players finally saw the end of the NHL's tyrannical C-form, the signing of which tied underage junior players to an NHL club. To get perspective on the power of the C-form to an NHL club, and what it would mean to a lesser light, the Boston Bruins, desperate to get Bobby Orr's parents to sign off on it, promised a then-staggering $10,000 signing bonus, a new car, and they'd pay for a new stucco job on the family home.

The NHL's inaugural draft took place in 1963, and the only players eligible for the draft were those who had not signed a C-form. Montreal selected Gary Monahan with its first pick that year, and six years later, the last of the C-form players had "graduated" into adulthood. Future superstars such as Rejean Houle, Gilbert Perreault, and Guy Lafleur were "free" to be picked first by whoever had the first choice from 1969 onward. Canada's young amateur hockey players were finally free of a sponsorship system that, when it didn't work, was akin to indentured servitude.

In May 1970, at its annual meeting in St. John's, Newfoundland, the CAHA further advanced the welfare of junior hockey by dividing the country's players into two groups. The Canadian Hockey League would now consist of teams from the three major junior leagues—the Quebec, Ontario, and Western loops—which would compete in a round-robin tournament at season's end for the Memorial Cup. All other junior teams would be classified as Junior A and would compete for the Centennial Cup. The division was a function of hockey's growth and success in Canada, as well as a need to refine the hierarchy of excellence at a time when doing that very thing was much on the national hockey brain.

the team 8–0 in 1965, even the team's players were resigned to the fall in the country's hockey fortunes. "We do the best we can, but we are no match for them," said centre Fran Huck. Defenceman Jack Bownass added, "We were sent over here without the equipment, and expected to do the job." Bill Stephenson, covering the game for *The Globe and Mail*, felt compelled to pile on to the self-recrimination, adding, "The Canadians were so lacking in aggressiveness against the Russians in the third period that the Soviet team eased up, possibly out of compassion for an inferior opponent."

One bright spot for the Canadians was the play of their rookie goalie, fresh out of Cornell University, who shut out the USA 1–0. Ken Dryden would go on to become a Hockey Hall of Famer, but before that, he would be a big part in the story of Canada's hockey redemption. But first another story had to end, and the news was delivered to Father Bauer and his team after the tournament's closing ceremonies by none other than Alan Eagleson, the NHL Players' Association director, now on the executive of Hockey Canada.

The nationals could consider themselves such for as long as they wanted, he said, and keep their scholarships, too. But Canada had won permission to use professionals as part of the next team they'd send to wrestle back the nation's hockey supremacy, and the meaning was clear to all. Father Bauer's idealist run was over. Little did anyone know at the time, but so, too, was Canada's international hockey presence. The country would not return to compete in world championships or the Olympics for nearly a decade.

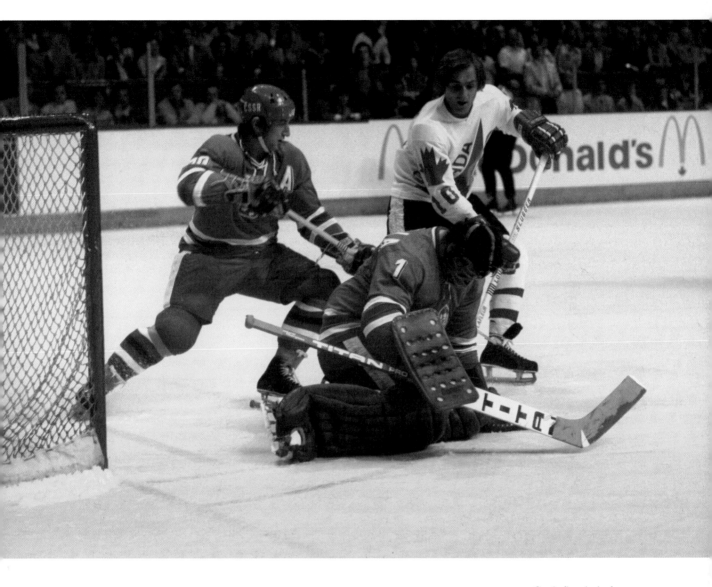

Guy Lafleur looks for a loose puck in a game against the Czechs. As the rest of the world caught up, it became clear that the only way to win the big tournaments was to make sure Canada's biggest stars were wearing the maple leaf.

CANADA SKATES AWAY FROM INTERNATIONAL PLAY

The poster for the world championship from which Canada withdrew due to a conflict with the IIHF. Canada's withdrawal shocked the international hockey world, and was a catalyst for the 1972 Summit Series.

On January 4, 1970, the Canadian Amateur Hockey Association rocked the country—and the hockey world—by announcing that Canada was withdrawing from international competition. "We will not return until the rules permit us to enter a team that is truly representative of Canadian hockey," said CAHA president Earl Dawson, after a hostile exchange with IIHF president Bunny Ahearne during an emergency meeting in Geneva. Canada was taking this action, Dawson continued, "so that we can play our best players, as all other countries do." And by best, Dawson was speaking of NHL supernovas like Bobby Orr, Gordie Howe, Phil Esposito, and Brad Park, players who would mop the ice with Europe's best. Or so the Canadian powers that be thought.

The drastic Canadian action had come as a result of Bunny Ahearne's perceived double-cross to Canada. At the 1969 IIHF annual meeting in Crans, Switzerland, it was the pragmatic Ahearne who cast the deciding vote to allow Canada to use minor-league pro players and reinstated amateurs (i.e., players who had returned to amateur play from professional leagues) in the world championships. The IIHF saw this concession as necessary to keep Canada coming to international tournaments, especially since the European players representing their countries were far from amateur, taking payment in the form of housing and subsidy to play hockey all year, for example, under the auspices of the Soviet Red Army.

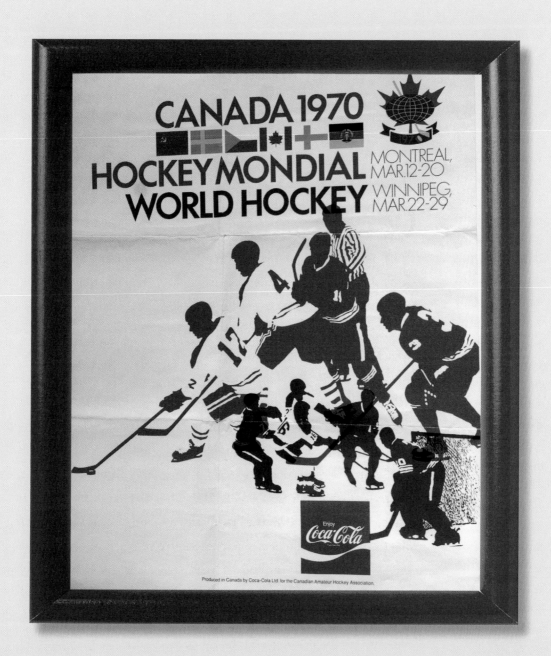

By winning this concession from the IIHF, Canada had not quite won the right to send its NHL elite to compete on the world stage, but it was a start. And for the first time ever, the IIHF was allowing Canada to host the tournament, so the Canadian delegation, which included CAHA president Earl Dawson and secretary Gordon Juckes, along with Hockey Canada's Charles Hay, Father Bauer, journalist and former MP Douglas Fisher, and Christopher Lang, a banker turned Hockey Canada executive, returned home planning a triumphal world championship for Montreal and Winnipeg in the late winter of 1970.

And then it all came crashing down on a Swiss Sunday morning in January. There had been rumblings at Saturday's meetings, but the Canadian delegation of Dawson, Juckes, Hay, and Fred Page of Vancouver thought they had worked out a compromise with the Europeans and the IIHF president himself on Saturday night. The Canadians had suggested an exhibition tournament in Canada in 1970 instead of an official world championship. In that way, they could have a year to get an official ruling from the IOC, one which they believed would counter that of Avery Brundage, who had ruled that any team that played against Canada, with its professionals, would not be allowed to play in the Olympics. Everyone agreed that it was an excellent compromise, and the CAHA representatives, Juckes and Dawson, were relieved. The CAHA did not want to pull out of international play, but as a sign of the power shift, Hockey Canada did want to exit, as a last resort, and it had the government's backing.

The Canadians were told that the general meeting was to start at 10:30 on Sunday morning, but when they entered the room, Bunny Ahearne officiously told them that the meeting had started ninety minutes earlier, and that all had been decided: Canada couldn't use professionals after all. The Soviets, fearing the loss of their hockey prestige if Canada sent professionals, had undercut all the agreements, and they invoked the IOC ruling as their justification.

It was the kind of hypocrisy that Hockey Canada wanted to stamp out, and so, when Canada withdrew, the IIHF relocated the world championship tournament from Canada to Sweden, for the Swedes had supported the Soviets, knowing they stood to gain the revenue that Canada would lose. The CAHA and Hockey Canada had hoped to make $500,000 from the tournament. "In Winnipeg alone there will be $300,000 worth of ticket refunds," said Juckes.

Canada's departure was, said irate Europeans, like the World Cup without Brazil. For six decades, the Canadian presence had represented the gold standard, the one that every team had dreamed of conquering. Even though Europeans had lately been beating Canada, and elevating their own hockey programs, the debt they owed to Canada was huge, and without the draw of a Canadian team, all international tournaments would lose their lustre.

As a result of Canada's stand, Father Bauer's national team was officially disbanded, winning its final game in Ottawa 2–1 against a Czech squad. Hockey Canada would now go into a restructuring of just how hockey needed to work from the grassroots up. Ironically, though Canada's withdrawal from the IIHF had shocked everyone in the hockey-playing nation, that shock became the catalyst for the 1972 Summit Series that would change Canada's hockey fortunes for the good.

HOW THE SUMMIT SERIES WAS MADE

Charles Hay and Gordon Juckes never believed in the Canadian government's boycott of international hockey, the fallout of the country's betrayal by the IIHF in 1970 when it reversed its ruling that Canada could use some professionals in its international teams. For the next two years, Hay, now the president of Hockey Canada, and Juckes, fulfilling the same role at the Canadian Amateur Hockey Association, made a dozen trips all over Europe to persuade the Soviets that it was in their best interests to play their best against ours.

Indeed, the 1972 Summit Series, the tournament that would change the hockey world forever, could be said to have originated through the three powerful forces: the IIHF betrayal, the Canadian resolve to end the IIHF's hypocrisy on the use of professional players, and the sheer determination of Charles Hay and Gordon Juckes to wear down the Soviets.

Signs of their success began to appear in 1971, when Canada's prime minister Pierre Trudeau made his first state visit to the USSR, and the Soviets hinted at a possible match between Canada's pros and their stars. The Soviets turned the hint into a taunt when their head coach Anatoli Tarasov, a disciple of Canadian hockey guru Lloyd Percival, announced that he would train his players to fight. Despite Father Bauer's efforts to play the game without the violence, it was a brutal assessment of what the world thought Canadian hockey had become.

Team Canada and the Soviet squad pause for their national anthems before doing battle in the 1972 Summit Series— the Cold War on ice.

Even so, the fact that the Soviets were entertaining the idea in public was a sign of things to come. Gary Smith, a young Canadian stationed at Canada's Moscow embassy, was assigned to find out just how serious the Soviets really were about this hockey contest by combing the newspapers for hidden messages. Before long, he was drinking vodka with *Isvestia* sports editor Boris Fedosov, and watching highlight film of the 1971 Stanley Cup final between Montreal and Chicago. When the Soviets witnessed Chicago superstar Bobby Hull in full flight, they were certain the Canadians had sped up the film.

In April 1972, Sport Canada director Lou Lefaive, the affable liaison between the federal government and Hockey Canada, along with Hockey Canada's president Charles Hay, board member Douglas Fisher, and CAHA president Joe Kryczka, a Calgary lawyer of Polish stock who understood Russian, attended the IIHF meeting in Prague during the world championship. Their mission was to hammer out the details of just how a series between Canada's pros and the USSR's best might work.

The Soviets were prepared to play under whatever conditions the Canadians wanted, as Soviet ideology believed their system, and therefore their players, to be the best in the world—exactly the same thing the Canadians believed about themselves. Even so, the Soviets strung the negotiations over several days of meetings, with Kryczka not revealing that he understood what they were saying to each other in their native tongue. He would debrief Hay on the unfiltered substance of it all at the end of each day, and afterward, assert that he believed they were just dawdling to get the best deal they possibly could for the eight-game series, with four games in each country, and with international referees, to be played that September.

When the negotiations were done, the Soviets hauled out a bottle of vodka at a morning meeting, and offered it to the Canadians. CAHA president Kryczka replied that it was too early in the day for Canadian lads to slug vodka, to which the lead Soviet delegate, Andrei Starevoitov, replied (through his interpreter), "You're Polish. Drink!" It was a salutary lesson in the Soviets' cunning, one which Canada would come to learn on ice.

So, too, would the Canadians learn the cunning of NHL Players' Association executive director Alan Eagleson, who was also a Hockey Canada board member. Eagleson was not part of the official delegation, and had not been part of the negotiations, but had showed up at the end of them to give the NHLPA's imprimatur to the agreement. He was the first to telephone journalist George Gross back home with the historic news—which thrilled the country—so the deal seemed to be his doing. It didn't matter, for almost everyone in Canada knew that come September, Canadian professional hockey players would reclaim the national game from its temporary residence in the USSR, and do it so convincingly that the world would forget the Soviet interregnum. But before that glorious restoration, Canada still had one more lesson left to learn from the Soviets.

Team Canada's coach, Harry Sinden (second from left), knew not to underestimate Soviet hockey, having seen its power as a player with the Whitby Dunlops at the 1958 world championship.

US AGAINST
THEM

The six-decade journey from the foundation of the Canadian Amateur Hockey Association, created to protect and develop the amateur game, came home to roost on a bittersweet reality: Canada's amateurs were not good enough to keep winning championships in the game the country had given to the world. Compounding that frustration was the fact that the world would not allow Canada to send Bobby Orr and Phil Esposito and Bobby Hull to teach the usurping Soviets a lesson they'd never forget. In September 1972, the stars finally aligned in Canada's glorious hockey firmament, for Canadian professionals would now be unleashed to restore national hockey honour by defeating the Soviets over an eight-game series—four home, four away—with no trophy but that of public adulation for the winner, who would be recognized as the world's true hockey champions.

As far as the country was concerned, it was a reality a long time coming. Canada had not won an international hockey championship since 1961, nor an Olympic gold medal in the sport since 1952. The years of winning just by showing up were long gone, and Father Bauer's attempt to create a national team from scholar-athletes only served to point out the need for a true national team: one made up of the very best, the ones who were paid for their talents.

That reality collided with another conflict roiling the pro hockey world in 1972. There were now two elite professional hockey leagues: the 55-year-old NHL and the upstart World Hockey Association (WHA), which would launch its first season that October. The WHA announced its bold intention to rival, if not supplant, the NHL, by wooing Chicago

Black Hawks star left winger Bobby Hull to play for Winnipeg with an unbelievable $1 million salary spread over ten years. At the time, the average NHL salary was $18,000 a year, and Hull's defection to the new league instantly defined the brand as rich and glamorous.

The NHL had not exactly embraced the idea of letting its players compete for Canada against the Soviets, for then as now, team owners worried about injuries—especially when thirteen of the league's sixteen teams were based in the United States. And they were certainly not going to permit the WHA to join this quest for hockey glory, because to do so would make the new league even more legitimate. NHL president Clarence Campbell, a Hockey Canada adviser, declared that the NHL refused to let Bobby Hull play on the Canadian team.

As a measure of the importance of the series to Canadians, and of Bobby Hull's stature as one of the greatest players the game had ever known, the national response to the NHL was loud and angry. Even though Team Canada's roster dazzled with the likes of Esposito and his goalie brother Tony, the speedy Yvan Cournoyer, and sleek Frank Mahovlich, the Canadians didn't have Gordie Howe, who had retired (temporarily), or Bobby Orr, who would travel with the team but not play due to recovery from a knee injury. Even so, to the Canadian public, it was Hull's omission that bordered on treason, and from water coolers to Legion halls, from letters to editors to talk radio to roadside billboards, from schoolrooms to Parliament Hill—even Prime Minister Trudeau joined in pleading Hull's case—people begged the NHL to relent. The NHL's resolve to stand fast was a further consolidation of the power that had been transferred from amateur to professional in the creation of Hockey Canada. The NHL owned the "best" and they would not let the country forget it.

So Canadians, in their powerful desire for a victory, focused on the delirious pleasure they would have watching that victory unfold in eight straight routs. It seemed as if their wish would be granted when Phil Esposito scored thirty seconds into the first game in Montreal, and Paul Henderson added another six minutes later. But Canadian coach Harry Sinden, who had played the Soviets as a member of the world champion Whitby Dunlops, saw that the speed and skill of the Soviets had only become better with time, and the country saw it, too, watching the Soviets work the puck with creativity and precision, their stamina and strength—both physical and mental—seeming to grow as the game wore on and they wore Team Canada down, convincingly winning the first game 7–3. As goalie Ken Dryden later recalled, "The Eight Straight gang was one down now and in desperate trouble."

Things got worse. Team Canada was booed in the warm-up to Game 4 in Vancouver (a city that was no stranger to bad hockey), and by the time it had ended with a 5–3 Soviet victory, they were booed off the ice. The Canadian professionals now had a 1–2–1 record, and their captain, Phil Esposito, sweat pouring off his face, made an emotional and defiant plea for understanding in a post-game interview that was broadcast and rebroadcast across the nation. "These Russians are great hockey players," he said. "Why not give them some credit and stop blaming us?"

The only good news in the national hockey nightmare was that the next four contests were "away" games. After a pit stop in Sweden, where the Canadians re-established their reputation as gangsters and thugs en route to a win and a tie, "Team Ugly" (as some now called it) arrived in the USSR to take back Canada's game from the Communists. And they were extremely talented Communists, with players like the superlative goalie Vladislav Tretiak and forward Valeri Kharlamov—already with three goals, one a game-winner, as was his lone assist—who could have easily played in the NHL. All Canada needed to do was win three of their next four games against a magnificent opponent, playing at home, who had already beaten them twice. But the Canadians had bonded in their Swedish interlude, and they had found their game. They would play that game full out, for after all, they had nothing to lose but what already seemed lost.

But this series meant as much to the Soviets as it did to Canadians. Not only did both nations love hockey, but the arrival of the Canadians was the first time in a long time that an invading force had landed in the USSR in the name of peace. Such as it was.

Coaches Make the Game

The Canadian Amateur Hockey Association began to deliver its first national hockey coaching program clinics in 1972 with the creation of the National Coaching Certification Program. Until then, various groups had offered hockey-coaching courses across the country, but this new program represented a combined effort on the part of the twelve branches of the CAHA, and the newly formed Hockey Development Council, to create a coherent program for all hockey coaches across Canada. Educators with some hockey background began to replace retired professional players behind the bench, and the hockey world saw the rise of professional coaches who looked at the game as a subject worthy of scholarly study—such as former high school math teacher Roger Neilson with his video studies; Dave King and his game scholarship; and Ron Smith, who learned the value of video as Roger Neilson's assistant. They are a few of the thousands of coaches who would teach the country's next generation of hockey players a new way of playing the game.

Team Canada's specially imported beer and beef went missing; players were awoken in the middle of the night by phone calls with no one on the other end; and Canada's jet-lagged 2,000 supporters were banned by the Soviets from public displays of fandom. But the team and the fans rallied together at this adversity, with the fans chanting "da da, Canada; nyet nyet, Soviet" during Team Canada's loss in Game 5. They still believed in the team, even though one more Canadian loss would mean that not even Canada's best could topple the mighty Soviets in a tournament. And maybe never would.

Whatever happened, Team Canada would never accomplish what fans hoped they would do. They would certainly not *humble* the Soviets. It was far too late for that. Now the Canadians were fighting for their lives, to prove they were as good as the Russians.

But high-pressure, life-or-death hockey was what the members of Team Canada played every spring. They still had to do what they came to the USSR to do: win three games just to maintain national honour. It seemed like an insurmountable challenge. But there wasn't a player in the room who hadn't come back from a stinging loss before, and there was no one there who hadn't been counted on back home to be the guy to hold his head high and lead. So, summoning the hockey-honed virtues of persistence, pride, and a willingness to "pay the price," Team Canada began to fight back, winning Game 6 and Game 7, thanks to goals by Paul Henderson, a dependable but unspectacular Maple Leaf, and to Bobby Clarke, a feisty diabetic who played for the thuggish

Philadelphia Flyers. When commanded by assistant coach John Ferguson to stop the Soviets' star left winger Valeri Kharlamov from skating rings around the Canadians, Clarke applied a two-handed slash to Kharlamov's ankle and broke it. To this day, Clarke's attack is considered a great criminal act in Russia, but to Team Canada, it was an example of doing what was needed to win.

A first-rate dramatist couldn't have imagined a more pulse-pounding ending to this transcendent moment in Canadian hockey history: the eighth and final game between Canada and the USSR, with the winner to take all. The Soviets, horrified by their change of fortunes, tried a little subterfuge by replacing Game 8's scheduled referee with a friendlier one. As a result, when a goal that tied the game for Canada was disallowed, Alan Eagleson—now an essential cog in Hockey Canada's wheel—tried to attack the Soviet timekeeper. In an extraordinary sequence of events, the Soviet militia took him prisoner, and the Canadian players then liberated him with their sticks and fists. Suddenly, an international hockey contest had literally become what it had always been at heart: the Cold War played out on ice.

The violence worked. Incredibly, Canada's disallowed goal was now allowed and the game was tied. And, with less than a minute left, Paul Henderson scored again for Canada. Canadians who saw his nation-saving goal will remember where they were. "Metro is wild with delirium: like end of WWII," crowed a headline from the *Toronto Star*, perhaps exaggerating the import, but not the feeling of national relief. Team Canada had restored—in the most dramatic fashion possible—the nation's game. But the end was just the beginning: once again, the world would want to take the crown from Canada.

It had been billed as Us versus Them, but in the end, it was a celebration of the game beloved by two nations that would become closer because of it.

THE INVENTION OF THE VISOR

It was late in a game on December 7, 1973, when Greg Neeld, an 18-year-old defenceman with the Toronto Marlboroughs, beat 16-year-old Kitchener Rangers defenceman Dave Maloney to the puck in the corner. Maloney tried to stop Neeld from stealing away with the puck by hooking him, but his stick slipped and gouged Neeld in his left eye. Neeld, rated the eleventh-best prospect in junior hockey, was being compared to Bobby Orr, but doctors couldn't save his left eye. His hockey career was nearly ended by an accident that should have been, given the physics of hockey, far more common. And that was now a problem that Greg Neeld wanted to address.

The only face protector then available for non-goalies was a CCM wire face mask, but Neeld couldn't see out of it, so, with the help of his father, an Air Canada pilot, he and his dad designed the world's first hockey visor. The Neelds' solution was ingenious: they snipped out the wire cage and replaced it with clear plastic. Greg Neeld returned to the Marlies as the first player to wear a visor on February 17, 1974, in a 4–2 loss to the Hamilton Red Wings, with Neeld moving up to left wing from his old defence position. "I wanted to relieve some of the pressure on him," said Marlies coach George Armstrong. "On defence, if someone got by him there was only the goalie left. On left wing, if someone beat him, he could rely on the defence and the goalie."

Manny Malhotra, who captained Canada's 2000 junior squad, would nearly lose his left eye after being struck in the face by a puck while playing for the Vancouver Canucks in 2011. After recovering from two surgeries to his damaged eye, Malhotra returned to continue his NHL career—wearing a visor.

Neeld played well enough with one eye to wind up drafted by the Buffalo Sabres in the fourth round of the NHL draft in 1975, but the NHL rules committee couldn't get a two-thirds majority of votes from member teams to allow Neeld to play in the league while wearing his visor. "I'm very upset that three Canadian teams voted against a kid who grew up in one of the cities (Vancouver) and played in another (Toronto)," said Buffalo general manager Punch Imlach.

Neeld would go on to have a professional career in the World Hockey Association, playing seventeen games for the Toronto Toros in 1975/76, and at the start of that season, the Canadian Amateur Hockey Association imposed rules to make facial protection mandatory in minor hockey. Forty years after Neeld's injury and invention, the NHL finally made all players entering the league wear visors, beginning in the 2013/14 season.

Greg Neeld turned tragedy into triumph by developing the helmet visor after losing his sight in one eye during a hockey game. The visor is now mandatory for all players entering the NHL.

THE CREATION OF THE WRIGLEY NATIONAL MIDGET TOURNAMENT

One of the legacies from the 1972 Summit Series was the CAHA's desire to see a national championship for midget teams—an age class encompassing players older than 15 and younger than 18—to test young Canadian players against the world. Or rather, to test them against the part of the hockey world that mattered: the USSR.

Partnering up with the chewing gum company, the CAHA created the Wrigley National Midget Hockey Tournament in 1974. Each of the CAHA's twelve branches would send a champion to the finals, with the tournament city earning a spot by virtue of hosting the party, as in the Memorial Cup. Wrigley would fly the teams to the tournament, kit them with uniforms, and award a $1,000 scholarship to the best player, as well as $25,000 to the CAHA for minor-hockey development. And as the grand prize for winning the tournament, the Wrigley champs were flown to the USSR to play a six-game series against elite Russian midget teams.

The Verdun Midget Maple Leafs won the first Wrigley championship, held in Oshawa, Ontario, in 1974. The tournament was televised across Canada by CTV, and when the Maple Leafs played the final game of their tour against Red Army in Moscow, an estimated 50 million to 100 million Soviets watched the game on TV, their collective memory fresh with Canada's defeat of the USSR two years earlier. Verdun lost that match

CANADIAN CENTENNIAL MIDGET HOCKEY CHAMPIONSHIP

KINGSTON, ONTARIO

MARCH 25 TO
APRIL 1, 1967

KINGSTON
COMMUNITY
MEMORIAL
CENTRE

A. C. A. H. A.
CENTENNIAL
PROJECT

SOUVENIR PROGRAM 50c

6–5, and the team won only one of its six games, outscored 59–21 by the Soviets. But the Midget Maple Leafs learned some things along the way.

The game that got them a mention in the House of Commons as having been "brutally assaulted and seriously wounded by some Soviet Midgets during a fight without equal in the history of hockey" came in their second match in Moscow. With Verdun losing 6–2 in the third period, Ron Harris took exception to being taken heavily into the boards. He pushed the Soviet player, who pushed back, and the gloves were dropped. A Soviet player left the penalty box to pile on the Canadian, and that was the signal for both benches to empty—save for the Canadian player who was serving a joint penalty with his now brawling Soviet counterpart, but he couldn't escape to join the battle because he had his arms pinned by the Soviet timekeeper.

The Soviets, failing to understand the rules of Canadian hockey brawls, kicked Canadian players with their skates, narrowly missing carving out John Bethel's eye. When order was restored, Bethel stitched up, and the teams had cooled off—helped along by an apology to the Canadians by Anatoli Tarasov—the Verdun Maple Leafs went back out on the ice and lost 9–2.

The Canadians returned home with their eyes—those not swollen shut—opened to the values of another world, where you could get reprimanded by Soviet guides for jamming your hands in your pockets at Lenin's Tomb, or for leaning against a priceless Rembrandt, but mainly by observing just what the Soviets did to win. "The highlight for me was a tour of the Central Army Sports Club in Moscow," said team captain Wayne Singleton. "I saw kids our age working out all the time. There was a bantam team lifting weights. They do as much work off the ice as on. I figure Canadian kids could do with a lot more practicing and conditioning."

The Wrigley Tournament eventually became the Air Canada Cup in 1979, and then, in 2004, the Telus Cup. The roster of NHL players who have passed through the tournament includes some of pro hockey's greatest players: Patrick Roy, Joe Sakic, Rod Brind'Amour, Kirk MacLean, Cliff Ronning, James Patrick, Roland Melanson, Kris Letang, Sidney Crosby, Dany Heatley, Daniel Brière, Denis Savard, Joffrey Lupul, and Al MacInnis, among many others.

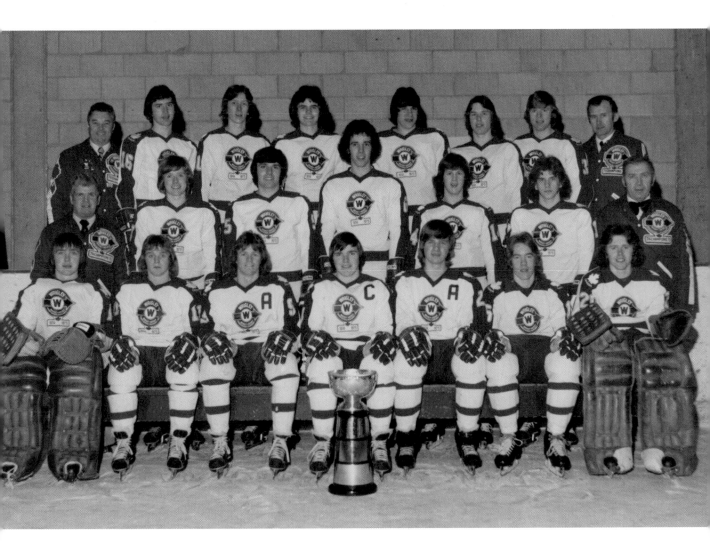

The Midget Tournament showcased players who would become some of hockey's greatest stars. This 1975 team featured future Hall of Famer Mike Gartner (back row, fourth from left).

THE 1976
CANADA CUP

The epic drama of the '72 Summit Series had left the hockey cosmos hankering for a world-class tournament that would truly feature the best teams on the planet. Hockey's world championships took place in the spring, when many of the best NHL players were competing for the Stanley Cup, and the Winter Olympics were still the province of "amateur" players. So Douglas Fisher, then head of Hockey Canada, and Alan Eagleson, having risen to be a key power player on the back of the NHLPA, negotiated with the Soviets in 1974 to keep the Canadian and Soviet best meeting in a world hockey tournament, played every three or four years, like the World Cup of Soccer. It would be called the Canada Cup.

And with more than $400,000 in prize money, the lure was potent for European teams to participate, especially those from behind the Iron Curtain. The Canada Cup was also a victory for the NHL's rival professional league, the WHA, whose players would now be allowed to compete, too, just as they had done in the 1974 Summit Series, a watered-down version of its predecessor, which the Soviets won. As far as the Canadian organizers were concerned, the inaugural Canada Cup would be a massive success— so long as the home team won.

The first Canada Cup was organized as a round-robin playoff, with the first two teams in the round-robin segment of the tournament to meet for a best-of-three final. The Soviets showed up with a depleted crew, minus five of the players who had made their 1972 team such a powerhouse, including their top forward line of Petrov, Kharlamov, and Mikhailov. The Soviets, who were still wounded by their 1972 loss, built in a pride-saving

Bobby Hull, who was banned from the Summit Series in 1972, celebrates a goal against stingy Czech goalie Vladimir Dzurilla in the 1976 Canada Cup.

escape clause should they lose again by leaving their star trio at home: a logic that made sense in a totalitarian society, but not on the ice. In a scenario rich with Canadian hockey history and tradition, the Soviets met Canada in the final game of the round robin in Maple Leaf Gardens on a Saturday night, and lost 3–1.

The home team's nemesis in the first Canada Cup proved to be the Czechs, who were backstopped by Vladimir Dzurilla, a pudgy 34-year-old who had been retired for four years. The Czechs shocked Canada with a 1–0 shutout win in the round-robin portion of the tournament, and so Canada met them with something to prove in the best-of-three series finale. Canada breezed through the first game in Toronto, winning 6–0, and looked to be making an equally easy conquest in Game 2. Montreal's hockey connoisseurs packed the Forum to the rafters to watch Canada race out to a 2–0 lead, which is when the Czech coaches put Vladimir Dzurilla back in goal. And back came the Czechs.

At the end of regulation time, the game was tied 4–4 and the last thing Canada wanted to do was to play a one-game winner-take-all match against the crafty Czechs. Assistant Coach Don Cherry, moonlighting from his job as coach of the Boston Bruins, had noticed the Czech goalie coming far out of his net to challenge shooters. "Anyone getting a breakaway, from now on try delaying a bit," he told Team Canada during the intermission. "Instead of shooting, take an extra stride or two so you have something to shoot at."

The Canadians came out hard in the first sudden-death overtime, trying to take advantage of the fact that the Czechs were starting the extra frame with a man in the penalty box. But the score stayed tied.

With a little more than eight minutes left in the first overtime, Serge Savard corralled the puck behind goalie Rogie Vachon. He quickly passed the puck up the half boards to Denis Potvin, who fed it to Lanny McDonald just inside his own blue line. McDonald dished off to Marcel Dionne at centre ice, and he passed it to Toronto Maple Leafs captain Darryl Sittler, who was heading down the left wing with speed. When Sittler breezed past the Czech defenceman, goalie Dzurilla did the only thing he could and came out far to cut off Sittler's angle. Sittler most likely wasn't thinking of Don Cherry's advice when his hockey instincts kicked in, and he faked a slap shot. Dzurilla took the bait, and the Leafs star skated around the sprawling goalie to pop the puck into the empty net.

Canada had won the world's first best-of-the-best hockey tournament, and like other Canadian hockey victories, it would serve only to whet the world's appetite to beat the country at its own game.

Team Canada celebrates winning hockey's first "world cup" in 1976. Many consider the '76 Canada Cup team to have been the best ever.

THE FIRST
OFFICIAL
WORLD JUNIOR
CHAMPIONSHIP

Team Canada debuts at the first official world junior championship in Czechoslovakia, Christmas 1976.

Part of Hockey Canada's mission was to focus attention on developing the country's young players, to make sure they stayed on top of the national game. CAHA executive Gordon Juckes worked passionately—and with no small amount of gold-dust diplomacy—to get the North Americans and Europeans to agree on an upper age limit for world junior international play, with the world's governing bodies deciding that a player could be no older than age 20 in the year that tournament was to be played.

And so, over Christmas 1976 into New Year's 1977, the first official World Under-20 Championships took place in Czechoslovakia, the tournament becoming another example of the radical shift in international hockey culture that resulted from Canada's decision to withdraw from international play in 1970.

When the Canadians said they wouldn't play, there came from that refusal the historic 1972 Summit Series, the Canada Cup, and now the new world junior tournament. So Canada was back in this new and improved game, but—amazingly—was still reverting to a strategy it used to great effect back in the olden days by sending the Memorial Cup champs, the St. Catharines Fincups, to wear the maple leaf. Clearly, such an approach had seen its day.

The Soviets, Czechs, Finns, Swedes, Poles, West Germans, and Americans all sent teams made up of their best under-20 players. The Canadians came out like teams of yore, blasting Poland 14–0, West Germany 9–1, and the USA 8–2. Led by the prolific duo of Dale McCourt and John Anderson, who would finish one and two, respectively, as top scorers in the tournament with a combined thirty-four points, the Canadians seemed primed for gold after beating the Finns 6–4 and the Swedes 5–3.

But on Christmas Day 1976, they ran into the reality of the Czechs. The best Canada could muster was a 4–4 tie, and once again, Canada was faced with a winner-take-all match against the undefeated Soviet Union. If Canada could vanquish the Soviets, they would win the gold.

The Soviets not only defeated that idea early on in the tournament's penultimate game on January 2, but they utterly crushed it, scoring six unanswered goals in the first period. No one scored in the second, and despite a spirited comeback by the Canadians in the third, their four goals were just enough to make the defeat seem respectable. The Soviets took gold, and Canada got silver.

Even so, a powerful new tradition had been created: the world junior championship tournament would become one of the most important dates not only on the Canadian hockey calendar, but on that of all the countries who wanted to be good enough to beat the Canadians. Once Canada started winning.

Team Canada warms up en route to a silver medal at the first world junior championship.

JUNIOR WORLD CUP
OF HOCKEY
1978

$2.00

WAYNE GRETZKY AND THE 1978 WORLD JUNIOR CHAMPIONSHIP

With the arrival of the world junior hockey championships (WJC), Hockey Canada officials also focused their efforts on creating a *brand* by conducting a marketing campaign. They couldn't do better than their 1978 world juniors poster boy, 16-year-old Wayne Gretzky in his first big-league international tournament. Better still was the fact that the WJC was being held in Canada—in the country's hockey temples of Montreal and Quebec City.

This time, Canada decided not to send a national champion, but instead they emulated the professionals and sent an all-star team featuring Ryan Walter, Rick Vaive, Rob Ramage, Bobby Smith, Mike Gartner, Curt Fraser, and Brad Marsh.

Gretzky scored a hat trick in Canada's 9–3 win over Czechoslovakia to propel them into the final round, but the skill and consistency of the Europeans won out in the last stages. Despite the fact that Gretzky led the tournament in scoring, Canada lost to Sweden and the USSR while once again beating the Czechs, which was good enough for a bronze medal.

Canada's coach, Ernie "Punch" McLean saw what the future looked like, and had a plan. He was going to convince Hockey Canada to send scouts to all three junior hockey finals in Canada the following March and April. "They would watch for the best 18-year-olds in the three finals.

Canada hosted the second world junior hockey championship in Montreal and Quebec City in 1978.

Sixteen-year-old Wayne Gretzky made his first "big league" appearance at the 1978 world junior championship. He led the tournament in scoring.

Those players, along with the nucleus of eight players that were with Team Canada this year would attend training camp two weeks or so after the Memorial Cup Final."

Even so, Canada would again send Memorial Cup winners to the world juniors until 1981, when the country finished in seventh place. That meant Canada's three points in the standings put it just ahead of last-place Austria, owners of zero points, and this woeful result finally got the attention of those within the CAHA who had been resistant to a national junior team. Once again, Canadian hockey was at a critical evolutionary moment: if the country wanted to regain its place at the top of the international hockey table, it needed to find a way to make excellence not the exception, but the expectation and the reality.

Team Canada's 1978 juniors in their blue, white, and red uniforms at centre ice in the home arena of the team that made *bleu, blanc, et rouge* synonymous with hockey excellence, the Montreal Canadiens.

THE LEGACY OF "DOC" SEAMAN

Daryl "Doc" Seaman was already a legend when he decided to do something to help Canadian hockey achieve the supremacy he remembered it having when he was a kid growing up in Saskatchewan during the Great Depression. Indeed, his philanthropic efforts were evident even then, when Seaman would "steal" from his family's pantry and take food down to the men camped by the railway tracks, riding the rails and looking for work that wasn't there.

After flying an astonishing eighty-two combat missions out of North Africa as a submarine-hunting pilot during World War II, Seaman became one of Canada's leading oil tycoons with his brothers, working the Alberta oil sands to create Bow Valley Industries, thousands of jobs, and a lot of money.

Seaman had agonized over the state of Canadian hockey during the dry spell before the 1972 Summit Series. "There was a feeling that we were not as skilled as the Russians and falling behind," Seaman recalled in his biography, *Staying in the Game*. "One brainchild Charlie Hay and I had in 1970 was to get back to the basics and develop the skills out in the community and put something back at the grassroots level."

That desire would dovetail with Seaman's co-ownership of the Calgary Flames, which he and fellow oilman Harley Hotchkiss wrangled from Atlanta to Calgary in 1980. The Flames' Project 75, created in 1980 and named to commemorate Alberta's seventy-fifth birthday as a

THE
DK (DOC) SEAMAN
TROPHY

WESTERN HOCKEY LEAGUE
SCHOLASTIC PLAYER OF THE YEAR

province, was a unique and ingenious idea. The wealthy executives discovered that a Canadian amateur sport association could own petroleum resources, tax free, so long as the profits went into amateur sport. "So we bought some oil and gas properties and donated them to Project 75," said Seaman.

Now known as the Seaman Hotchkiss Hockey Foundation, the organization has played a profound role in Canada's international success by building community arenas, supporting the development of coaches and referees, and offering hockey scholarships to worthy players. More than that, the Project 75 initiative became a long and fruitful result of the drought before the '72 Summit Series, and part of the awakening afterward. Soon, the country would begin to see the tangible results of Canada's efforts to win back its game, thanks to "Doc" Seaman's priming of the national hockey pump.

Daryl "Doc" Seaman (left) proudly wears the sweater of the team that he helped so much to achieve excellence. Doc's brother B.J. Seaman stands beside him with Harley Hotchkiss (right).

THE PROGRAM
OF EXCELLENCE

At the Canadian Amateur Hockey Association annual meeting in St. John's, Newfoundland, in May 1981, the CAHA had seen enough. After years of watching Canada's erratic annual international hockey improvisation swing between the occasional triumph and the frequent reality of coming away less than golden, the CAHA—and Canadians—figured there must be a better way, and they had a plan. They wanted to start a national program to develop Canada's best hockey players. The driving force behind this plan—and many others to come—was CAHA president Murray Costello. He had played centre at Toronto's St. Michael's College, and then in the NHL for Chicago, Boston, and Detroit, and he also had a law degree. Costello had also been a hockey executive, with the Seattle Totems of the WHL, and an arbitrator with the World Hockey Association. In 1979, he became the CAHA's first paid president, and he would be visionary in creating the foundation for the modern Canadian national hockey program for men and women. It was called the Program of Excellence.

It was not an easy sell. The first part of the plan called for Canada's junior leagues to send their best players—identified by CAHA scouts in regional tournaments—to a summer tryout camp for the national junior team that would play in the world junior championship. The second part of the plan would then see these same junior teams lend their best players to the national junior team in the middle of the season. And on top of that, they proposed creating an under-17 feeder system for the national team.

The Western Hockey League, the Ontario Hockey League, and the Quebec Major Junior Hockey League did not immediately raise the flag

When the arena in Rochester, Minnesota, didn't have a recording of Canada's national anthem, the 1982 gold medal–winning junior team belted it out themselves.

and join in the quest. Teams were concerned about losing their best players at a critical time of the season, and maybe also about losing those top players to injury. Through Costello's perseverance and pedigree, they eventually agreed to give it a try, especially since the junior leagues would each have a seat on the Program of Excellence's policy committee.

And so the first true Canadian national team went forth to Rochester, Minnesota (with some games in Manitoba and Ontario), to play for junior gold in 1982. Under the coaching of Dave King, who drilled his squad in how to play "international" hockey—a clean Canadian check would get a penalty, a European spear or slash to the Canadian players would not—the Canadians won their first game against Finland 5–1. They weathered a two-goal third-period comeback by Sweden to win 3–2, and then they beat teams by scores that Canadians who could remember teams from a half century earlier would find familiar: 11–3 over West Germany, 11–1 over Switzerland, and most satisfying of all, 7–0 over the Soviets, giving the Soviet team the worst thrashing in its junior history.

Led by left winger Mike Moller, defenceman Gord Kluzak, and goalie Mike Moffat, the Canadians came into the final game against Czechoslovakia with a guaranteed silver medal. But they hadn't come to Minnesota under the inaugural auspices of the Program of Excellence to go home second best.

And then, Canada was on the wrong end of a 2–1 score as they entered the third period. The Canadians came out hard, and Marc Habscheid and Mike Moller put Canada up by a goal. But the Czechs tied it up, and that's how it went into the record books. The Canadian team had outscored its opponents 45–14 while compiling a 6–0–1 record to claim first place in the round-robin tournament. And it was enough for Canada to win the gold medal.

When it came time to play the national anthem of the champions, there was a technical problem—or worse, the Rochester, Minnesota, arena didn't actually have a copy of "O Canada." In the end, it didn't matter. The Canadian players linked arms on their blue line to belt out the anthem themselves, thus creating an iconic moment for the first golden triumph of the Program of Excellence. It would be a national moment of triumph that Canadians would come to expect with each new year.

Top:
Three years after the foundation of the Program of Excellence, Canada celebrates its first world junior gold medal.

Bottom:
The 1982 Team Canada world junior gold medal was a historic moment in the nation's hockey life, one meriting its own hockey card.

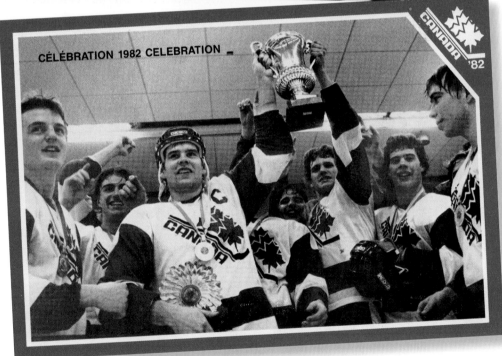

CÉLÉBRATION 1982 CELEBRATION

PART 3

THE AGE OF EXCELLENCE,
1984–PRESENT

In this third section, we follow the payoff of all the hard work done in the preceding decades to produce the Program of Excellence and, as a result, a resurgence of Canada's international hockey power up to the present day—and beyond. Because of Canada's excellence in the game it gave to the world, the world has measured its own excellence by Canada's standard. As a result of Canada's success, the competition that Canada faces has become steadily better. So, in no small way, the Age of Excellence is also Canada's gift to the world.

CANADA'S
FIRST SPENGLER

World War I's reach extended deep into the twentieth century when Canada arrived in Davos, Switzerland, to compete in its very first Spengler Cup competition in 1984. Canadian players had been competing in the Spengler from the very beginning of the tournament in 1923, when it was created as a way to help heal the wounds of World War I, which had stopped all international sporting competition with its global carnage.

Dr. Carl Spengler, of Davos, had donated the trophy as a magnanimous gesture to allow Germany and Austria back into the game, as both countries had been banned from official IIHF competitions in the culture of blame that followed World War I. Spengler's father, Alexander, had come from Germany to Davos as a political refugee in the mid–nineteenth century, after the failure of the March Revolution of 1848, in which he had taken part as a student. Upon receiving his medical degree in Zurich, Alexander became a doctor in the farming village of Davos, nestled in the pristine air of the Swiss Alps, and made an astonishing discovery: the village was totally free of the deadly tuberculosis then ravaging the world.

Spengler promoted Davos as a spa, beneficial to people with lung ailments, and soon the town had become a destination for the tubercular and the literary—Robert Louis Stevenson, Arthur Conan Doyle, and Thomas Mann all were inspired by it. So, too, were Canadian hockey players, who had been enjoying the town's splendid natural ice when they would descend from Oxford and Cambridge universities to give the Europeans a lesson in Canada's game.

Team Canada's Derrick Walser (right) celebrates a championship-game goal with teammates Tyler Seguin, Patrice Bergeron, Ryan Smith, and Jason Demers. Canada would go on to win this game and the 2012 Spengler Cup.

The first Spengler Cup match in December 1923 did what it was supposed to, seeing a team from Austria—Wiener EV—play Berliner SC from Germany. Oxford University, stocked with Canadian players, including future Canadian prime minister Lester B. Pearson and governor general Roland Michener, won the first Spengler Cup against Berlin. That tournament didn't finish until New Year's Day 1924, due to heavy snowfall and avalanches, and indeed its scheduling between Boxing Day and New Year's Eve was the thing that kept Canadian hockey teams away from it for fifty years (after Oxford's Canadians won the Spengler in 1923, 1925, 1931, and 1932), until Canada began playing internationally during that winter sojourn with the advent of the world junior championship.

The 1984 Canadian team, the country's first official entry, was composed of Canadian players on Christmas break from their European club teams, or from their colleges. After six days of getting to know each other on and off the ice, the Canadians unleashed a 64-shot attack on a West German team to win 3–1. After defeating host club Davos 9–2, the Canadians met the Soviet club team Khimik Woskresensk in the match to determine which team would emerge from the final round with the best record, and so win the trophy.

The Soviets were leading 3–1 after two periods, but Canada's captain Ron Plumb, a former Hartford Whaler, scored early in the third period. Don McLaren got his second goal of the game with 1:48 left, and a minute later, Plumb broke in alone on the Khimik goalie Leonid Gerasimov, deked him out of position, but seemed to be too far past the net. Plumb made a desperate reach and he poked the game-winner into the net much to the delight of the 5,111 pro-Canadian fans in the arena. "I've won championships before," said Plumb, "but it's never been as sweet as this."

Team Canada won
its first Spengler Cup
in 1984.

THE 1984
CANADA CUP

In September 1984, Team Canada, like many a Canadian team before it, had a hockey score to settle, one packed with history and betrayal and general humiliation. In 1976, Canada had staged the first Canada Cup tournament as an expansion of the 1972 Summit Series. Instead of being a two-team competition, the Canada Cup would invite pros and amateurs alike to compete for the latest iteration of world hockey supremacy, played in summer, when the world's top professional hockey league, the NHL, was not in session.

Montreal Canadiens defensive superstar Larry Robinson was part of the all-star cast that comprised Canada's 1984 Canada Cup team.

Canada won the first Canada Cup in 1976, but the second one, in 1981, had been a problem from the start. The tournament, originally scheduled for 1980, had been delayed a year by the Soviet invasion of Afghanistan. Even so, the Canadian squad had Scotty Bowman behind the bench, who had coached Montreal to five Stanley Cup titles, and a 20-year-old rising superstar named Wayne Gretzky, who had set an NHL scoring record in 1980/81 with 164 points. Complementing Gretzky was an all-star cast featuring Guy Lafleur, Mike Bossy, Bryan Trottier, Denis Potvin, Clark Gillies, Ray Bourque, Marcel Dionne, Larry Robinson, and Bob Gainey, among others.

The Soviets had been rebuilding their national team, and the 1981 version saw only eight players back from the previous Canada Cup squad. When Canada defeated the Soviets and their high-octane offence, led by a new trio of 21-year-olds, Vladimir Krutov, Igor Larionov, and Sergei Makarov (later dubbed the KLM Line), in the last game of the opening round by a score of 7–3, fans across the country were confident that winning the second Canada Cup was going to be a mere formality.

After defeating the USA 4–1 in the semi-final, the Canadians once again met the Soviets, who had defeated the Czechs by the same score.

It was as if the Soviets had somehow found a different team since they last played Canada four days earlier. Canada outshot the Soviets 12–4 in the first period, but couldn't put the puck past Vladislav Tretiak, who had cagily been left on the bench by Coach Viktor Tikhonov in the earlier loss to Canada.

Nor could the Soviets score on Mike Liut, until five minutes into the second period. Canada tied the game three minutes later, but the Soviets turned up the heat, stifling Gretzky, the tournament's leading scorer, and putting another seven pucks past Liut.

The shock to Canadian pride rippled far and wide, but the epicentre was Montreal, where NHLPA boss Alan Eagleson refused to allow the Soviets to take home the trophy they had just won. The Soviets stashed the Canada Cup in a hockey bag and tried to sneak it onto their bus, but Eagleson got wind of it and led the charge to retrieve it, throwing punches en route. Inventing a rule on the spot, Eagleson insisted that the trophy had to be won three times before it could become the property of the winner, and he stole it back from the Soviets, even though he and Prime Minister Trudeau had handed it over to the victorious USSR team at centre ice of the Montreal Forum. A group of embarrassed Canadians, led by Winnipeg trucker George Smith, had a replica made and presented it to the Soviets in a ceremony in Winnipeg attended by 4,000 people. It may be Canada's game, but we weren't going to be sore losers (except for Eagleson). There would always be next time.

Despite undergoing a lengthy training camp in preparation for the 1984 Canada Cup, the team had problems, the biggest one being its composition. The presence of Wayne Gretzky and Mike Bossy and a host of NHL stars mainly from the dynastic—and rival—Oilers and Islanders created team turmoil, but after an expected win against West Germany (in their first and only Canada Cup appearance), Canada tied the USA, lost to Sweden, and despite beating the Czechs, lost their final round–robin match to the hated Soviets 6–3. It was another national moment of hockey angst. But there was still a shot at redemption.

Alan Eagleson, whose planning of the playoff format the last time saw a one-game, winner-take-all rout of the Canadians by the Soviets, returned to a system where the top four teams made it into a semi-final round. It seemed like fortuitous clairvoyance, as Canada had barely made the cut, having finished in fourth place in the round robin.

And in fine dramatic fashion, Canada's semi-final opponent was the Soviet Union. Canada dominated the first two periods, but managed to register only a 1–0 lead because Vladimir Myshkin, who had replaced the retired Tretiak, was channelling the departed Soviet super-goalie. And then, just as they had in their last Canada Cup triumph, the Soviets broke out of their shell and scored twice in the third period to take the lead. But Canada's Doug Wilson, a Chicago Black Hawks defenceman, tied the game late in regulation time to put Canada in the position of playing sudden-death hockey against the Soviets. At 12:29 of overtime, Mike Bossy deflected a Paul Coffey shot past Myshkin, and the country exhaled. Canada had squeezed into the final to play the Swedes in a best-of-three series.

The Swedes came into the final riding a 9–2 victory over the United States, having scored on their first four shots. But Canada took heart from the tough win against the Soviets, and defeated them 5–2 in Game 1, and then gave everyone a scare by nearly blowing a 5–0 lead in Game 2 to win the match 6–5, and the 1984 Canada Cup.

Mark Messier was part of the Edmonton Oiler contingent on Team Canada in 1984—and conflict would ensue between them and their dynastic rival New York Islanders on the team.

Team Canada won the 1984 Canada Cup by defeating the Soviets then vanquishing their new rivals, the Swedes, in a best-of-three final.

THE 1986
WORLD JUNIORS
GO FOR GOLD
AT HOME

In 1985, Canada had won the world juniors gold in the kind of way no Canadian team wants to win world championships: on goal differential, after finishing with an identical 5–0–2 record with the Czechs. Both teams had tied each other and the Finns. The Finns could have snatched the gold from Canada by beating the Soviets by at least eight goals, but they wound up on the losing end of a 6–5 game against the USSR, who took the bronze. Canada had scored more goals than the Czechs, so gold was theirs.

The 1986 world juniors were held in Hamilton and Burlington, Ontario, and the Canadian team had been built to win the tournament decisively, through size, strength, and skill that would put victories in the win column. "Tough, abrasive and talented, the swashbuckling Canadians are dominating this tournament," reported *The Globe and Mail*, and the team's early games were throwback scores to the country's dominating days of yore: 12–1 over Switzerland in their opener, followed by an 18–2 thumping of West Germany, a 5–2 win over the USA, and a 9–2 rout of Sweden.

Only Finland had made it close, losing 6–5 to a Canadian team stocked with future NHL talent. Craig Billington and Sean Burke shared goaltending duties, with Burke earning two shutouts; Terry Carkner and

All alone with the puck at the side of the Americans' net, Shayne Corson was Canada's top scorer in the tournament, but although he scored in the final game against the Soviets, it wasn't enough for gold.

Sylvain Côté patrolled the Canadian blue line with thundering efficiency; Joe Nieuwendyk centred Shayne Corson and Jim Sandlak as the tournament's top scoring line; and Mike Stapleton centred Scott Mellanby and Luc Robitaille, a late replacement for injured Stéphane Richer, who used his last-minute chance to catapult himself from the 171st overall draft pick into a Hall of Fame career with the Kings and Red Wings.

Canada was accused of both piling on bodies and padding the score, but in a series whose round-robin format decreed that the winner—in the case of tied teams—would be the one with the best goals-for-and-against differential, the Canadians were leaving nothing to chance. So when Canada met the USSR on January 2, both teams were the only two unbeaten squads, with identical 5–0 records. Canada, however, had the better goal differential to date: 50–12, versus the Soviets' 34–10. Even though both teams had one more game remaining after playing each other, everyone knew that this match was really the gold-medal game.

All 17,369 seats in Hamilton had been sold well in advance, and fans, many of them in Team Canada's red and white sweaters, bore signs echoing the 1972 Summit Series: "Da, da, Canada; nyet, nyet Soviet." When Jim Sandlak dumped Alexander Semak into the visitors' penalty box and Shayne Corson scored for Canada, it looked very much like yes, yes, the Canadians were on their way to gold. But the Soviets answered back with four straight goals, and Canadian brawn was no match for Soviet speed. "Canadians insist they learn something whenever they play the Soviets," wrote legendary sportswriter Trent Frayne the morning after Canada's loss of both game and gold. "Surely what they discovered last night was that they'd better learn to fly."

Despite his disappointment at losing the gold medal to the Soviets, Luc Robitaille—a late selection to the team—used the tournament to show the world his formidable hockey talent.

THE PUNCH-UP IN PIESTANY

The team of self-described "knuckleheads" who represented Canada at the 1987 World Junior Championship in Czechoslovakia arrived at the tournament looking to teach the Soviets a lesson after Canada's loss of the gold to them the year before at home, in Hamilton.

This edition of the Canadian team featured players who would go on to stand out—for a variety of reasons—in the pros: Brendan Shanahan, Luke Richardson, Mike Keane, Glen Wesley, and Theoren Fleury, being some of the marquee names on the twenty-man squad, nineteen of whom would go on to play in the NHL. And the 1987 world juniors would be remembered not for its slapshots, but for its punches.

The players on the squad, coached by the Scottish-born, hard-nosed Bert Templeton of the St. Catharines Fincups, were not exactly the poster boys imagined by Murray Costello and Hockey Canada when they created the Program of Excellence. The players broke curfew, they enjoyed as much Czech pilsner as they could pack away, and generally behaved like the rowdy teenagers that they were on an Eastern European road trip.

On the ice, the Canadians started out by beating the Swiss 6–4, but the curve quickly went downhill when they tied the Finns 6–6, and lost to the Czechs, 5–1. They reversed the slide with a gift of an opponent in Poland, whom they beat 18–3, and followed up with 6–2 and 4–3 wins over the USA and Sweden. So by the time the Canadians entered their final game on January 4, they could take back the gold by beating the Soviets by more than four goals, and better still, the Soviets couldn't win anything. The USSR had played a disastrous tournament, and the team entered its game against Canada with a 2–3–1 record.

Theo Fleury was part of the impressive roster that came home disappointed in 1987. Like many from that team, he would get another shot at gold wearing the maple leaf. Here, he waves the flag after winning the gold medal in Utah, 2002.

Some observers claimed that it was this nothing-to-lose attitude on the Soviet team that would lead to Canada making "the most disgraceful exit from a world tournament in this country's hockey history." Indeed, a pall of doom shadowed the Piestany arena at the beginning of the second period, when players and fans observed a moment of silence in respect for the four Swift Current Bronco players who were killed when their team bus crashed five days earlier in Saskatchewan.

For the next five minutes after the announcement, the game took on a funereal tone, sluggish and moody, before the two teams traded goals. By the time the infamous "Punch-Up in Piestany" began, the Canadians were winning 4–2. The catalyst for the violence was a collision between a Soviet player and Team Canada's Everett Sanipass, which resulted in a fight. Then an unpenalized two-handed slash to Theoren Fleury by a USSR player started another fight. When a Soviet player left his team's bench, the bench-clearing melee ensued, with at least twelve separate fights taking place. Eventually, the Norwegian referee—chosen for neutrality rather than competence—and the linesmen left the ice (later claiming they were told to do so by the IIHF), and arena officials turned out the lights to try to end the brawl, which exhausted itself after twenty minutes amid fans' whistles of derision and chants of, "We want hockey!"

"The majority of fault lies with the officials, and to some extent, the Soviets, for starting it," said Canada's minister for amateur sport and fitness Otto Jelinek. "Canada has been painted awfully unfairly. Maybe the Canadians lacked a little bit of discipline, but emotions can run high … you really can't blame the kids."

People were blaming the coach, Bert Templeton, who had a reputation in junior hockey circles as an agitator. A cartoon in the *Toronto Star* showed the Soviets in their dressing room, planning second-period strategy in front of a chalkboard. "Don't worry comrades, we've found their weakness," says the bushy-browed Soviet coach, his pointer aimed squarely at a caricature of Bert Templeton in boxing gloves.

Polish linesman Julian Gorski tries to break up Canada's Everett Sanipass and the USSR's Sergei Shesterikov during the Punch-Up in Piestany.

Others blamed Canada's hockey culture, but one lone voice rose above the outrage in clarion defence of the Canadians. Indeed, it was the Punch-Up in Piestany that launched Don Cherry into his orbit as Canada's coach, when he told the CBC's Brian Williams that the Soviet coach "will be drinking water and bread in Siberia after this game. But he's got nothing to lose. Send 'em out, have a little thing. But Canada's going to end up with the short end of this, I'll tell you."

Cherry would turn out to be right. The IIHF held an emergency meeting with the second period unfinished, and with a vote of seven against Canada's lone vote, declared the game null and void. Both Canada and the USSR had been expelled from the tournament, and both would be leaving the world juniors with nothing. Fifteen years after the Summit Series, the country's rivalry with the Soviets was even hotter, and both countries now had another match to avenge. Their chance would come that summer in the 1987 Canada Cup.

THE FIRST WOMEN'S TOURNAMENT

Sharon Sanderson thought she'd never play hockey again. She was a passenger in a car on her way to a hockey meeting in 1981 when a drunk driver slammed head-on into her vehicle, killing her driver and nearly killing Sanderson, a defenceman for the Hamilton Golden Hawks of the Ontario Women's Hockey Association. Her right foot was pinned and its tendons exposed; both lower leg bones were broken; her pelvis was cracked; her front teeth almost severed her tongue; and her liver was lacerated. "They had three hours to put my femur back together before there was nerve damage," she said, "but my leg is one inch shorter."

A year after the accident Sanderson was back on skates, and in April 1987, she was playing for Team Canada in the world's first Women's Hockey Tournament, which made history at the North York Arena in the Toronto area. The Golden Hawks, as champions of Canada, represented the country as Team Canada, while Ontario also had a team in the tournament, reflecting the strength of Canadian women's hockey.

Switzerland, Japan, the Netherlands, the United States, and Sweden all sent teams to compete in the tournament, with the Swedish team getting a little help from a fellow hockey player in Toronto. "Borje Salming helped to sponsor our team to come here," said Maria Hedlund, a 19-year-old Swedish defenceman, grateful both for the gesture from the Toronto Maple Leafs star, and for the chance to play against the world's best. "In Canada and the USA, the women's hockey is better than in Sweden."

While historic, the tournament was also "unofficial" in that it wasn't sanctioned by the International Ice Hockey Federation. That, though,

The first "official" women's world hockey championship took place in Ottawa in March 1990.

was part of the plan in staging it, for it allowed women's hockey officials to strategize on how to finally give women their place on international ice.

Fran Rider, president of the Ontario Women's Hockey Association and chair of the tournament, held meetings with delegates of other countries, including Britain, China, Australia, and West Germany, in addition to those competing, to expand opportunities for women's hockey around the world. Even so, there was one place where the opportunities shrank: on the ice, with each period lasting just fifteen minutes. "Most countries are not accustomed to twenty-minute periods," said Rider. "Only Switzerland is."

It didn't matter to the Canadians, who more or less romped through the tournament, racking up scores last seen posted by the men's teams in the 1920s and '30s. Both Team Canada and Ontario scored nineteen goals each against the Netherlands, while Ontario beat the Swiss 16–0, and Canada thumped Japan 11–0.

The toughest competition the Canadians faced was, not surprisingly, from the United States. Team Canada beat the USA 2–1 in the round-robin portion of the tournament, while Ontario lost 4–2 to the Americans. They redeemed themselves in the semi-finals with a 5–2 win over the USA, to put them in the final against their countrywomen, Team Canada.

More than 1,000 fans turned out to watch Canada take a 1–0 lead on a first-period goal by Janet Stone, and so it remained until the third period, when Colleen Kohen added another. When Ontario's Angela James— soon to become a pillar of the national team—took a slashing penalty with a minute left, Canada's Kelly Weaver scored on a power play, and Shirley Cameron, another star in the making, added an empty-net goal to seal the 4–0 win for Canada. Team Canada won the first Hazel McCallion World Cup, named in honour of the legendary mayor of Mississauga and women's hockey pioneer.

"We opened a lot of eyes about women's hockey," said Team Canada captain Marion Coveny. West German delegate Wolfgang Sorge agreed. "I will report what I have seen to [IIHF president, Günther] Dr. Sabetzki," he said. "I am sure he will support women's hockey."

Top:
Team Canada—to their horror—were given pink uniforms to wear at the 1990 Women's World Hockey Championship. Fans embraced the look, cheering the Pink Ladies to victory.

Bottom left:
A program from the first official women's world hockey championship. The multiple languages on the program reflect the multinational competition.

Bottom right:
Team Canada's main rival—even at the first official world championship—was the United States, which Canada defeated in the gold-medal game.

1990 Women's World Ice Hockey Championship

Championnat Mondial Féminin de Hockey sur Glace, 1990

SOUVENIR PROGRAM
Souvenir Program
Minnesprogram
Programme Souvenir
Souvenirprogramm
Muisto-ohjelma
記念プログラム
Programm zum Andenken an
Women's World Ice Hockey Championship 1990

THE 1987 CANADA CUP

They have been called the "greatest three games ever played," which is indeed an extravagant claim when it comes to Canadian hockey. But the 1987 Canada Cup takes on legendary status because of just how Canada's tough victory affirmed the Canadian way of playing to win in the sport that the country had invented.

Team Canada was led by Wayne Gretzky and Mario Lemieux, playing together for the only time ever on the same line, and they were supported by an all-star group of players that included Gretzky's Stanley Cup–winning Edmonton Oilers teammates Grant Fuhr, Mark Messier, Paul Coffey, and Glenn Anderson.

Gretzky scored Canada's first goal in the round robin, which wound up in a 4–4 tie with the Czechs at the Saddledome in Calgary. After beating the Finns, the USA, and the Swedes, Canada met the Soviets in the final game of the round robin, and Gretzky saved the day with a goal in the final three minutes of the game at Hamilton's Copps Coliseum, to salvage a 3–3 tie for Canada.

The Soviets and Canada made it through the semi-finals to meet again in the three-game final, with both teams itching to show the world what a hockey champion looked like. The Canadians erased a 4–1 Soviet lead in the second period to send the first game into overtime, which the Soviets won, 6–5. The second game went into overtime as well, but this time it was the Soviets who had played catch-up, after Mario Lemieux, assisted by Wayne Gretzky, had staked the Canadians to a 3–1 lead. With the score tied at five in the second period of overtime, Gretzky notched

Edmonton Oilers' Hall of Fame goalie Grant Fuhr makes an acrobatic save in the 1987 Canada Cup.

his fifth assist of the evening and Lemieux his hat trick when he scored the winning goal at 10:07 to give Canada the 6–5 victory.

The Canada Cup had come down to a one-game, winner-take-all match at Copps on September 15—and shades of a game played in September fifteen years earlier coloured the beginning of the must-win game. The Soviets looked to have been underestimated by Canada once again as they raced out to a 3–0 lead in the first eight minutes of the opening frame. Still, that left fifty-two minutes for the Canadians to regroup, and by the time the third period began, Canada had a 5–4 lead.

The Soviets tied the game with less than eight minutes left, and it looked, incredibly, as if the third and final game was heading into overtime as well. With less than two minutes left on the clock, Dale Hawerchuk won a faceoff in the Canadian zone and passed the puck to Gretzky, who took off down the left wing. Canadian defenceman Larry Murphy skated along with Gretzky, acting, it would turn out, as a decoy. When Soviet defender Igor Kravchuk, the last man back, dropped to block the pass that he thought Gretzky was going to make to Murphy, Gretzky deftly fed the puck back to Lemieux, who was as surprised as the sprawling Soviet.

"I thought he was going to pass the puck to Murphy," the 21-year-old Lemieux said. "That other defenceman went for Wayne and that left me free. As I skated in, I saw that the top shelf was open. I was just trying to find a hole."

Lemieux fired a rising wrist shot into the top right corner over the shoulder of Soviet goalie Sergei Mylnikov, and Canada had won the 1987 Canada Cup.

"We wanted to keep Gretzky under control," said a resigned Soviet assistant coach, Igor Dmitriev, after the defeat, "but because he plays centre, and then left, and then right, and everywhere else, it is very bad for your team to play when one player chases him around."

It was Wayne Gretzky though, with characteristic modesty, who put his finger on the Canadian victory by invoking the virtues of Canadian hockey. "We might not have as much talent as they do," he said, "but it's the trademark of Canadians to work hard. We won it on guts and desire."

Top:
Wayne Gretzky hoists the 1987 Canada Cup.

Middle:
Mario Lemieux powers past the Soviet defence. Lemieux would score the 1987 Canada Cup winning goal.

Bottom:
Team Canada's 1987 Canada Cup roster was stocked with Edmonton Oiler talent, which helped Oilers Wayne Gretzky and Paul Coffey connect on the ice.

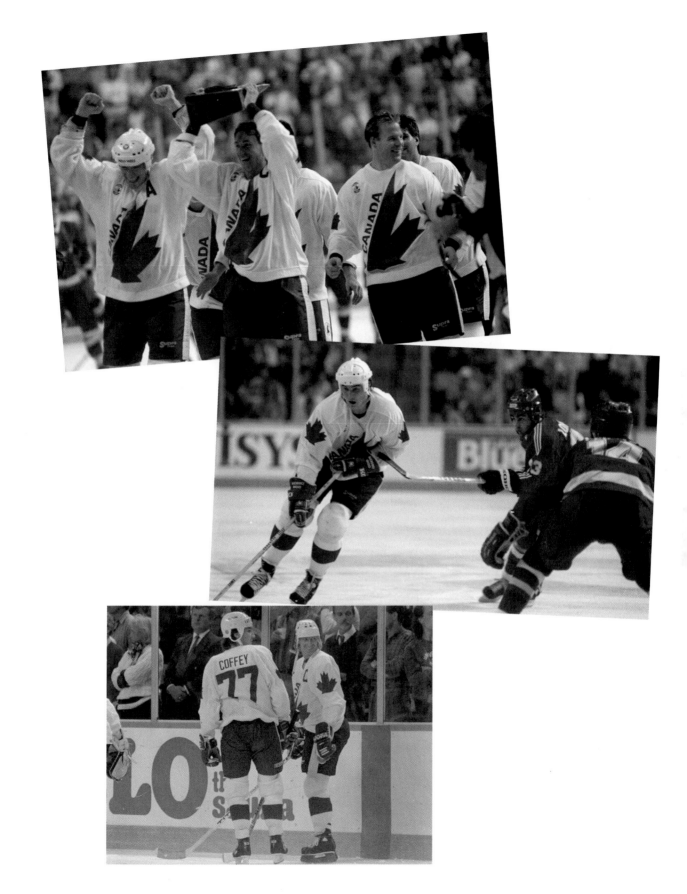

THE 1988 WORLD JUNIORS REDEMPTION

Theo Fleury had been on the ice for the Punch-Up in Piestany in 1987, and now as captain of the Canadian squad, it was his and Team Canada's mission at the 1988 World Junior Championship to redeem the name of the Canadians who felt they had been suckered by the Soviets in the last tournament. The fact that the 1988 juniors were taking place in Moscow sweetened the desire for revenge—but also the possibility for even greater humiliation.

Hockey Canada made sure that the team and their coach Dave Chambers understood the meaning of the Program of Excellence: discipline would be the order of the tournament, both on and off the ice.

"We are looking for control with intensity and emotion," Chambers said. "We want to make sure we don't overdo it so we are not a bunch of passive nice guys."

The round-robin tournament format would see the top three teams winning medals. As far as the Canadians were concerned, their true gold-medal game fell on New Year's Day 1988 when they played the Soviets. Canada went up 2–0 on goals by Fleury and Trevor Linden, a lead they carried into the second period when the USSR finally found a way to beat Jimmy Waite, who had been superlative in net. Canada added a third goal, which proved to be the winner, as the Soviets, despite adding another goal and swarming Waite, couldn't tie the game.

Canada had two games left, against Poland and West Germany, and

Team Canada celebrates redemption after winning the 1988 world junior gold medal.

in winning them won the gold medal, but the players knew after beating the Soviets they had done what they set out to do. "For a year I figured the Russians took away something very special that belonged to me," Fleury said. "The world championship gold medal." With 8–1 and 9–1 wins over the Germans and Poles, the Canadians had their gold medal—and redemption.

Even so, there were worries at home that despite Canada's success internationally, the players who were needed to stock a program of excellence were in danger of running into short supply. The Canadian Amateur Hockey Association's statistics showed that, between 1980 and 1986, peewee registration (up to age 12) was down 25 percent, bantam (age 15) down 38 percent, and midget (age 17) down 47 percent.

Among the reasons for the steep decline—argued from ice rinks to boardrooms—were both the high cost of hockey, in terms of equipment and travel, and a dearth of talent: teenage players were now allowed on NHL teams. As a result, minor-pro leagues, as well as those offering intermediate and senior hockey, were disappearing. "One of the biggest reasons for the drop at the bottom of minor hockey is that there are fewer places for them to go at the top," said Vern McCallum, secretary-manager of the Ontario Minor Hockey Association.

"We have perhaps created an elite of the elite," said Brent Ladds, president of the Ontario Hockey Association, in assessing the results of a demanding, high-performance program designed to build hockey excellence. But it also came with a cost. "If we start to kill the dream [of players] too early, we discourage people from playing hockey."

Though the banner behind Canada's 1988 world junior team lists two gold medals, this squad added a third in Moscow.

THE 1988 OLYMPIC WINTER GAMES IN CALGARY

Chicago Blackhawks draft pick Trent Yawney —one of the few NHLers on Team Canada— defends against Finland at the 1988 Calgary Olympic Winter Games.

In 1986, IIHF president Günther Sabetzki had announced that the 1988 Olympic Winter Games in Calgary would be the first truly "open" Olympics for hockey players. "Canada can use Wayne Gretzky if it wants to," he said. The NHL said differently, with its president, John Ziegler, arguing that NHL fans (especially season-ticket holders) would not tolerate being deprived of star players while the Olympic Games were going on.

Alan Eagleson, executive director of the NHLPA, took another view, one echoing the need for commitment argued by Father Bauer, national team visionary: "It's remote to assume that a Gretzky would be available. [Coach] Dave King would want players with him for more than just the three weeks of competition. We've learned that you can't take a team of players eliminated from the various teams in the NHL on Monday and expect them to beat the Russians on Tuesday. But if you could get some of these guys involved for six months, it would be interesting."

As a result, Canada did not send an A-list of NHLers to the 1988 Winter Games. Those players who did sign on to Canada's Olympic hockey project had to leave their professional leagues for the season in exchange for the glory of wearing the maple leaf and $12,000 (they had to pay their own living expenses). Andy Moog, a Stanley Cup–winning goalie with the Edmonton Oilers, was sitting out the season due to a contract dispute, and was the biggest name on the team. His number

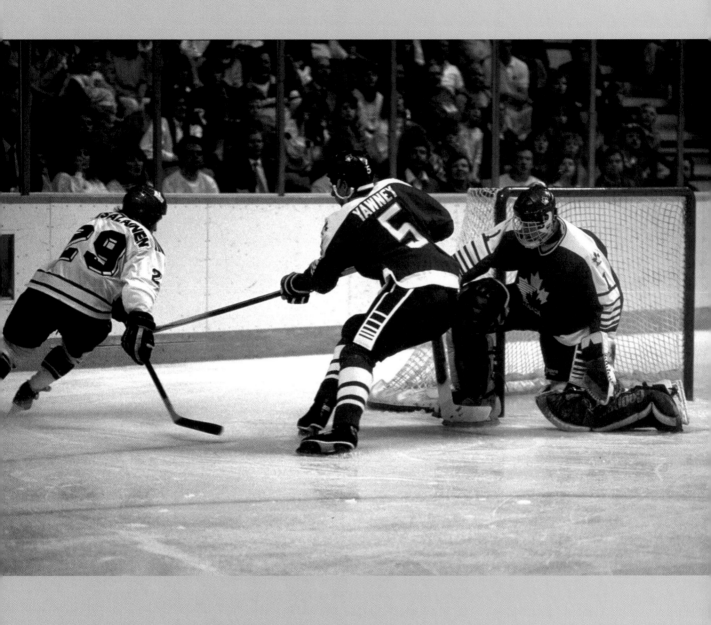

two, Sean Burke, had been the second-round draft pick of the New Jersey Devils in 1985, while team captain Trent Yawney was a third-round pick of Chicago the year before. Both Burke and Yawney would have long NHL careers.

Calgary's brand new reverse hyperbolic paraboloid known as the Saddledome was the biggest Olympic hockey venue to date, seating 20,016 fans, with an ice surface that could expand to international size. The twelve teams were divided into two groups, playing a five-game round-robin tournament. The top three teams from each group would advance to the medal round, with results from the previous round counting in their statistics—a calculation that had robbed Canada of an Olympic medal in 1964.

The 1988 Canadian Olympic hockey team was built on the model created by Father David Bauer—a true national team that trained together for months before the Olympics. The team made it to the medal round, but after a loss to the Soviets, it finished fourth.

Team Canada made it to the medal round, but ran into reality against the Soviets. The Canadians played a strong first period, but forty-five seconds into the second, the USSR broke the scoreless tie with a wraparound goal, then added another on a power play that Frank Orr colourfully reported had been awarded "when a comrade took a dive that would have earned him no worse than a silver medal at the Summer Games. Everyone in the house saw the splash except the Finnish referee Antti Koskinen, one in a series of things Antti didn't notice."

Canada had to open up its game, a strategy for which the team had not been built, and eventually went down 5–0 to the Soviets, who would wind up taking the gold medal, with Canada finishing in fourth. Even so, now

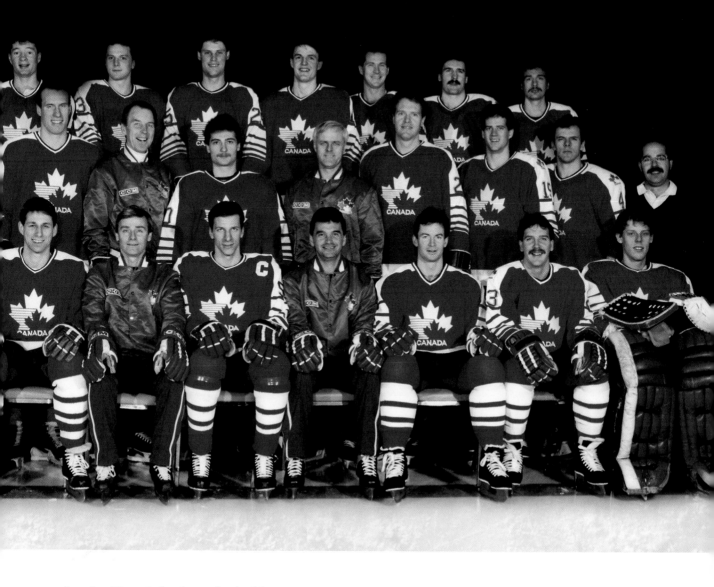

that the Olympic hockey rules had been reset, Canada would bring its best back
to the Olympics in quest of a gold medal it had not won since 1952. But other
changes would be coming, too, with the fall of the Berlin Wall, and the crumbling
of the Iron Curtain. Eastern Bloc players, who had been prevented from leaving
to compete in the NHL, would soon be playing in the world's best hockey league.
Some of the newly liberated countries that came to the fore after the Soviet
breakup would also hunger for hockey gold. The international game was only going
to get tougher for Canada.

JUSTINE BLAINEY

On April 17, 1982, Canada's *Constitution Act* became law, another historic stage in the country's self-definition as it loosened its colonial ties with Britain. Within that constitution was a *Charter of Rights and Freedoms*, expressing just what it meant to be a Canadian, with a powerful declaration of the rights of the person in section 15: "Every individual is equal before and under the law and has the right to the equal protection and equal benefit of the law without discrimination and, in particular, without discrimination based on race, national or ethnic origin, colour, religion, sex, age or mental or physical disability."

In spring 1985, 12-year-old Justine Blainey, a 5'1", 100-pound defenceman, made the Toronto Olympics, a boys' team in the third tier A division of the Metro Toronto Hockey League (MTHL), winning a place from among more than sixty other competitors. Her coach, Dan D'Amario, rated her the Olympics' sixth- or seventh-best player. "She is very competitive, wants to learn and has good basic skills in skating and shooting. She skates backwards as well or better than anyone her age in the A level. She will be a regular with us, most likely on right defence."

Like Abby Hoffman a generation before her, Blainey wanted to play in a boys' hockey league because they offered higher levels of competition. However, under existing Canadian Amateur Hockey Association rules, integrated hockey was permitted up to age 12 only—and only in areas where no girls' teams were available. Blainey was out of luck.

So, in September 1985, Justine Blainey took her case to the Supreme Court of Ontario to ask the court to order the Ontario Hockey Association

Justine Blainey's desire to play hockey at the highest level—with boys—took her all the way to Canada's highest court and advanced the country's human rights law.

to compel the Metro Toronto Hockey League to let her play. Also, the judge was asked to declare section 19(2) of the *Ontario Human Rights Code*, the section that permits sex discrimination in sports, unconstitutional. The court was further asked to issue an injunction so Blainey could play while the investigation continued.

The OHA's lawyer John Findlay argued that females, particularly those who had gone through puberty, were not equal to males in size, physiologically, nor equal in strength or aerobic capacity. In an argument rife with irony, he argued that the 3,500-member Ontario Women's Hockey Association would collapse—while that organization itself feared invasion by men if the sex segregation was removed.

Blainey lost the initial round, and the case moved through the courts all the way to the Supreme Court of Canada, which declared on June 26, 1986, that it was unconstitutional for the Ontario Hockey Association to prevent Blainey from playing with boys' teams. The Court also said the clause in the *Ontario Humans Rights Code* allowing for sex segregation in sport was unconstitutional.

Blainey's fight was not over, for she now had to convince the Ontario Human Rights Commission that the OHA regulation keeping her off the boys' team violated a section of the code guaranteeing no discrimination based on sex. The OHA's response was to state that girls were still not allowed on boys' teams.

Finally, on January 8, 1988, the Ontario Human Rights Commission ordered the MTHL East Enders to let Blainey play for the team, even though, said general manager Bruce Secord, a majority of East Enders players' parents voted against having Blainey on the team. Nevertheless, a week later, the now 15-year-old Blainey—who had celebrated her birthday on January 11—pulled on her black-and-gold number 55 sweater of the East Enders Ticats and skated out to become the first girl to legally play in the MTHL.

Playing at Forest Hill Arena in front of a boisterous crowd of 200—many of them from the media—Blainey held her own, and even took a punch on the chin. "She can play," said Shawn Wilcox, a bantam A player from another team, watching with his mates from the stands. "If she's good enough and can take the heat, why not?"

Not everyone was thrilled by this breakthrough in Canadian human rights. "This is a circus," said MTHL president John Gardner as he surveyed the reporters waiting for Blainey to emerge from her private dressing room after a 3–1 loss. "It's not fair to the team."

Blainey, however, was not bothered. "All around, it was a great day," she said after the game. "Hopefully, I can play the rest of the season, and hopefully, if I am big enough and strong enough, I can play next season, too."

Thirteen-year-old Justine Blainey raises her skates in victory after the Supreme Court of Canada rejected an Ontario Hockey Association bid to keep her from playing on a boys team, June 27, 1986.

THE 1990
WORLD JUNIORS

Canada went to the 1990 World Junior Championship in Helsinki on the back of a fourth-place finish the year before, and like many a Canadian team before them of late, they went to atone for the failure of their recent hockey ancestors.

With a squad featuring 16-year-old Eric Lindros, along with Stu Barnes, Kris Draper, Patrice Brisebois, and Stéphane Fiset in goal, Team Canada was looking to cruise comfortably into the medal round. After nearly losing their first game to the USA, they built on that 3–2 win to waltz past the Poles 12–0 and the Norwegians 6–3 before hitting a roadblock called Finland on December 30, 1989, whom they played to a 3–3 tie in Helsinki.

Canada's next game was on New Year's Day against the Soviets, and as had become the custom for both countries, it was a gold-medal match for the players—even though not for the tournament. Fiset had been in goal a year earlier when the Soviets had humbled the Canadians 7–2 in Fairbanks, Alaska, en route to winning the 1989 world juniors.

When the Soviets took a quick 3–0 lead in the first period, Fiset thought he was back in the Alaskan nightmare. "I said to myself, 'Oh no, not again.' But after our guys got a couple back I made that save on Bure and that did more for my confidence than anything else could have. I figured then that maybe we had the chance to beat the Russians if I didn't give them anything more."

Fiset had robbed speedy Soviet wizard Pavel Bure, who had deked him out of position and fired the puck homeward, only to have a diving Fiset block the shot with his arm and save the goal. Though the Soviets took a 3–2 lead into the second period, the Canadians scored three goals in that frame and added another in the third to win 6–4.

The Canadians followed up that emotional win by having a ninety-six-second mental breakdown two days later in their game against Sweden, which saw them blow a 4–2 lead in the third period, helped by a phantom penalty—so common to Canada in international play—to lose 5–4. Now the Canadians had to beat the Czechs in Turku in their final game, and hope that the Swedes could beat—or at least tie—the Soviets, which would give Canada the gold medal.

The Czechs—who had the firepower of Robert Reichel, Bobby Holik, and Jaromir Jagr—scored first, but Canada came back with two goals in the second period to take a 2–1 lead. But they knew that back in Helsinki, the Soviets were beating the Swedes by a goal. During a play stoppage with ninety seconds left, the Canadians got an assist from the public address system when the rink announcer declared that Sweden had done the unthinkable: they had tied the Russians 5–5, with one second left on the clock. If Canada could win this game, they would win the gold medal because they had already beaten the Russians. But the Czechs knew that if they could get two quick goals, they could win the gold, as they would finish with more points than Canada.

Reichel, Holik, and Jagr didn't leave the ice, coming hard at the Canadians as Fiset kept the puck out of the net and time ticked off the clock as if it had been slowed down to cause maximum agony to Canadian hearts. "There was a faceoff in our end late," recalled coach Guy Charron. "It was to the right of Fiset. I had been using Stu Barnes for those faceoffs because he's a right-hand shot. Kris Draper asked me if he could take the faceoff; he told me he could win it." Draper won the faceoff, the Canadians killed the clock, and Canada had won gold.

Or maybe not. Shortly after the game, Team Canada's coaches learned that the Soviets were protesting the final Swedish goal, saying they had video that proved the puck went in the net after time had expired. Canada's coaches didn't breathe a word of this brewing disappointment as the team made the 200-kilometre drive to the awards ceremony in Helsinki. By the time they arrived, tournament officials had viewed footage that showed the Swedes had put the puck in the Soviet net at 19:59 of the third period, and the Soviets had no footage to counter that. It had not been a straight line to the pinnacle, but Canada's juniors were once again champions of the world.

The 1990 edition of Team Canada's juniors badly wanted to avenge their humiliation at the 1989 World Junior Championship. After coming from behind to defeat Pavel Bure and the speedy Soviets, they vanquished the Czechs to win gold.

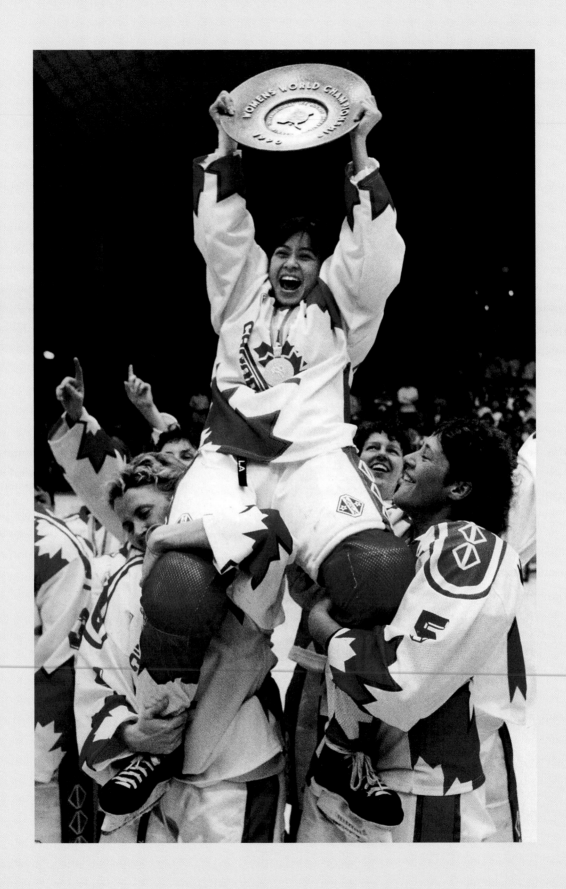

SHIRLEY CAMERON

Shirley Cameron dared to hope when she helped to found the Edmonton Chimos women's hockey team in 1973 that the day would come when women from around the world would have a tournament of their own. Indeed, hope was the best strategy, as almost a decade later, Cameron, a 29-year-old letter carrier for Canada Post, had to "call in sick" so she could travel to Brantford, Ontario, to play in the inaugural Canadian women's national championship tournament in 1982. As a junior employee, she couldn't rearrange her vacation schedule and hoped that no one would notice her absence.

When the Chimos won silver in the tournament after losing to Ontario in overtime, and Cameron, a centre, scored seven goals and eight assists in six games, the media took notice, and so, too, did Canada Post when they read about her exploits in the *Toronto Sun* after a reporter who promised not to use her story about how she had to get time off to play the tournament broke his promise.

"I got suspended and probably if that happened nowadays I probably would have gotten fired," Cameron said. "But at that time they suspended me for a week. So it cost me a week of my wages."

Finally, after decades of struggle to prove that the women's game was more than a novelty, women's teams from Sweden, Finland, Norway, West Germany, Switzerland, Japan, the United States, and Canada converged on Ottawa in March 1990 to show the world their game for the first time at an elite level. The first official IIHF Women's world championship had arrived. Shirley Cameron was there, along with France St.-Louis, both of

Susie Yuen is hoisted by her teammates after the Canadian women's team defeated Team USA to win the first women's world hockey championship in Ottawa.

them as pioneers of Canadian women's hockey, to mentor young players like Geraldine Heaney, Angela James, Vicky Sunohara, Judy Diduck, and Laura Schuler, who would form the core of Canada's women's team for years to come.

At the beginning of the 1990s, 7,500 women and girls played in leagues affiliated with the Canadian Amateur Hockey Association, while another 18,000 played for high-school, university, or recreational teams. And as a statement of how far the women's game had penetrated popular culture, TSN televised four games nationally in 1990, and about eighty-five journalists from six countries covered the most important tournament yet in the history of women's hockey.

Even so, the organizers made the Canadian team wear pink uniforms, and offered one hundred "beauty makeovers" as draw prizes. Despite their loathed uniforms, by the time the tournament was over, the "Pink Ladies" had outscored their European opponents 32–1 and thrashed Japan 18–0.

"Women's hockey is not the pyjama party you might imagine," wrote the correspondent for *Sports Illustrated*, whose coverage of the event was testament to the stature women's hockey had achieved. "They know how to play the game. Their breakout plays are the same ones used in the NHL, their passes are short and crisp, their skating strong and their puck-handling skills extraordinary."

The Canadians did what Canadian teams had done for so long in international play—crush the early opposition. In the round-robin portion of the tournament, Canada beat Sweden 15–1, West Germany 17–0, and Japan 18–0. Canada's semi-final match against Finland was a rally in pink, with the 4,416 fans receiving pink and white pompoms at the door, the arena workers in pink shirts, and a costumed pink flamingo driving the Zamboni, which had ten plastic pink flamingos decorating its hood.

The Canadians took a comfortable 6–3 lead into the third before letting down their guard, and suddenly the Finns scored twice to knock Canuck goalie Denise Caron out of the game with an injury in the fifth-goal scrum. Caron had to be fitted with a neck brace before being removed on a stretcher, and the injury shocked the Canadians into throwing up a wall around backup

Cathy Phillips, who didn't face a shot in the final six minutes.

"Was I worried?" asked Canadian coach Dave McMaster after the game. "I'm soaking wet."

The team was ecstatic, now one win away from a championship on home ice. "Winning women wear pink!" shouted forward Heather Ginzel, whose two-goal performance won her the game MVP award. "And you know what? A gold medal on these uniforms is going to look awesome!"

After spotting two goals to the United States in the championship game, the Canadians turned it on to the delight of the more than 8,000 fans in Ottawa's Civic Centre. They outshot the USA 40–15 and scored five unanswered goals to win the gold in a rugged, physical match that showcased

the skills and heart of the tournament's two best teams—and it began a fierce rivalry.

"How are they going to keep us out of the Olympics now?" asked Dave McMaster after the win, referring to the bid to have women's hockey admitted to the 1992 Olympic Winter Games. "This was as big a victory for women's hockey as it was for Canada. And it will only get better from here."

In July 1992, the IOC voted to include women's hockey in the Olympics starting in 1998. It was too late for Shirley Cameron, who retired as a player in 1992 in order to coach. As a testament to her excellence in playing and developing the women's game, the winner of the annual ten-game super series between Alberta's top two teams—the Chimos and the Calgary Oval X-Treme—is awarded a trophy named after her, the Cameron Cup.

Goalie Denise Caron celebrates her 1990 IIHF women's hockey championship gold. To her left is France St.-Louis, who went on to be awarded the Order of Hockey in Canada and served as chef-de-mission in Sochi.

THE 1991
WORLD JUNIORS

It looked as if Team Canada had ruined TSN's party. The fledgling Canadian sports network had taken over broadcasting the world junior championships from the CBC, and in 1991, at home in Saskatchewan, TSN had all seven of Canada's games scheduled to air. Canadians had responded, turning on and connecting with the kids wearing the maple leaf to create almost instant destination television over the Christmas holidays from that moment on. And then Team Canada met the Czechs.

The Canadians, featuring Eric Lindros in his draft year, had rolled along in their first five games—hitting a speed bump against Doug Weight and the USA, whom they tied 4–4—on their way to cruising over the Swiss 6–0, Norway 10–1, Sweden 7–4, and the Finns 5–1. As they headed into a game against the Czechs on January 2, 1991, the Canadian juniors knew that their opponent had lost to the Swedes and was without eligible stars like Jaromir Jagr and Bobby Holik, as they were now otherwise engaged in the NHL.

The Czechs were not planning to become Canadian roadkill, and took a 2–0 lead. Canada had come back to defeat the Swedes and tie the USA, and once again, they began the climb out of a hole of their own making, though the Czechs were fighting back. Pat Falloon scored for Canada with fifteen seconds left in the first period, but Jozef Stumpel restored the Czechs' two-goal lead. Canada scored again, the Czechs responded, Mike Craig answered back, and then, with forty-nine seconds left in the second period, Craig set up Eric Lindros for the tying goal. In the third period, the duo connected again when Lindros won a faceoff in the Czech end, and set up Craig to put Canada up 5–4.

Team Canada's loss to the Czechs at the 1991 World Junior Championship in Saskatchewan nearly ruined the party—but a little help from Finland got them into the gold-medal game against the Russians, where they sealed the deal.

The Czechs tied the game on a power-play goal late in the third, and then with just over two minutes left to play, Martin Rucinsky scored the game-winner for the Czechs. It looked as if Canada had lost a gold medal at home without even having had the chance to play the Soviets. Their hopes rested on the slimmest of miracles: the Finns defeating or even tying Pavel Bure and his teammates on January 3. If the Finns could pull it off, then the Canadians could win gold by beating the Soviets the next night.

Saskatchewan had endured ten days of brutally cold temperatures, and so the Canadians stayed put in their Saskatoon hotel while the Finns played the Soviets in Regina. As TSN had other commitments that night, the network did not broadcast the game, but it did send live updates, which the players followed like kids at a peewee hockey tournament, the doors to their rooms open, and players wandering back and forth, anxious about the result, and fearing it, too.

But fourteen minutes into the second period, the Finns had an improbable 4–0 lead on the Soviets at the Regina Agridome before an astonished, if sparse, crowd. Back in the hotel, Team Canada was ecstatic. "We were going crazy," recalled centre Kent Manderville. "But we also knew the lead wasn't safe, not with all the firepower [the Soviets] had, especially Bure."

Bure, who would finish as the leading scorer in the tournament, potted a hat trick to put the Soviets up 5–4 with less than ten minutes left in the game. As Team Canada had feared, the Soviet arsenal had been unleashed, and their golden hopes were just that. They couldn't expect a gift like they'd received the year before, when the Swedes scored against the Soviets with one second left to give Canada the gold.

No, they couldn't. This time, the Finns scored with a fluky backhand with 15 seconds left, to tie the Soviets 5–5. Now Canada could win gold by beating the Soviets. And the Soviets could win gold by tying the Canadians.

It looked, once again, as if Canada was going to be disappointed. With a little over five minutes left in Canada's final game, and with a sold-out Saskatchewan Place and more than a million Canadians tuned in to watch the triumph, the two teams were tied 2–2 after Canada had blown a 2–0 lead.

With the play looking to come out of the Soviet zone, and a Soviet player floating at centre ice hoping for a breakaway pass, Canadian coach Dick Todd shouted at defenceman John Slaney—part of a "no-name" defence corps that had taken its media lumps—to back out of the Soviet zone. Slaney didn't hear the coach, focused as he was on knocking the puck down.

"I was able to stop it and shoot towards the net and it found holes in the traffic," Slaney recalled modestly, about the goal that won the gold for Canada and would have had the arctic winds howling through the arena if the celebration in the stands got any more roof-blowing raucous, as fans sang "O Canada" over and over again. "We had a terrific bunch of kids who made up for their weaknesses with big hearts," said Todd. "Sure, it looked a little bleak on Thursday night, but this is a very tough, well-balanced tournament, and anything can happen."

After blowing a two-goal lead in the final, Team Canada rallied with a late goal against the Soviets to win the 1991 World Junior gold medal in Saskatoon.

THE WORLD CUP OF SLEDGE HOCKEY

More than a century after the first indoor hockey game in Montreal, the sport had swept the planet. Australia and South Africa had become IIHF members in the 1930s. And Israel and Turkey joined up in 1991, the same year that saw East and West Germany leave the IIHF, as they no longer existed now that the Berlin Wall had come down and the reunification process was underway. Not only had Canada's game become global, but it had also triumphed over obstacles of class and gender—and in 1991, players with physical challenges were formally admitted to the world of international hockey.

The first world cup of sledge hockey was held in Oslo, Norway, in 1991. Sledge hockey had been invented by wheelchair-bound athletes in Sweden in 1961, and it slowly made its way to North America. In 1979, Dick Loiselle, a former director of Toronto's 1976 Paralympics, had brought back a sled from Europe, one given to him by Rolf Johansson, a Paralympic gold medallist in wheelchair track and field, and one of the inventors of sledge hockey. Four years later, in 1983, Canada held its first national sledge hockey tournament, in Medicine Hat, Alberta.

Each sledge hockey team has six players on the ice, including the goaltender. In order to be eligible for competition, sledge hockey players have to have a permanent disability that prevents them from playing

Greg Westlake joined Canada's sledge hockey team in 2003 and soon emerged as one of the country's hockey stars, winning gold and bronze Olympic medals at Torino and Sochi.

hockey on skates, such as amputation of the leg or foot, paralysis, joint immobility, or cerebral palsy.

Players are strapped into a metal frame that rests on two regular-sized skate blades and is high enough to allow the puck to pass underneath. Sledge hockey players use two 75-centimetre-long hockey sticks, with spikes on one end and blades on the other. They use the spikes to power the sledge across the ice, and the slightly curved blade to play the puck.

In the first sledge hockey world cup, Sweden lost for the first time in twenty-five years to Team Canada, who would win the championship. As with the first exhibition of ice hockey in the Olympic Games, sledge hockey would not become official for another three years. Nevertheless, Canada now had one more hockey gold medal to add to its international collection, and other countries had one more Canadian team to beat to take it away.

Sledge hockey was introduced to the world in 1961. In 1983, Canada held its first sledge hockey tournament.

Canada's Marc Dorion (left) and Norway's Tommy Rovelstad collide during the bronze medal round at the 2010 Vancouver Olympic Winter Games.

THE
FUTURE OF
HOCKEY IN 1991

In mid-November 1991, the federal government hosted a conference in Toronto's Sutton Place hotel to once again examine the state of the national game. The Open Ice Trust saw stakeholders—pros, amateurs, collegians—convene to examine how Canada's game could be made better. One of the issues occupying the conference was hockey violence, especially in the younger leagues.

The Open Ice Trust concluded that what had been lost in hockey was the pleasure of playing. In order to save hockey, it needed to become again what it had always been at its untainted heart: fun.

Creativity, skill, and fair play were emphasized at hockey camps and in kids' leagues. Schools, too, such as Edouard-Montpetit, a "sport etude" school in Montreal, changed the way they taught hockey. Students had to maintain a 75 percent average to stay on the team, and while they played hockey, they needed to learn self-reliance and solutions through making and fixing mistakes. It would be about self-discovery through learning— not about rules, or intimidation and violence.

Canada went back to the hockey drawing board in 1991 to see how the game could be made better. The answer was to go back to the basics: hockey should be played for fun. From that, all good things would come.

THE 1991 CANADA CUP

The 1991 Canada Cup saw even heavier expectations placed on Team Canada to once again prove supremacy in the national game, even if Patrick Roy, Mario Lemieux, Joe Sakic, Ray Bourque, and Steve Yzerman were not on the team. Coming off two straight tournament wins in 1984 and 1987, Canada's roster depth could boast a team of Wayne Gretzky, Mark Messier, Luc Robitaille, Brendan Shanahan, Al MacInnis, Paul Coffey, Steve Larmer, and 18-year-old Eric Lindros, a team touted to score the Canada Cup hat trick.

Even the Soviets were predicting a Canadian win, in a characteristically cold-blooded way. "I'm not only a journalist but also a scientist," said Eugeny Potenkin, a reporter with the USSR's *Sports World*, and "by computer analysis, we have determined that the Soviet national team gets a mark of 2,100. The Canadians get 1,100. But because the Canadians are playing at home, we double the score. That brings them to 2,200—100 points more than the Soviet Union. So Canada wins."

And yet, once again national expectation and Soviet computers ran into reality when Canada met Markus Ketterer, a hot goalie, in their first game against the Finns in Toronto, and the best they could achieve was a 2–2 tie. The Canadians bounced back with a series of convincing 6–3 and 6–2 wins over the USA and the Czechs, and a 4–1 win against Sweden. Canada's other tie was against the USSR, which, despite the Soviet computer's prediction of a vastly superior team, had a depleted lineup, and due to the imminent political implosion of the USSR, was making its last appearance as the USSR in a major hockey tournament. The final

The Great One stands beside the Next One, 18-year-old Eric Lindros, as the duo prepare to lead Canada to victory in the 1991 Canada Cup.

edition of Team USSR would finish the 1991 Canada Cup in second-to-last place in the round robin.

The Canadians went into their semi-final against Sweden as if it was Game 7 of the Stanley Cup final, according to the man who was a late addition to the team and who would become celebrated for his Game 7 heroics. "It's a sudden-death hockey game," Mark Messier said, after a team workout at Maple Leaf Gardens. "You really have to play a disciplined game because there are so many things that can happen, like a bad bounce or a bad call ... in sudden death."

Canada played a perfect game, beating the Swedes 4–0, and winning a spot in the best-of-three final against the USA. Disaster seemed to strike Canada in Game 1, when the USA defenceman Gary Suter—who had been suspended from the 1987 Canada Cup for retaliating to a Soviet spear by breaking his stick across a USSR player's face—cross-checked Wayne Gretzky from behind, smashing his face into the glass. The hit, which Canada's head coach Mike Keenan called "illegal," aggravated a two-year-old back injury, and Gretzky was out not only for the series but also for a month of the soon-to-follow NHL season.

After winning the first game 4–1, the Canadians were careful to avoid talk of scalp-hunting Suter in Game 2. "I'm sure if you talk to Gretz, the first thing he'll say is make sure we go out and win," said Brendan Shanahan. "We're not concerned with Gary Suter. We're not going to waste a month of preparation just to get even."

In the end, it all came down to Gary Suter. With less than eight minutes left in Game 2, with the teams tied 2–2, the USA was in the last thirty seconds of a sharp-looking power play that had already generated five scoring chances. When Suter tried to keep the puck in the Canadian zone, he banged it off the shin of Steve Larmer, who was off to the races. Suter couldn't catch Larmer as he raced down the ice, drew US goalie Mike Richter out of the net, and tucked a backhand through the 5-hole. Larmer added an empty-net goal on another Suter error, and Canada had won its fourth and last Canada Cup. The tournament that had begun as an outgrowth of Canada's epic series against the Soviets in 1972 had needed to become global in scope and sensibility. And as a sign of its success, it would next appear in 1996 to proclaim what it had become: the World Cup of Hockey.

Canada defeated Team USA in a best-of-three final to win the country's fourth—and final—Canada Cup. Here, Bill Ranford and Eric Desjardins keep the puck away from American sniper Brett Hull.

THE 1992 WINTER OLYMPICS

When Canada went into its second "pro team" Olympics at Albertville, France, in 1992, the pundits were reminding fans to keep their expectations in perspective. "This being the Olympics and all it's okay to dust off the cliché and say Canada is going for the gold," wrote Bob McKenzie in his *Toronto Star* column, "but remember that the bronze medal is the legitimate goal and measure of success in 1992."

The bronze medal? Our goal? Indeed, Canada's last Olympic hockey medal had been a bronze at Grenoble in 1968, when Father Bauer's national team was singing its swan song. Team Canada, under coach Dave King, had failed to win a medal as amateurs in Sarajevo in 1984, nor with the addition of professionals at home in Calgary in 1988.

The 1992 version wasn't exactly a team stocked with dazzling NHL talent, but rather with players who didn't fit, for one reason or another, in the NHL. Sean Burke, the goalie, had wound up out of favour in New Jersey; Joe Juneau had insulted the parsimony of Boston by demanding a one-way contract; no one would take Toronto forward Dave Hannan in a trade; and 18-year-old Eric Lindros had offended all of Quebec by refusing to play for Marcel Aubut's NHL Nordiques, promising to play anywhere but Quebec City until he was eligible for the amateur draft again in two years. The fact that Lindros, who had won a Canada Cup playing with the pros and a gold as a junior in Saskatoon in 1991, had not led the Canadian junior team to gold in Germany earlier in 1992—indeed, the team hadn't even won a medal—made people expect, if not demand, even more.

And yet, both with and against expectation, Team Canada played

A poster for the sixteenth Olympic Winter Games in Albertville, France, in 1992.

its way into the gold-medal match by defeating Germany 4–3 in a quarter-final shootout—the winner scored by Lindros—and then, after blowing a 2–0 lead against the Czechs in the semi-final, scoring two third-period goals to make it to the golden game against the Unified Team—which was what the Russians were calling themselves now that the USSR was no more.

Once again, Canada was meeting the Russians in a world championship game, much to the surprise of many. And yet, after two periods, and thanks to the superlative play of the goalie Burke, the score was 0–0. "In the dressing room, I told the players we were now starting a twenty-minute game for the gold medal," said Coach King. "And you know, even when they got the first goal, we were still confident."

In the end, Canada's 3–1 loss gave the country its first Olympic hockey medal in twenty-four years, and the colour of that medal was one step closer to the colour that mattered most. "The difference between gold and silver is very fine," Canada's captain Brad Schlegel said. "We were very close to winning the thing." It would take another decade, and heartache, before winning the thing would happen again.

Top:
Canada wasn't expected to do much at the 1992 Olympic Winter Games in Albertville, France. Despite negative predictions, the Canadians won the silver medal.

Bottom:
Goalie Sean Burke's superlative play in the 1992 Olympic Winter Games propelled Canada into the gold-medal game against the "Unified Team"—what remained of the Soviet Union post-breakup.

CANADA'S
WOMEN WIN
THE WORLD

I n April 1992, eight teams of the best female hockey players in the world descended on Tampere, Finland, 178 kilometres north of Helsinki, to compete for gold in the second edition of the women's world championship tournament.

Canada had won the inaugural title in 1990, and so automatically qualified for the 1992 tournament, as did the United States. The top five European women's teams were also included, and rounding out the group was China, playing in its first international tournament.

The Chinese were also Canada's first opponent, and the Canadians found them a challenge. "The Chinese were very aggressive, quite big, and not so well disciplined," said Canadian team manager Glynis Peters. "We had a hard time to do what we wanted to because they were all over the ice." All over the ice, perhaps, but taking twelve penalties and managing just thirteen shots on Canada's Marie-Claude Roy, who backstopped Team Canada to an 8–0 win, with France St.-Louis and Karen Nystrom notching two goals apiece.

The Canadians, favoured to win the tournament, followed their rout of China with a 10–0 trouncing of Denmark, and a 6–1 win over Sweden. After dispatching the host Finns 6–2 in the semi-final, Canada faced its chief rival, Team USA, on April 26 in the gold-medal match.

"Nancy Drolet and Danielle Goyette are quickly becoming as domin- ant in their sport as Wayne Gretzky and Mario Lemieux are in theirs,"

Team Canada defender Geraldine Heaney would win the 1992 Women's World Hockey Championship award as the tournament's best defenceman.

was the Canadian Press assessment in describing Drolet's hat trick and Goyette's goal and three assists as the duo led Canada to an 8–0 thumping of the USA. Other players who would long wear the Canadian colours also chipped in, with Angela James adding two goals, and 19-year-old Manon Rheaume posting the shutout.

Canada's second consec-utive world gold medal marked the quarter pole of an eight-straight women's world championship triumph for the country, which continued until the USA defeated Canada 1–0 in a shootout in 2005.

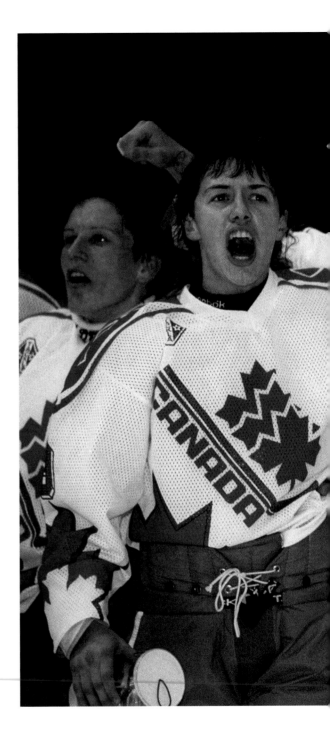

Canada's women celebrate their second world championship with an exuberant rendition of "O Canada."

MANON RHEAUME PLAYS IN THE NHL

Manon Rheaume made history when she appeared in goal for Tampa Bay during an NHL exhibition game in 1992—and by back-stopping Team Canada to two women's world hockey gold medals.

Just five months after starring in the women's world championship, Manon Rheaume played in an NHL game for the expansion Tampa Bay Lightning on September 23, 1992. Some called it a publicity stunt, suggesting that Tampa's GM Phil Esposito wanted to create some excitement around a new NHL franchise. But Rheaume had played with the boys before, and indeed, her father had even disguised her as a boy to play when she was a child. In 1983, while Justine Blainey was about to launch in the courts her fight to play with the boys, Rheaume had become the first girl to play in the Quebec International Pee-Wee Hockey Tournament, and she had also played in the Quebec Major Junior League. For the Lightning on this day, Rheaume made seven saves in her first-period exhibition game outing against St. Louis, surrendering two goals. The image of her in net, playing in the world's premiere hockey league, inspired another generation of girls to take up hockey. And Rheaume would continue to inspire by leading the Canadian women's team to a world championship the following year.

CANADA'S JUNIORS BEGIN A GOLDEN RUN

In late December 1992, the Team Canada juniors came to Gävle, a picturesque fishing village more than 300 kilometres north of Stockholm, to avenge a nasty ghost from the year before. In the 1992 World Junior Championship, the Canadians had finished sixth out of eight teams, just ahead of host Germany and the Swiss team. The humiliation of that tournament saw an almost complete reset of the Canadian squad, with only three returning players from the debacle of '92. One of those players was centre Tyler Wright, who gave his teammates a rousing address about how things went bad in Germany, and how they could prevent the same fate by knowing their chief opponent, Sweden, and the best player on the Swedish team, Peter Forsberg.

The Canadians already knew about Forsberg because they had his derisive words about them taped to their dressing room wall. "They are not so good," Forsberg sneered after watching Manny Legace backstop the Canadians to a 3–0 win over the USA in their first game of the round-robin tournament. "We are going to beat them. We are better skaters. They play tough, but it's a bigger ice surface and they're going to have problems with that. They may be good, but they are not so tough."

The Swedes had already beaten an undisciplined Canadian squad 8–5 in an exhibition game, scoring seven of their goals on the power play. Forsberg had sat out that game with the flu, but he would have a huge impact on the tournament, centring Markus Naslund and Niklas

275

Sundstrom, with the trio combining for thirty goals and sixty-nine points—and Forsberg alone had thirty-one points. The Canadians had talent, too, with top prospects Alexandre Daigle, Chris Pronger, Chris Gratton, Paul Kariya, and Rob Niedermayer being the first five selections at the NHL draft that coming June.

The Gävle Arena was made of pine and its walls featured images of Canadian geese—the emblem of the town's third-division hockey club—and Team Canada took that as a talisman going into its second game of the seven-game tournament, for the Canucks' opponent was Sweden. The winner of this game would surely control the tournament to win round-robin gold.

The Canadians played the first period as if afraid to lose, and were lucky to be down just 1–0 after twenty minutes, thanks to the goaltending heroics of Manny Legace. During the first intermission, head coach Perry Pearn refocused his team's perspective by reminding them of Forsberg's dismissive comments, and thus inspired, Canada bolted to a 3–2 lead after two, and ultimately a 5–4 victory. "I would like to know what Peter Forsberg thinks about our team now," Pearn shot back after the match.

The Canadians rolled through their next game, defeating Russia 9–1, eking out a 3–2 win over Finland—Legace faced forty-five shots in that one—and then meeting Japan on January 2. "If we were to lose to Japan, it would be one of the most monumental upsets in the history of sports," Coach Pearn said. "We're Canadians. They're Japanese. At the best of times in international hockey, they're almost too polite to us because of where we come from. And this game is for the gold medal."

The Japanese were rude enough to score one goal to Canada's eight, and with that win the Canadians could afford to blow a game to the Czech and Slovak Republics two days later and still win the gold. They finished with an identical 6–1 record to Sweden, but while Sweden had the better goal differential, Canada had beaten the Swedes. With that victory, Canada's juniors began a five-year golden rule of the WJC. The Age of Excellence had truly arrived.

Despite the Swedes having a better goal differential, Canada beat the Swedes on their home ice to ensure a junior gold medal.

THE 1994
WINTER GAMES

The 1994 Olympic Winter Games in Lillehammer, Norway, provided another historical moment for Canada's national hockey team. When the country returned to international hockey competition in 1980, the Canadian team still followed the model created by Father David Bauer, building a team of amateurs over time and seasoning them with regional games. Even when professionals were allowed into the Olympic mix in 1988, Canada's team remained largely amateur, as it was again in 1992 and here in 1994. But now, with the NHL "dream teams" being allowed in the next Olympics, the feeling was that the true end of an amateur era had arrived.

The IOC had changed the format so that summer and winter games now alternated every two years to avoid the staging of both in the same year, and as a result, Canada had seized a chance to avenge its 1992 gold-medal loss to the Unified Team in France by making a golden statement in Norway. Team Canada's lineup featured NHL talent in Chris Kontos, a veteran winger, and Paul Kariya, the first-round draft pick of the Anaheim Ducks, along with Corey Hirsch, who saw his relegation to Canada's national team by the New York Rangers as a demotion.

The team's most unusual NHL addition was Vancouver Canuck Petr Nedved, who had defected from his home state of Czechoslovakia at a 1989 midget tournament in Calgary when he was 17. Nedved had received his Canadian citizenship in 1993, and being engaged in an acrimonious contract dispute with the Vancouver Canucks, was free to play in the Olympics for Canada, though his motives were questioned.

"Canada is my home, now and forever," he said at the time. "I wanted to be free, and Canada has made it possible. I am thankful to the country."

Coached by Tom Renney, the Canadians sprinted out a 7–2 win in their first pool game against Italy, after taking a meagre 2–1 lead into the third period. "Why give them a chance?" asked Chris Kontos. "We want to send a message to other teams that we mean business."

Team Canada went out and sent a 3–1 *billet-doux* to France, and then Nedved scored on a penalty shot to help his new *confrères* grind out a 3–3 truce with the USA. Canada continued to win through its Pool B games, and after defeating the Czechs and the Finns in the medal round, wound up playing Sweden for gold.

"Place your bets, guys," Tom Renney yelled at the Finns after Canada had defeated them in the semi-final. "Put your money on Canada." Renney was taking a shot at the Swedish coach, Curt Lindstrom, who owned a betting shop in Stockholm, and had loudly pointed out that the Swedes were favoured at 9:2 odds to win gold, while Canada was a long shot at 7:1.

In the end, it came down to a kind of gambling. Sweden scored in the first period, no one scored in the second, then Canada went ahead in the third with goals by Paul Kariya and defenceman Derek Mayer. Canadians could taste the country's first Olympic hockey gold medal in forty-two years, and then, with less than three minutes to go in the game, Canada took a penalty, and Sweden, inevitably to Canadian hearts, scored on the power play. Overtime solved nothing, and so the gold-medal game would be decided by that most dubious of sports solutions, a shootout.

Both teams scored twice on their five shots in the first shootout round, and when Sweden missed on its first sudden-death shot, Petr Nedved had a chance to win gold for his adopted country. Nedved had Swedish goalie Tommy Salo beaten, but the puck rolled off his stick before he could shoot. Peter Forsberg scored on his shot, and when Salo stopped Paul Kariya, Sweden had won the gold on the equivalent of a penalty shot.

The Canadians had defeated the Germans the same way in 1992, but the shootout format was not popular with the players. "We didn't lose a hockey game," said goalie Hirsch. "We lost a shootout."

Despite the fact Forsberg's goal would one day feature on a Swedish postage stamp, the Swedes also had a sense of loss, one foretold by their very success. "What this means is the North American pros are going to come shopping and more and more people are going to go away," lamented Swedish forward Roger Hansson. "Look at what happened to the Russians. All their best stars went to the National Hockey League. It's very tough for them to get it back together."

While Canadians were taking consolation in their silver medal, the Russians were lamenting their alarming fall from the summit. They had lost the bronze-medal game 4–0 to Finland, making it the first time since they debuted in the Olympics in 1956 that no Russian player had stood on the medal podium.

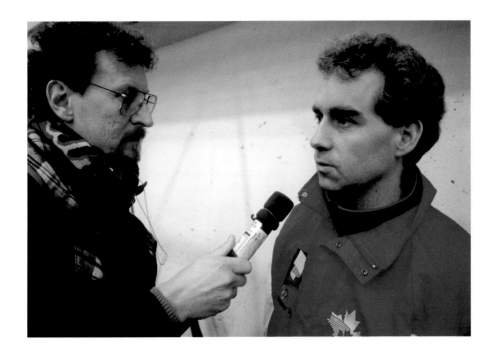

Hockey Canada president and CEO Tom Renney coached Team Canada at the 1994 Olympics. Despite going into the tournament as a long shot, Canada was still disappointed to come home with silver.

THE 1994 WORLD CHAMPIONSHIP

After their heartbreaking gold-medal loss to the Swedes in an overtime shootout at the 1994 Olympics, Canada wasn't taking any chances three months later at the IIHF world championship in Milan. The Canadians had not won a gold at the worlds in thirty-three years, and now, stocked with a full roster of NHL talent from teams that had not made the Stanley Cup playoffs (or gone deep in them), they didn't want to leave anything to chance.

"I think there is every reason to practise the shootout," said Canada's coach, George Kingston, who had learned the hard way as coach of the Olympic team in February. "We've practised it about five times. We want to be ready."

As it turned out, Canada would need its shootout skills after breezing past Sweden 6–0 in the semi-final. Having played the Finns to a 1–1 draw, and failing to win the game in overtime, Canada once more went for gold in the series of penalty shots that the IIHF and the IOC thought brought excitement and drama to a championship game in a way that playing until someone scored in sudden-death overtime would not.

Canadian goalie Bill Ranford was beaten twice in round one, while Luc Robitaille and Joe Sakic scored for Canada. Robitaille scored again in the sudden-death shootout round, and Ranford saved the next Finnish attempt. Canada had won its twentieth world title in the same manner that they had just lost Olympic gold. "I think we should play sudden-death overtime until it's won," said Canada's Jason Arnott. "Hockey is a team competition, not a contest of individual skills."

Paul Kariya, Brendan Shanahan, and Jason Arnott (left to right) celebrate Canada's first world championship in thirty-three years.

THE 1996
WORLD CUP

After the 1991 Canada Cup, the tournament morphed into the World Cup in 1996, but as far as Canadian fans in Ottawa on September 8 were concerned, the only final to the series that they wanted to see was a rekindling of the old days, with Canada versus Russia. But on that Sunday night, the Russians were being outhit, outworked, and outplayed by Team USA in the semi-final, the winner of which would meet Canada, who had beaten Sweden in double overtime the day before.

"I expected some booing of our team and [Brett] Hull," said Team USA's coach Ron Wilson, like Hull, a dual citizen of Canada and the United States. Fans had chanted "traitor!" at Hull because the Canadian-born player chose to play for the USA—after he had been rejected by Canadian coaches in 1986. "But I felt it was mean-spirited. I can understand from a patriotic point of view, having a little fun. But it wasn't a light-hearted booing. There were fans throwing beer at our bench at the end of the game."

Canada was lucky to be in the final, after struggling against Germany, and getting a break from a Swedish shot hitting the post in semi-final overtime. And after the USA dominated play in the second period of the first game in Philadelphia, scoring two goals to take a 2–1 lead, Canada managed to summon luck again, when Mark Messier fired the puck toward Claude Lemieux, speeding in on US goalie Mike Richter, with less than a minute left in the second period.

Lemieux collided with Richter, knocked the puck into the net, and then Canada took the lead when Theoren Fleury scored a goal in

Team USA's Bill Guerin is rammed into the boards by Canada's Adam Foote during the first period of Game 3 of the World Cup finals in Montreal, 1996.

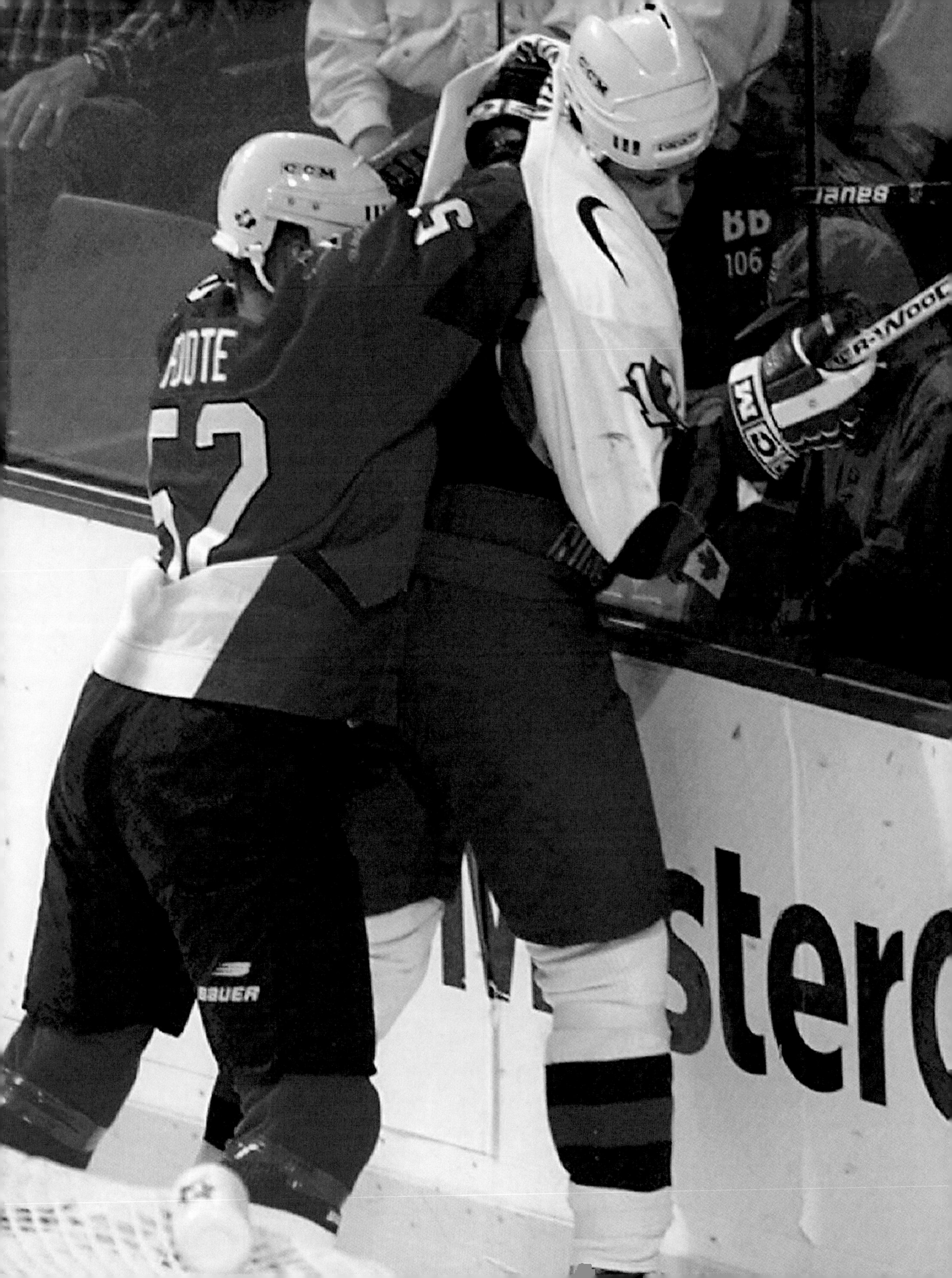
CCM
BAUER
106

A Canadian Hockey Marriage

The hockey landscape changed for the better once again when Hockey Canada merged with the Canadian Amateur Hockey Association in 1994, eighty years after the CAHA's founding in 1914. The idea behind the merger was to create the Canadian Hockey Association (CHA), which would govern all levels of national and international play. This merger promoted even greater cohesion in Canada's national hockey cosmos and led to the establishment of a Centre of Excellence in each of Calgary, Vancouver, Toronto, and Saint John to develop the nation's hockey talent from the frozen ground up.

the third. It looked as if the result would stand, but Canada's Eric Desjardins accidentally put the puck in his own net while trying to tuck it under goalie Curtis Joseph with 6.3 seconds left.

When Steve Yzerman won the first game for Canada ten minutes into overtime, it seemed, with the series returning for its final two games to Montreal, that Canada was riding its luck all the way to the title. Team USA rode its own luck, fending off Canadian domination and getting a couple of controversial goals—and a back-breaking wrist shot from Brett Hull that snapped the twine in the last game—to combine with superlative play between the pipes from Richter to stun the Canadians and their country by winning both games 5–2.

The morning after saw a country in shock, with media pundits declaring that Canadian hockey was in a state of crisis. In truth, Team USA had learned its lessons from Canadian hockey, and handed them back to the teacher. The Canada Cup was no more, the World Cup had begun, and Canada was characterized by naysayers as just another country in the hockey world with the new Number One living south of the forty-ninth parallel. For proud Canadian hockey players, it was a ranking that was just temporary, and incentive to remind the world that Canada would never be "just another country" when it came to hockey. Soon, they would get their chance.

Canadians were counting on Mario the Magnificent to vanquish the USA in the 1996 World Cup—as he had done in 1987. It was not to be, as the USA shocked Canada to win the tournament.

SPEAK OUT

On January 2, 1997, one of Canadian hockey's darkest and saddest stories came to the first of its several endings when former junior hockey coach Graham James pleaded guilty to 350 counts of sexual assault against Sheldon Kennedy, a player James had recruited to the WHL's Moose Jaw Warriors when Kennedy was a 15-year-old in 1984, and also Theoren Fleury, whom James sexually assaulted from age 14.

In 1996, Sheldon Kennedy, then a Calgary Flame and teammate of Theo Fleury, went to his coach for help about the damage James had done to him, which was destroying his life and his professional performance. The Flames sent Kennedy to a therapist—a hypnotherapist, who missed the point.

"They wanted to relax me and calm me down," said Kennedy. "They never talked about the Graham thing. They talked about scoring goals. That was the least of my worries."

After revealing all to his wife, Kennedy filed a police complaint that summer. Fleury also filed a complaint, though he would not publicly identify himself as the other complainant until 2010. Kennedy and Fleury revealed that James had abused them from 1984 until 1995, with the abuse continuing after both men had become professional players.

Graham James, who coached the Swift Current Broncos (and Sheldon Kennedy) to a Memorial Cup victory in 1989, was sentenced to three and a half years in prison.

"The fault is mine alone," said James upon sentencing, while Sheldon Kennedy wept on his wife's shoulder. "I'm truly sorry this happened."

And yet the fault was not James's alone, but part of a system that

Hockey Canada's goal is to help players become not only better athletes but better people. Sheldon Kennedy (seen here playing for the Swift Current Broncos) exemplifies both.

refused to believe—or ignored—evidence of his terrible crimes against minors over whom he had power. "I heard some things about Graham," said Edmonton Oiler Todd Marchant, who had played eighteen games for James in 1992/93. "If you heard the rumours, it was hard to believe [what you were hearing]. You can't really believe it, and maybe people chose not to believe it."

The Canadian Hockey Association gave James a lifetime ban, and people across Canada wondered what could be done to stop sexual predators from joining the game in the future. "Hockey, sport in general, we tend to look at as somewhat pure," said Dave Branch, president of the Canadian Hockey League, the umbrella organization representing Canada's three junior leagues. "When something happens in our game that's distasteful, yes, it really hits a nerve."

Canadian Hockey Association president Murray Costello called it a "red light" and said the CHA would propose screening programs for coaches at its semi-annual board meeting at the end of January 1997. While Costello acknowledged there would be privacy issues, he thought public knowledge of CHA screening would function as a pre-emptive strike: "Those types, with those tendencies, wouldn't bother applying."

The CHA was not alone in having a predator in its midst, and while James got away with his crimes for a long time, the CHA took sweeping action to ensure the safety of all players and coaches by creating a stringent screening program not just for coaches but for trainers and managers of minor hockey teams across Canada. Hockey has always been about fun, but the shock of the Graham James saga showed how important it was to write into policy exactly what it is *not*. The CHA developed policies making it clear that it will tolerate no bullying, harassment, abuse, or neglect, whether physical, emotional, or sexual, of any participant in any of its programs. The CHA expects every parent, volunteer, and staff member to take all reasonable steps to safeguard the welfare of its participants and protect them from any form of maltreatment.

As part of that commitment, the CHA teamed up with the Canadian Red Cross to develop the Speak Out program to prevent bullying, harassment, and abuse in hockey across Canada. It is a comprehensive system of workshops, resource materials, screening processes, and branch and association initiatives all focused on ensuring that our game is as fun and—most urgently—as safe as those who love it know it should be. Everyone associated with the game is held to the standards of conduct laid down by Speak Out: coaches, managers, parents, players, and administrators. Anyone who is part of our game is held to the same high standard.

Speak Out has proven so effective that it serves as a model for other sports. Today the program continues to set the bar for conduct in athletics, and it has expanded into the Respect in Sport Program, which is an online educational tool to train youth leaders to recognize, understand, and respond to issues of bullying, harassment, and abuse. The development of the Respect in Sport Program was spearheaded by Sheldon Kennedy and associate Wayne McNeil in partnership with the Red Cross. It serves not only the sports community but also schools and the workplace.

Kennedy devotes his time to helping victims of abuse, and he is one of the leading voices in the field worldwide. Kennedy spoke passionately in front of a United States congressional committee on sexual abuse of children after the Penn State University football incidents shocked the United States. Sport is about bringing out the best in kids and in communities. That's why it's always shocking when it brings out the worst.

THE 1997
WORLD JUNIORS

While Canada's World Cup loss in September 1996 to the USA might have caused gnashing of Canadian teeth about the fate of the hockey nation, the 1997 World Junior Championship in Switzerland had the country counting on the kids to make it right. The team that head coach Mike Babcock said "weren't especially talented at all," certainly looked to be living up to that label after tying both the Czechs and the now-dreaded USA in the round-robin tournament, and knocking off the so-called easy teams, the Swiss and the Germans, with the hardly overpowering scores of 4–1.

But like many teams not blessed with all-stars—though Joe Thornton and Daniel Brière were the two notable exceptions—they learned how to play together as a team to beat the Slovaks, then the Russians, to put themselves in a position to get World Cup revenge on the USA in the gold-medal game.

Boyd Devereaux, who had scored the tying and winning goals for the Canadians in their semi-final come-from-behind win against the Russians, scored eight minutes into the second period, and it was good enough to give Canada a win, with Brad Isbister adding the insurance early in the third period.

"We win together today, we walk together forever," said Mike Babcock, invoking Fred Shero's famous exhortation to the Philadelphia Flyers when Babcock spoke at an impromptu media conference at Pearson Airport on the team's victorious return home. Canada's win marked the fifth straight gold medal at the world junior championships, but Babcock's notion of "forever" would take on an unintended irony in years to come. It would be nearly a decade before Canadian juniors again heard their national anthem on the world stage.

Mike Babcock coached a workmanlike team to 1997 World Junior gold. It would be nearly a decade before Canada would see junior gold again.

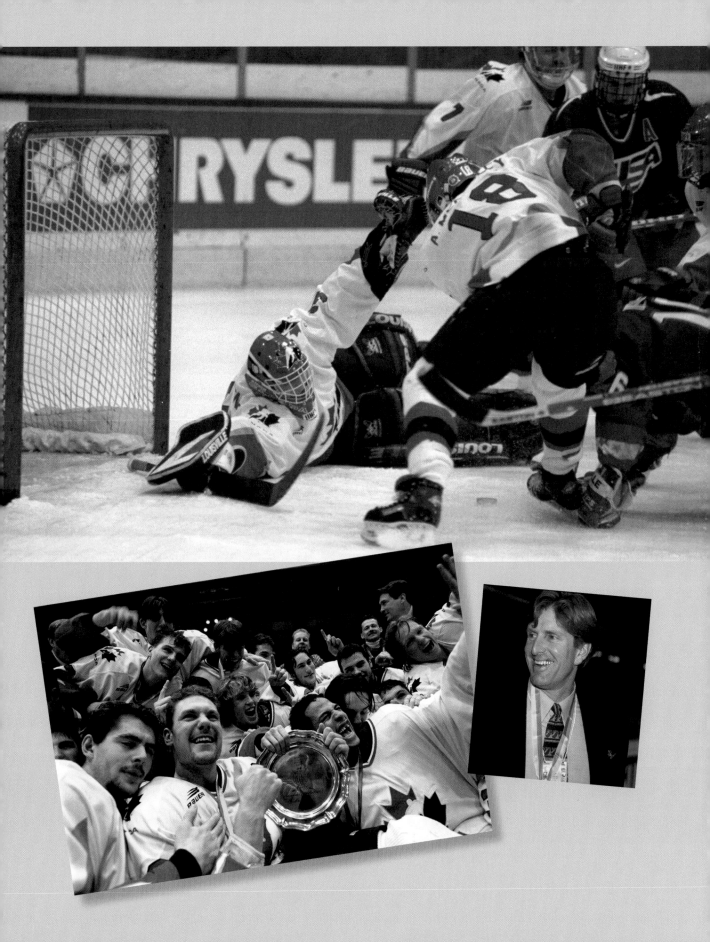

ALAN
EAGLESON

In January 1998, a Canadian hockey icon plummeted in disgrace, though not in his own eyes. Alan Eagleson, once the most powerful man in hockey, stood in a courtroom and pleaded guilty to robbing the people for whom he had worked. And in one final irony, the man who had done so much to put Canada at the top of the international hockey world, through tournaments like the 1972 Summit Series, the Canada Cup, and the World Cup, played his last game in the other team's rink: a Boston courtroom.

Thanks to the work of Russ Conway, a Massachusetts investigative journalist, Eagleson was charged in March 1994 by US authorities with thirty-two counts of racketeering and embezzlement relating to his work as head of the NHL Players' Association. Two years later, the RCMP charged him with eight counts of fraud and theft, alleging that Eagleson stole or defrauded more than $200,000 from Hockey Canada, the NHL, and the NHLPA.

The list of Eagleson's alleged crimes is a long one, but ranges from mismanaging client funds and information— for example, failing to tell Bobby Orr that the Bruins had offered him 10 percent ownership of the team, or taking huge fees from players to represent them in insurance claims that he knew had already been approved—to lying about revenues from inter-national tournaments, then diverting funds to his private company, to stealing from the players and their pension fund.

Eagleson, though, taking a page from his own slippery playbook, had worked out a plea with the US and Canadian authorities. So when he stood in a Boston courtroom and said the words that thousands of players had

Alan Eagleson (right) watches the 1984 Canada Cup game with Montreal Canadiens managerial genius Sam Pollock.

longed to hear, he was pleading guilty to only three counts of mail fraud. The judge ordered him to pay the US equivalent of a $1 million Canadian fine ($697,810.09) and sentenced him to eighteen months in prison, which would make him eligible for parole after six months served. And the Eagle would serve his time in Canada.

Even so, the moment was cathartic for several generations of former NHL players. "I just want to say, 'Thank God for the United States of America' because this never would have occurred in Canada," said Carl Brewer, one of twenty former NHLers in court that day to see justice begin to be done.

Indeed, Eagleson's place as a pillar of Canadian society included membership in the Order of Canada, service as an elected member of Ontario's legislature, presidency of the Ontario Conservative Party, winner of the Lester B. Pearson Award for international peace in recognition of his service to the game of hockey globally, and honoured member of the Hockey Hall of Fame.

Eagleson was stripped of his Order of Canada, and so, too, of his place in the Hall of Fame. The latter gesture seemed more than a touch like airbrushing the photograph, for he "once did the state some service" as Shakespeare's Othello ironically put it. His portrait might have hung there as a reminder for the generations to come, the way the portraits of the once mighty hang in galleries so that children may ask if they were good, or bad, and learn the truth. One thing the players never heard Eagleson say was the other two words they longed to hear, to atone for the pain and suffering that he had caused to so many: "I'm sorry."

Alan Eagelson was a power in Canadian hockey for more than three decades until his crimes against the people he represented were exposed by an American journalist, and he was convicted by a US court. Here, Eagleson returns home victorious to Canada from the 1972 Summit Series with Tony Esposito (left) and Paul Henderson.

BOB
NICHOLSON

On April 5, 2014, Bob Nicholson stunned the hockey world by announcing his resignation as the president and chief operating officer of Hockey Canada, the non-profit organization he had helmed since 1998. Characteristic of his light touch, Nicholson joked at the press conference that, after a glance at the financial pages, "I saw that gold had just gone up, so I thought it was the right time to make this announcement."

Bob Nicholson (centre) displays Team Canada's "lucky loonie" alongside hockey legends Wayne Gretzky (left) and Mario Lemieux (right).

On Nicholson's watch, Canada won forty-four gold medals in hockey. Hockey Canada also became financially healthy under Nicholson's shrewd handling of the men's world junior championships, as his support of non–North American clubs with money and resources served to bring bounty back to Canada when the tournament rose to become one of hockey's signature annual events.

Nicholson, like so many executives in the hockey world, played the game himself at a high level of competition. As a forward with the Junior A Penticton Broncos, he was part of the team that won the 1973 BC Junior Hockey League and BC–Alberta Championships. He attended Providence College on an NCAA hockey scholarship, and he then served as technical director with the BC Amateur Hockey Association from 1979 to 1989.

Nicholson became vice-president of programs with the Canadian Amateur Hockey Association from 1990 to 1991, then senior vice-president of the Canadian Hockey Association from 1992 to 1998, managing all national men's teams, national women's teams, and developmental programs, and overseeing international and national event marketing

and licensing. He also served on the IIHF Coaching Committee as well as several sports advisory committees.

While his Hockey Canada legacy touches many levels of the sport, what he wanted most upon his departure was for people to remember where the hockey journey begins.

"I want it to be about kids, kids playing the game," Nicholson said. "If we have a lot of kids playing the game, we're going to win gold medals."

Bob Nicholson with Canadian women's hockey legend Danielle Goyette.

Bob Nicholson and
Jayna Hefford celebrate
Canadian women's
Olympic hockey gold
at Sochi, 2014.

THE MEN'S QUEST FOR GOLD AT NAGANO

Ten years after professional hockey players had first appeared at the Calgary Winter Olympics, the 1998 Nagano Olympics saw the arrival of NHL "dream teams." Canada, which had not won an Olympic gold medal in men's hockey since 1952, had golden visions dancing across the country, not unlike the nation's confidence before the start of the 1972 Summit Series.

Indeed, the drought had been so long that the last time Canada had triumphed, *Hockey Night in Canada* was about to begin its rookie season on television, and the NHL had just six teams. Now, with twenty-six teams competing, Canada was, like other iterations before it, going to reclaim the national game with a Hall of Fame kind of NHL lineup featuring Wayne Gretzky, Joe Sakic, Brendan Shanahan, Martin Brodeur, Patrick Roy, Steve Yzerman, Al MacInnis, Scott Stevens, Eric Lindros, and a cast of all-stars.

The Canadians started off with an easy 5–0 romp over Belarus, then scored three goals in the second period to beat the Swedes 3–2. In the final game of the first round, they flexed their muscles over their new chief rival, the USA, with an easy 4–1 win.

After defeating Kazakhstan 4–1 in the quarter-final game, the Canadians met the Czechs for the right to compete in the gold-medal game. After playing the first period as if they were still enjoying their previous day off, the Canadians picked up their game. So did the Czechs, but after two periods, neither side could get the puck past the goalies: Patrick Roy and Dominik Hasek. Midway through the third period,

Czech Republic goalie Dominik Hasek stops a penalty shot by Canada's Joe Nieuwendyk in the shootout during the semi-final game at Nagano, Japan.

Czech defenceman Jiri Slegr blasted a slap shot past Roy, and as the clock ticked down, it looked as if Slegr's first point of the tournament would be the game-winner.

And then, with a little over a minute to play, and after a game-saving stop by Hasek, Eric Lindros passed the puck from behind the net to Trevor Linden, who was in the lineup because of a knee injury to Joe Sakic. Linden fired the puck home and the game was going into overtime.

A ten-minute overtime period solved nothing and, once again, Team Canada would stake its fate on a shootout (which the NHL would adopt to resolve regular-season games in 2005). The Czechs scored on their first shot, when Robert Reichel put the puck past Roy. It was all they needed, for when Hasek stopped all of Canada's shooters—Theo Fleury, Joe Nieuwendyk, Eric Lindros, Ray Bourque, and Brendan Shanahan—the Czechs had won the game, and would go on to take the 1998 Olympic gold medal with an equally stingy 1–0 win over Russia.

"Woe Canada" lamented a headline in *The Globe and Mail*; "Canada Loses Olympic Shocker" shouted a banner in the Olympic Extra section of the *Toronto Star*. Pundits from couch potatoes to water-cooler experts to newspaper columnists questioned Canadian coach Marc Crawford's decision to use Ray Bourque in the shootout instead of hockey's greatest player, Wayne Gretzky, but Bourque was famously accurate on penalty shots, and Gretzky was famously average.

Gretzky's first international game had come in 1977, when he played in the world juniors, and now, two decades later at the end of his career, he had come here to win the only award that had eluded his talent: an Olympic gold medal. "It's tough to swallow when you play a tournament where you actually don't lose a game and you're going home," Gretzky said after the loss, forgetting in his disappointment that the Canadians still had a shot at the bronze. But there would be no medal of any colour after the Canadians lost the bronze-medal game to the Finns. The failure of Team Canada's dream team had made the Olympic drought even worse. Just what would it take to put Canada back on the summit where they had once, and for so long, stood in solitary triumph?

Even Patrick Roy couldn't propel Canada into the gold-medal game at Nagano. His one miss during the semi-final shootout was enough to advance the Cezchs, who won the gold.

WOMEN AT NAGANO

The 1998 Winter Olympics finally admitted women's hockey to the games, and just as Canada's men had entered favoured to win, so did the women. But the team was playing not just for the maple leaf they proudly wore for the first time as Olympians, but for teammate Danielle Goyette, who had learned two days before the games began that her father had died of Alzheimer's disease back home in Saint-Nazaire, Quebec, where she had learned to play hockey on its frozen ponds.

Silver was the colour of tears for Canada's women at Nagano, Japan.

It was a devastating case of déjà vu for Goyette. Three years earlier, she had learned her mother had died, just before the final of the national championships. Rather than leave the team for the funeral, Goyette scored all three goals to give Quebec a 3–2 win over Ontario.

So, Goyette, who had been a member of Canada's national team since 1991 and had celebrated her thirty-second birthday less than a week earlier, dedicated her first-ever Olympic game to her father, and came out and scored the first-ever Olympic goal for Canada's women, adding another two goals to lead them to a 13–0 victory over Japan.

In addition to Goyette's hat trick, rising 19-year-old phenom Hayley Wickenheiser—a multi-sport athlete who would also play soft-ball for Canada in the Summer Games—inspired Team Canada with her bright, creative play and added two goals, while eight other Canada players scored in the easy win.

Despite the onslaught, the Canadians had trouble with China, before Goyette broke the 0–0 tie in the second period, assisted by Wickenheiser,

with what turned out to be the winning goal in a 2–0 Canadian victory. Goyette added two more goals in a 5–3 win over Sweden, and the insurance goal in Canada's 4–2 victory over Finland.

Team Canada seemed to be coasting into the medal round, up 4–1 at five minutes into the third period against its fiercest rival, Team USA, in the final game of the preliminaries. Then the USA scored six unanswered goals and won the game 7–4. It was one of those pivotal moments in sport where the momentum shift, both physically and psychologically, was staggering, made cruelly personal when a US player said to Goyette, "Dedicate that to your dead father" in the handshake lineup at the end of the game.

It was no surprise that Canada and the USA would meet for the gold-medal game. Keying off their two recent wins against Canada (the USA had won the Three Nations Cup for the first time in 1997), the USA scored twice on the power play before Goyette got Canada's women on the scoreboard, and herself into the Olympic record books as the scorer of the country's first-ever women's gold-medal-game goal. It wasn't enough, and after the USA added an empty netter, the Canadians sobbed with the silver medals around their necks as their now mortal hockey enemies celebrated their victory.

And yet Canadian coach Shannon Miller put the moment into proper and generous historical perspective when she watched Team USA's captain Cammi Granato getting her gold medal. "I had pure joy that an Olympic gold medal was going around the neck of a female hockey player. I was disappointed it wasn't us, but I was so glad to see a woman being honoured for playing hockey here."

Team Canada's handshake lineup with Team USA at Nagano was far from sporting as the competitive tension between the two teams turned cruelly personal.

BILL HAY
AND THE
HALL OF FAME

In July 1998, the Hockey Hall of Fame continued a family tradition by appointing Bill Hay as chair and CEO. Hay's father, Charles, who had been critical in the formation and success of Hockey Canada, had been inducted into the Hall in 1974. Now his son would serve as guardian of a pillar of Canada's national culture for the next fifteen years.

In selecting Hay to lead the Hall, the trustees were also selecting a man whose hockey pedigree was superlative enough to have him ripe for election himself to the Hall as a player. He had played junior hockey with the Regina Pats, scoring seventy-eight points in sixty-two games. After a brief stint at the University of Saskatchewan, Hay dropped out, and instead of reporting to the Montreal Canadiens, who owned his NHL rights, showed his singularity of vision by hitchhiking to Colorado, where he convinced Colorado College to give him an athletic scholarship while he completed a degree in geology.

Hay intended to join his father in the family oil business, but he thought first he'd give the life of a professional player a go, and when Chicago bought his NHL rights from Montreal for $25,000 in April 1959, he began a brief but illustrious career as a Black Hawk, winning the Calder Trophy as rookie of the year, and the Stanley Cup in 1961.

The 6'3" centre played between Murray Balfour and Bobby Hull, a trio dubbed the Million Dollar Line for their comparatively high salaries and their golden touch around the net. Teammate Stan Mikita said it was

Bill Hay starred in the NHL, then as a chair and CEO of the Hockey Hall of Fame, he turned his talents to developing the game he loved.

Hay's leadership ability that pushed the Hawks to an NHL championship. "The trick in making us a winner was getting the team working. This is where a leader comes in and Billy Hay was just such a leader."

Hay retired from pro hockey at age 31 to join the family business, but he never left the game. He was part-owner and team president of the Calgary Flames, and served for seventeen years on the Hockey Hall of Fame's selection committee, and eighteen years on the board. Under his guidance, the Hall launched two major expansions, including a $750,000 World Hockey Zone in 2005, financed by an IIHF donation of $1.2 million of profit from the Salt Lake City Olympics, and he developed strong partnerships with Hockey Canada, the IIHF, the NHL, and the NHLPA.

Hay was also instrumental in seeing the Hall of Fame induct its first female members in 2008.

Bill Hay speaks at a Hockey Hall of Fame induction ceremony. He was the driving force behind the inclusion of women in the hall's pantheon in 2008.

THE OPEN
ICE SUMMIT

Ken Dryden was no stranger at protecting Canada's game at important hockey summits. Here he is surrounded by Soviet players on September 2, 1972.

In August 1999, the Molson Open Ice Summit convened in Toronto to sort out what could be better about hockey, especially with the country's Nagano hockey wounds still raw. For three days, more than a hundred of the key figures in Canadian hockey, representing the National Hockey League and its teams, as well as minor-hockey parents, coaches, association branch presidents, and Canadian Hockey Association board members and administrators, met to talk about how the Canadian game could improve.

"Why don't we pass more and better? ... Why do we play so many games and practise so little? ... What about the body contact in our game, the stickwork, hits, and fighting?" asked Ken Dryden, rhetorically, in his opening speech to the delegates. The Hall of Fame goalie, author, hockey philosopher, and, at the time, president of the Toronto Maple Leafs, challenged the delegates with the idea that hockey's next century depended as much on what the country did off the ice as on it.

The delegates responded to the challenge with a brilliantly simple strategy: bring back shinny for 8-year-olds. As with the ancestral pond game that had launched the organized hockey now at the centre of introspection, there would be few rules, a loose structure, with players rotating positions so that everyone could gain experience, and with no such thing as a mistake.

Wayne Gretzky and his father Walter attended the opening day of the Summit, and perhaps encapsulated all that anyone ever needed to remember about how to play Canada's game. "When I was 10, my love was

Saturday morning," said the superstar son. "Skate from 8 to 5, come home and watch *Hockey Night in Canada*. I didn't do it to practise or say I'm going to make the NHL. That was my love. That's what we have to do." And, the hockey dad added, "They've got to remember that it's got to be fun. If it's not fun they won't get any better, and when they get to be 14, they'll quit." Wayne Gretzky agreed. "Get the kids understanding they should do it for love, and everything else will fall into place."

Wayne Gretzky is hugged by his father, Walter, during the pre-game ceremonies for Gretzky's last game in the NHL on Sunday, April 18, 1999, in New York City. Both Wayne and Walter have been strong advocates for the game.

Sledge Hockey
Strikes Gold

By 2000, sledge hockey had held its own world championships, run under the auspices of the International Paralympic Committee. The sport had become an official Paralympic event in 1994 at the Winter Games in Lillehammer. This 2000 world championship was held in Utah, as a "test" event in preparation for the 2002 Salt Lake City Winter Olympics. Six nations took part, and the Canadians avenged their gold-medal loss to Norway at Nagano by beating the Norwegians 2–1.

Canada's Paul Rosen makes a save against Japan during second-period semi-final sledge-hockey action at the 2010 Winter Paralympics in Vancouver on March 18, 2010.

WOMEN AT
SALT LAKE CITY

Canada had come to the 2002 Olympic Winter Games in Salt Lake City with hockey gold in sight, and quite literally, too. Canadian icemaker Trent Evans had buried a golden loonie at centre ice of the E Center hockey arena, a temporary marker to begin with, but an act of defiance when colleagues objected and asked him to remove it. Evans agreed, but then in an act of Canadian stealth hockey magic, daubed yellow paint over the buried loonie and let it lay where he had planted it.

As talismans tend to be more effective if you know that you have them, Evans reported his mission to Hockey Canada's boss Bob Nicholson, who relayed the story to Team Canada execs. And then Evans delivered the news to the Canadian women's team, who had entered the 2002 Olympic Games as superheroes out to right a grievous wrong. They had lost gold in Nagano to their archrivals, the USA, who had cruelly mocked a player for mourning her dead father. Now, Canada's women could draw on the power of the buried golden loonie to propel them to Olympic gold.

The Canadian women, as expected, breezed through the opening round by defeating Kazakhstan, Russia, and Sweden by a combined score of 25–0. After falling behind 3–2 to the Finns in the semi-final, the Canadians scored five unanswered goals in the third period to put them in their second Olympic gold-medal game against the usual suspects: Team USA.

This time, though, Canada came into the gold-medal game as underdogs, having lost eight straight pre-Olympic matches to the USA. Before the game, a nasty rumour swirled that Team USA, its perfidy

Jayna Hefford scores the gold-medal-winning goal for Canada at the 2002 Salt Lake City Winter Olympics.

knowing no boundaries, had trampled on the Canadian flag in their dressing room. The desire for Canadian revenge was now as hot as the loonie buried beneath the ice was cold.

Even so, it seemed to Team Canada that the worst kind of reason was holding them back from victory: the American referee. She had called thirteen penalties against Canada—eight of them in a row—while issuing only six to the home team. Canada had scored first, when Caroline Ouellette put the puck past the US goalie less than two minutes into the game, and after the US tied it on a power play, Hayley Wickenheiser gave Canada the lead it would never relinquish.

Canada's golden women point out their secret weapon—a Canadian loonie—buried at centre ice at Salt Lake City.

Jayna Hefford scored for Canada midway through the third period, and goalie Kim St-Pierre held off the US after they notched another power-play marker and pulled their own goalie late in the game. Canada's women took the game 3–2 and had won their first Olympic gold medal.

"For those of us who were there in Japan, it's been a long four years," said Hefford. "But it's all worth it after tonight."

Canada's women's team celebrates their first-ever Olympic gold medal after a 3–2 win over their archrival, Team USA.

MEN AT
SALT LAKE CITY

I t had been fifty years since Canada's men had stood on the Olympic podium to receive their hockey gold medals. In Salt Lake City in 2002, not only did Team Canada have the golden loonie buried beneath centre ice at the E Center, and the inspiration of the Canadian women's hockey gold, but they also had Wayne Gretzky.

Even though Gretzky had retired as a player in 1999, the disappointment of not even winning a medal of any colour at Nagano still rankling, Gretzky had become head of Team Canada in 2002, charged with putting together a team that would come home with gold.

On paper, the Canadian team looked unbeatable, with Mario Lemieux the captain of a squad featuring veterans in their prime, like Steve Yzerman, Joe Sakic, Brendan Shanahan, Eric Lindros, and Martin Brodeur, along with the next wave of superstars in Paul Kariya and Jarome Iginla, supported by a stellar group embarrassing in its depth and talent.

On the ice, however, the Canadians began the tournament with a 5–2 loss to Sweden after Curtis Joseph let in a couple of soft goals, and followed that with a shaky 3–2 win over Germany, which had won the right to play vaunted Canada by emerging, with Belarus, from the preliminary round—a round that Canada and five other hockey powers were exempted from playing. The critics weighed in: the Canadians had been embarrassed by the Swedes, and were "lucky" to beat the Germans, with *The Globe and Mail* sounding moderate when it put in the boots: "They were nervous early and it showed, with players falling down on breakaways, fanning on shots, missing easy plays, looking more like rec-league players than Canada's finest talent."

Team Canada captain, Mario Lemieux, pops the cork upon ending a fifty-year Olympic gold drought in Salt Lake City in 2002.

After Canada responded to its growing chorus of alarmed "must-win-this-game" critics by tying the Czechs 3–3, Wayne Gretzky fired back.

"It's comical listening to some of the things being said right now," the usually mild-mannered Gretzky blasted in a fifteen-minute tirade. "It almost sickens my stomach to turn on the TV because I'm such a proud Canadian and such a fan of our game and very proud of all the players in our locker room."

He was also referring to suggestions swirling through the US media that team veterans were unhappy with Pat Quinn's coaching, and that Mario Lemieux was going to pack up his gear and head home. "[The Americans] are loving us not doing well," he said. "They loved us and the [bad] start we had. It's a big story for them."

The US media turned up the negative volume on talk radio, and the nasty rhetoric in print. "Could it be more obvious that old blondie is cracking under the pressure?" mused a Pittsburgh sportswriter about Gretzky. "Every time his face flashes on TV during these games, it looks as if he's passing a kidney stone."

Despite the doom forecast for Canada and the mocking of Gretzky as no longer the Great One but the "Great Whine," the team still remained the one to beat in the eyes of the world. "Everybody wants to beat Canada because everybody thinks they have the best team," said Finland's superstar Teemu Selanne, in advance of their quarter-final against Canada. "It's like playing the Stanley Cup champs."

Canada took heart from Gretzky's circling of the wagons and the players brought their best team out against the Finns, defeating them 2–1 in the quarter-final, with Martin Brodeur now Canada's go-to goalie. After Belarus shocked the hockey world—and the Swedes—by scoring on Sweden's Tommy Salo with a fluky slapper from just inside centre ice to win their quarter-final 4–3, Canada got its first lucky bounce. Instead of playing the team that had skated all over them, they played a team they could beat 7–1.

More than 10 million Canadians watched the gold-medal match between Canada and the USA. Shots of Gretzky in the stands, looking like a nervous parent, showed the strain of the mission: he and Pat Quinn had guided to this moment with pluck and patience and skill and a little luck, but losing wasn't an option.

The USA scored first, but Canada's tying goal was symbolic of the outcome: Chris Pronger passed to Mario Lemieux in the slot, and Lemieux put his stick on the ice to play the puck, US goalie Mike Richter bit, then Lemieux raised his stick and let the puck go through his legs and onto the stick of teammate Paul Kariya. The game was suddenly tied on a piece of Mario Magic, and it would send Canada flying, showing its depth and desire as the team pulled away to a 5–2 win. And of course, it was much more than that.

"Now we can finally say we have passed the torch on," said Eric Paterson, who had won Canada's last Olympic hockey gold as an Edmonton Mercury in 1952. "I just hope it's not another fifty years."

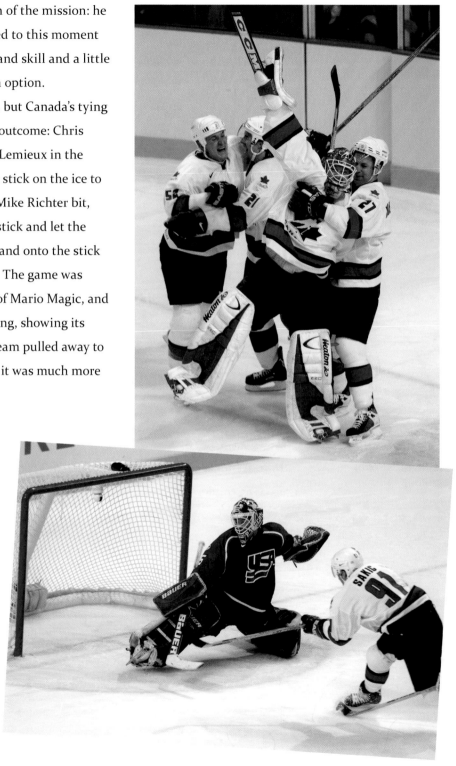

Joe Sakic scored two of Canada's five goals as Canada's men celebrated the country's return to the gold podium in Salt Lake City.

MEN'S UNDER-18 TEAM

The first national men's under-18 team was created in 1981 as part of the Program of Excellence. For the first ten years of the program, the under-18s engaged in exchange camps with the United States to hone the skills of their best young players. In 1991, the Japanese Ice Hockey Federation started the Phoenix Cup, a four-nation tournament that was designed to improve Japan's international hockey program. Canada won silver to the Soviet gold in the first tournament, and then took gold the following year.

The IIHF began their international men's under-18 tournament in 1999, though Canada did not participate in the first three years of the tournament, which took place in April, when many of Canada's best players were then still playing for their junior teams. The Canadians entered the under-18 competition in 2002, and finished a disappointing sixth. The team that arrived in Russia in April 2003 was determined to add some golden lustre to Canada's most recent entry on the international stage, especially with nascent stars like Ryan Getzlaf and Brent Seabrook in its ranks.

Canada didn't exactly dominate the opening round, emerging from Group B tied in second with the Czechs with 2–1–1 records. Only host Russia was undefeated at 4–0, but when Slovakia eliminated the Russians in the semi-final, and Canada followed their 8–1 quarter-final rout of Sweden with a 2–1 win over the USA, the Canadians could win gold by beating the Slovaks.

On April 22, 2003, in the historic city of Yaroslavl, Russia, the Canadians made history themselves when goalie Ryan Munce stopped all twenty-five Slovak shots and Ryan Getzlaf scored an insurance goal as Canada took its first under-18 gold medal with a 3–0 victory.

Ryan Getzlaf checks a Norway player during the 2008 IIHF championship, Getzalf's debut for the senior men's team. He would lead the tournament with eleven assists and his 14 points would be second overall. He had always been an impact player for Canada, scoring four points to help Canada's Under-18 team win its first gold medal in 2003.

THE 2004
WORLD CUP

The 2004 World Cup was only the second instalment of the world
tournament that had grown out of the Canada Cup, and last time
it was staged in 1996, the USA had shocked Canada by winning it. This
time, things would be different, said Wayne Gretzky, the team boss who
was still fresh off masterminding Canada's 2002 Olympic gold medal in
men's hockey.

The Canadian squad saw some returning vets from the 2002
Olympic championship team, so Martin Brodeur, Joe Sakic, and Steve
Yzerman welcomed Joe Thornton, Martin St. Louis, Shane Doan,
Dany Heatley, Brad Richards, Brenden Morrow, Patrick Marleau, Kirk
Maltby, and Kris Draper—none of whom had ever represented Canada
at this level of international play before. And then there was greybeard
Mario Lemieux—about to turn 39 years old, who had survived cancer,
retirement, and resurrection—who pulled on the maple leaf one last
time to lead Canada in his final international tournament.

In an effort to make the World Cup worldlier, the eight teams were
divided into two pools, with the first round of matches as well as the
quarter-finals taking place in Europe and North America. Even so, some
observers saw it as the Team Canada Invitational Tournament, for the
Europeans had a punishing travel schedule, while the Canadians had
only to shuttle between Toronto and Montreal.

The Canadians once again started modestly, squeezing out a 2–1 win
over the USA, then beating the Slovaks 5–1, and the Russians 3–1. They
faced the Slovaks again in the quarter-finals, and dispatched them 5–0
before facing the Czechs in the semi-final.

Mario Lemieux notched
five points in six games
as he played his last
international tournament
for Canada in the 2004
World Cup.

The Canadians went up 2–0, but the Czechs tied it. Canada regained the lead, but then dozed off and the Czechs tied the game six seconds later. That left goalie Roberto Luongo, a player able to win a tight game or send it wildly off in the other direction (and who looked shaky on the first and third Czech goals), to turn it in Canada's favour by shutting out the Czechs from then on, thus allowing Vincent Lecavalier to come to the rescue three minutes into overtime.

Even team boss Gretzky was worried. "It's great to be in the championship game again, representing our country," he said. "The problem is, I can't get on the ice and do anything about it, so it's a little nerve-wracking."

The Canadians vowed to play a full sixty minutes in the final against Finland, but it didn't take that long. Shane Doan scored at the 34-second mark in the third period to make it 3–2 Canada, and that was the final score to give the Canadians their first World Cup.

"Hockey is Canada and to score that goal in Toronto where hockey means so much ... it gives me chills," said Doan.

But it was Mario Lemieux, Canada's fourth leading scorer, who put a longer perspective on where the game had been, and where he saw it going, reminiscing after this victory that the best hockey he ever played had been back in the 1987 Canada Cup. "The speed of the game, the talent level of the players, the style of play we played back then—there was not a lot of hooking and grabbing, and every game finished 6–5. It was a different game back then, a different era, and I was glad I had a chance to play in both."

The day after Team Canada's World Cup triumph, the NHL locked players out in the absence of a new collective bargaining agreement, one thwarted by pro hockey's old nemesis: money. The players wanted to earn what the market would bear; the owners wanted to implement a salary cap. And that was all the playing that Lemieux or any of his teammates would do that season, for there would be no NHL in 2004/05. In a day, they had gone from champions of the world to unemployed NHLers.

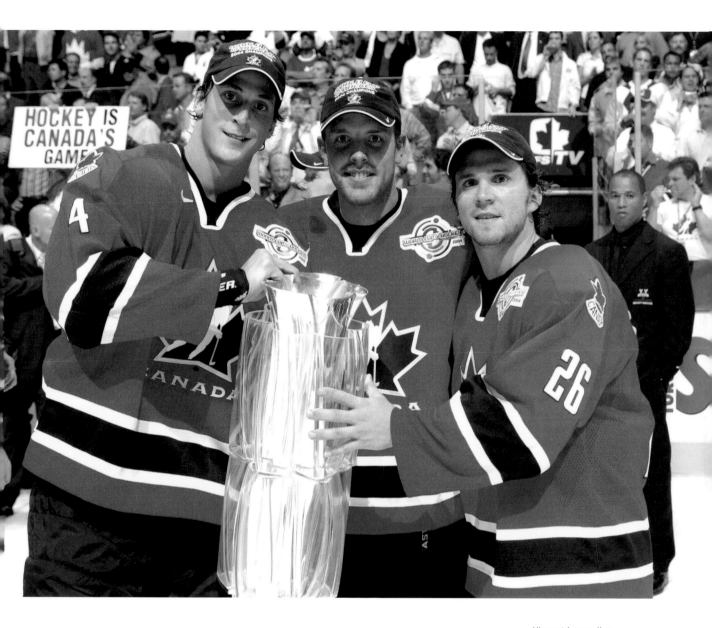

Vincent Lecavalier,
Brad Richards, and
Martin St. Louis (left
to right) transferred their
Tampa Bay chemistry
into a 2004 World Cup
championship for Canada.

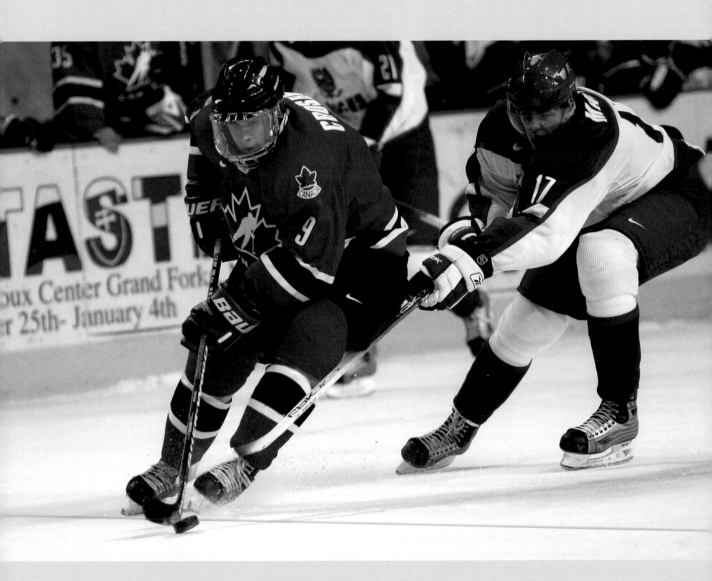

THE 2005 WORLD JUNIORS

The 2005 World Junior Championship saw Team Canada ice its best squad ever, thanks in part to the NHL lockout. Brent Sutter's squad had twelve players with experience in the NHL, and it had players like Patrice Bergeron, who had already played a season with the Boston Bruins. It also had a dream team of Corey Perry, Ryan Getzlaf, Brent Seabrook, Dion Phaneuf, Jeff Carter, and Sidney Crosby.

So Team Canada entered the tournament riding a seven-year gold-medal drought with even heavier expectations on their shoulders than Canadian squads usually wear, but the team relished the chance. "A lot of us have been waiting for this chance for a whole year now," said defenceman Shawn Belle, who was part of the squad the year before that blew a 3–1 third-period lead to lose gold to the United States. "You don't get a lot of second chances in life."

The Canadians made the most of this do-over, cruising through the tournament with a 6–0 record, and outscoring their opponents 41–7 with only the Slovaks managing to score more than one goal against them (and they scored three).

In the gold-medal game, Team Canada faced the Russians, fifteen of whom had been drafted by NHL teams. Gone were the days of the Russian team members being stoic and disciplined comrades; this incarnation was a hot-dogging crew of swaggering ruffians, led by Alex Ovechkin who trash-talked during the 2003 Russian gold-medal win over Canada in Halifax. Ovechkin had also questioned the untested Canadian goalie, Jeff Glass, every chance he got, and he and his teammates had behaved

Sidney Crosby fights off a check by Evgeni Malkin at the 2005 World Junior Championship.

like hooligans in their 7–2 semi-final win against the USA, taunting the Americans at their bench even upon scoring into an empty net.

Canada's response was to pound Ovechkin every chance that they got, with Dion Phaneuf acting as chief Ovechkin tenderizer. The physical punishment chased the Russian showboat from the game in the fifth minute of the second period, and the Canadians built their 3–1 lead—having scored on their first shot of the game—to grind the Russians into the ice with a 6–1 thumping.

It was the 135th victory for Canada at the world championships, and the country's eleventh medal. But it was also a victory for sportsmanship. "They are gold medallists because they deserve to be," said coach Brent Sutter, "not only by the scores but because they acted like professionals in every aspect."

The Canadian junior team celebrates the country's eleventh gold medal in Grand Forks, North Dakota, in 2005.

MEN IN
TORINO

In February 2006, Canadians were anticipating a golden reprise for the men's Olympic hockey team in Torino, Italy. The team looked like champions as well, with Pat Quinn back behind the bench as head coach, and players who knew how to win, such as Joe Sakic and Martin Brodeur, coming back to the Olympics from their 2002 triumph. Best of all, Wayne Gretzky was once again the team's general manager, a magic pair of hands who would guide them safely to gold.

It had been a tough year for Gretzky. His mother had died just before Christmas, and his grandmother just after the new year. And right before Torino began, reports surfaced that Gretzky had been caught on wiretaps talking to Rick Tocchet, his assistant coach in Phoenix, about how Gretzky's wife Janet could avoid being implicated in a gambling scandal that had resulted in New Jersey police charging Tocchet with money laundering, conspiracy, and promoting gambling.

"If I did one thing that would embarrass Team Canada or the country or hockey, I would resign," Gretzky said. "It didn't happen."

Then there were critics of Gretzky's team selection, leaving out young stars like Sidney Crosby, Jason Spezza, and Dion Phaneuf, but including Todd Bertuzzi, an erratic power forward best suited to the smaller NHL ice surface. And then there was Bertuzzi's baggage. "The worst poster boy for Canadian hockey imaginable," said one columnist about Bertuzzi, who was talented at annoying officials and teammates with his surly demeanour and penchant for taking bad penalties. That, and the fact he had attacked Steve Moore from behind in a game in Vancouver two

years earlier, an assault that broke Moore's neck and ended his career. Indeed, Moore's lawyer had filed a $19.5-million lawsuit against Bertuzzi while the Olympics were underway, making Bertuzzi an even bigger distraction.

"I dealt with a lot of this back in Vancouver," Bertuzzi said, "and I don't want to or need to drag it over here for this team."

At first, everything seemed fine, with the top-ranked Canadians doing what was expected: defeating Italy 7–2, and Germany 5–1. Things went sideways fast, with back-to-back 2–0 losses against Switzerland and Finland. Suddenly, the team seemed to be in disarray, though assistant coach Ken Hitchcock said it was really just a failure to understand the level of intensity that comes with representing your country.

"There's a difference playing against a Finnish player in the NHL, and a Finnish player with his flag on his back," Hitchcock said. "We're not playing against NHL players. We're playing against a bunch of flags."

Which was exactly the thing people were worrying about: that the players wearing the maple leaf weren't good enough or didn't care enough to uphold the 2002 reboot of Canada's golden Olympic tradition. "When you put on the Canadian jersey," said forward Dany Heatley, "you're expected to win."

The Canadians rallied with a trip to visit the British Columbia pavilion—a log house—and suitably stoked with a reminder of the pioneer spirit that made a country out of rock and ice, narrowly beat the fourth-ranked Czechs 3–2 to win a berth in the quarter-finals against the Russians, who had come into the tournament ranked seventh (out of eight teams).

The Russian team had been put together by executive director Pavel Bure, who had lit up the NHL as the Russian Rocket with the Vancouver Canucks. Bure took a page from his own playbook, and stocked his lineup with fast, edgy, supremely talented young players like Alex Ovechkin, Evgeni Malkin, and Pavel Datsyuk. It would make a difference, and the young Russians played that much harder than the older Canadians, and showed a level of maturity and desire far beyond that of their Canadian contemporary Rick Nash, who was benched repeatedly.

So, too, would Todd Bertuzzi make a difference, and in a way that those who knew his play in Vancouver knew too well. With no score in the game, Bertuzzi ran a thoughtless pick play on a Russian defender behind the Russian goal, and was penalized. It took Alex Ovechkin thirty-five seconds to score. The Russians would add another goal on a late power play, and Canada would not score any goals at all, making them scoreless in eleven of their last twelve periods of hockey. And now, they were going home.

"I take full responsibility for what happened," said Gretzky after the loss, and soon enough, others were joining in the chorus of blame, which in turn blended with the chorus of dire predictions.

Team Canada coach, Pat Quinn, is confounded by his high-octane 2006 Olympic squad's inability to score.

"Losing at hockey is always an option, but not one Canada really likes to excuse, especially when $97 million worth of hockey talent gets blanked, shut out, skunked in three of its last four games of a lost Olympics," wrote Cam Cole, in one of the most generous assessments. "So on this inauspicious occasion, with our heroes climbing on a funereal flight home to face the pitying glances if not the outright misery of plenty of disillusioned hockey fans across the nation, it is only fair to give the most disgusted of those fans their due. They called it. Wayne Gretzky must wear this, and so must the other members of Team Canada's brain trust, because they would not listen to the voice of Canada speaking to them, and they stubbornly had their way."

Gretzky, for his part, was looking to the next game, the way an athlete does after disaster. "We'll be around in 2010," he said. "This country is too proud, and the kids who play hockey in our country are too good. Our team will be back." Wayne Gretzky, however, was not.

WOMEN IN TORINO

The Canadian women's Olympic hockey team showed up in Torino in 2006 with several items on their agenda. They wanted to avenge a heartbreaking 1–0 loss to the USA in the 2005 worlds, and to defend their 2002 Olympic gold medal. But they also knew it was the "passing of the torch" that had become such a trope in Canadian hockey, the image having come from the pen of Lieutenant Colonel John McCrae, a Canadian physician and poet in World War I, mourning the loss of his friend. The old guard was done, the new guard was rising, and a golden hand-off was the order of the day.

The Canadians had gone 8–2 against their rivals, the USA, in pre-Olympic exhibition, and they fully expected to meet the women in the red-white-and-blue sweaters in the gold-medal match. But after Sweden stunned everyone by vanquishing the USA in the semi-final, the Canadians had to stay focused to make sure they didn't give the gold away out of surprise.

Canada had romped to the gold-medal final by outscoring its opponents 42–1, including an 8–1 first-round victory over the team they were about to meet. While the imbalance was redolent of the old days of Canadian men's hockey, it also reflected a troubling lack of parity in the women's game: there was Canada and the USA, and then there was everyone else. To the Canadians, it was not a cause for pity.

"We certainly want to be respectful," said team captain Cassie Campbell. "But at the same time, we can't lose sight of why we're here, and that's to win gold."

Canada's women redeem the country's hockey honour in Torino, Italy, with a 4–1 win over Sweden to take the Olympic hockey gold medal.

Canada took an early 2–0 lead on goals by Gillian Apps and Caroline Ouellette. Cherie Piper and Jayna Hefford added two more in the second, and Canada cruised to a 4–1 golden victory.

"It's a different feeling than 2002 because we didn't go through the same adversity," said Cassie Campbell. "The feeling this time is just, wow, it's over ... and this team will never be together again."

It would be the last Olympics for Campbell, as well as for Vicky Sunohara, Cheryl Pounder, Gillian Ferrari, and Katie Weatherston. The most emotional farewell was to—and from—40-year-old Danielle Goyette, who had scored Canada's first-ever goal in an Olympic gold-medal game in 1998, when the women had won silver.

Goyette lingered on the ice after the game, waving the flag saved from the women's golden triumph at Salt Lake City in 2002.

"They had to push me off the ice," she said. "I was emotional because I know this is something that won't come back."

Not the Olympics, maybe. But Goyette would be back, for one more chance at a gold medal at the world championship in 2007.

Captain Cassie Campbell proudly displays her second Olympic gold medal—and marks the end of an era. The Canadian women's team would lose many veterans, Campbell included.

THE 2006 WORLD JUNIORS

The 2006 World Junior Championship in Vancouver was doubly golden for Canucks fans—Team Canada sailed undefeated through the tournament to win its second straight gold medal, and Canada's defenceman Luc Bourdon, whom the Canucks picked in the first round of the 2005 draft, was named an all-star of the tournament.

"Luuuc, Luuuc!" the fans would holler whenever Bourdon touched the puck. "It was really exciting for him," recalled defence partner Kris Letang. "It was pretty much his building. For him, it was a chance to show them he was going to be ready to play in the NHL. He was already a leader."

Team Canada talked about playing to its identity during the tournament, one forged on four tenets: superb goaltending, relentless forechecking, physical brawn, and suffocating defence. "To me, defence isn't just about playing well in your own zone," said head coach Brent Sutter. "Defence is about being solid and not turning pucks over in bad areas."

With Letang, the heavy-hitting Bourdon would join a defence corps starring Marc Staal and Cam Barker to shut down the Russians, defying Russian Evgeni Malkin's modest prediction the Russians would easily take the gold. Despite facing a fifteen-shot barrage in the first fifteen minutes, Justin Pogge was perfect in net—Canada got the winner when Steve Downie scored at the end of the first period, even though they would go on to add four more in their 5–0 victory.

For the final two minutes of Canada's golden triumph, the fans in Vancouver stood and applauded the players, saluting yet another Canadian gold medal. Little did they know that they were also saying farewell to the Canucks' star-in-the-making, Luc Bourdon. Two years later, Bourdon's great promise was snuffed out when he was killed in a motorcycle crash near his home in northeastern New Brunswick at age 21.

Luc Bourdon celebrates a goal at the 2006 World Junior Championship in Vancouver. Canucks fans were delighted by the play of their rising star, but tragically, Bourdon was killed two years later in a motorcycle crash.

CASSIE CAMPBELL

On October 14, 2006, Cassie Campbell, who had twice captained Canada's women to hockey gold medals at the Olympic Games, made another kind of history: she became the first woman to do colour commentary on *Hockey Night in Canada*, when the regular commentator, Harry Neale, was stuck at home in Buffalo due to bad weather. Campbell, already an icon to female players everywhere, was scheduled to work the Calgary Flames–Toronto Maple Leafs game in her role as a reporter for *HNIC*. When she got the phone call eight hours before game time, Campbell thought the hockey boys were having fun with her. "I thought it was sort of a jokey play on a rookie," she said. "Then I realized they were serious."

She had done colour commentary for women's games on TSN, and so Campbell prepared for the assignment during the day by studying players and possible storylines, and an hour before air time, an *HNIC* producer walked her through video analysis. Then it was showtime.

Once play-by-play announcer Bob Cole said, "'Cass, we're going to make history' ... then it sunk in," Campbell said. "And I thought 'wow.'"

Campbell indeed made history, handling the assignment with the cool confidence she had always exhibited while making history on the ice as Canada's gold-winning captain in Salt Lake City and Torino.

Cassie Campbell made history by taking her hockey smarts from the ice to the broadcast booth to become the first female colour commentator on *Hockey Night in Canada*.

THE 2007 WOMEN'S WORLDS

The Canadian women entered the 2007 World Hockey Championship at home in Winnipeg riding high on their golden success at the 2006 Olympics, but hoping, as ever, to meet their rivals in the final, something they were deprived of by the Swedes at Torino.

Canada and the USA had met in all nine of the women's world championship finals to date, with the scoresheet tilted heavily in Canada's favour: 8–1. But it was the one win by Team USA that still rankled, a 1–0 victory in a shootout at the last world championship before the Olympics.

The Canadians had their chance in the qualifying round, taking their two wins and 17–0 goals-for-and-against record in those two games into a match against the USA with the Yanks' two wins and 18–1 GFA. In honour of the first women's world championship, Team Canada sported the same pink uniforms that their pioneering sisters had worn in 1990. At the end of the first period, members of that team were honoured at centre ice to the delight of the 15,003 fans in the MTS Centre—the largest audience in history to watch a women's ice hockey game.

There wasn't much for the fans to cheer about in the second period, with Canada trailing 4–2, until Hayley Wickenheiser took a cross-ice feed from linemate Gillian Apps and wired the shot over the outstretched glove of the US goalie. Apps tied the game less than three minutes later, and that was the result that stood at the end of sixty minutes. As they

had done the last time they had met, the two teams would be deciding this match with a shootout.

Hayley Wickenheiser skated in on the US goalie, gave her a couple of fakes, then slid the puck between her pads to score the game-winning goal, as none of the Americans could score on Charline Labonté.

"I think it was a nice game for us to win for those women who brought the game to where it is today," Wickenheiser said afterward.

Canada met the USA three nights later for the gold medal before another sellout crowd, and this time there would be no shootout. After a scoreless first period, Jennifer Botterill scored for Canada fifty-eight seconds into the second frame, with Jayna Hefford adding another midway through the game. Hayley Wickenheiser already had four shots on goal to her name when she took a pass from defenceman Delaney Collins and stickhandled the puck into the net.

Danielle Goyette, now 41 years old and back for another possible "last game" (which would come in 2008), scored Canada's fourth goal—and her sixth of the tournament, trailing only Hayley Wickenheiser, who would be named MVP, as she had been at Torino. Sarah Vaillancourt added another goal late in the third period as the Canadians, to the delight of the home crowd, thumped the USA 5–1.

More than 120,000 people had bought tickets to watch the women skate to gold, eclipsing the record 90,000 tickets sold three years earlier when the women's world championship was held in Halifax. And while the Canadians had won gold in the top division of the women's hierarchy, that spring saw four other divisions of women's international competition take place among twenty-four other nations in tournaments held in Japan, North Korea, England, and Romania.

Hayley Wickenheiser's shootout goal against Jessica Vetter in the qualifying round was a prelude to her goal in the gold-medal-game victory against the USA, which gave Canada its ninth world championship in ten tries.

THE
LEGACY OF
ED CHYNOWETH

In April 2008, the men's under-18 tournament saw a Canadian squad rich with talent: Jake Allen was in goal, and the firepower of Jordan Eberle, Taylor Hall, and Cody Hodgson was up front, all under the experienced tutelage of Pat Quinn. Canada beat Denmark and Germany in the preliminary round, but lost to Russia, before shifting gears to beat Slovakia 6–0 and head into the quarter-finals with a 3–0–1 record and second place in Group A, three points back of the undefeated host squad Russia.

It was the kind of bounce-back game that Ed Chynoweth would have liked. As one of the founders of Hockey Canada's Program of Excellence, and one of the most influential hockey people in Canada, Chynoweth's life had been devoted to making this kind of tournament possible. He became the Western Hockey League's first full-time president in 1972, and remained there until 1995, working to bring all three of Canada's major junior leagues under the Canadian Hockey League banner. He was chair of several Memorial Cup tournaments, helped create the expansion junior team the Edmonton (now Kootenay) Ice, and was also at the heart of bringing together the Canadian Amateur Hockey Association and the Canadian Major Junior Hockey League to form a joint committee that would oversee and operate Canada's world junior team program.

When the 2008 under-18 tournament began, Chynoweth was in the end stages of fighting cancer. On April 22, he died in Calgary, aged 66,

Ed Chynoweth was a driving force behind many of amateur hockey's successes in Canada, including the creation of the national junior team. Here, Ed honours Maurice Tanguay (left) as the Canadian Hockey League Executive of the Year for 1999–2000.

just a day before Canada's gold-medal game against the Russians. In his honour, Canadian players wore "ED" stickers on their helmets and posted his name on the Canadian bench.

And then they took his spirit onto the ice. The Canadians came out charging, quickly silencing the 10,000 fans cheering for the home team with a short-handed goal early in the first period. It was over from that moment on, though Jordan Eberle would score twice, Taylor Hall once, and Jake Allen would backstop his team to an 8–0 rout of the Russians. Cody Hodgson would win the tournament scoring title with two goals and ten assists.

Canada had won its second under-18 gold medal. The life's work of Ed Chynoweth could not have received a better salute.

Ed Chynoweth shares a laugh with another Western Canadian hockey legend, Pat Quinn, who won the Memorial Cup as an Edmonton Oil King in 1963.

The 2008 under-18 team celebrates its gold-medal win—dedicated to Ed Chynoweth—against Russia.

IIHF
100TH
ANNIVERSARY

To celebrate its 100th birthday, the IIHF celebrated the country that gave the world the game by hosting the men's world championship in Canada for the very first time in May 2008. Canada was able to mount a powerful roster, as only four NHL teams were left playing in the Stanley Cup playoffs. So Rick Nash, Dany Heatley, Patrick Sharp, Jonathan Toews, and Duncan Keith were available to headline a team that was predicted to become the first host country since 1986 to win it all at home—"home" in a vast country being the tournament venues in Quebec City and Halifax.

But there was a co-favourite to win the tournament: the team from Russia. In disarray after the restructuring of the USSR, the Russians had last won the world championship in 1993. Since then, they had made it to the podium three times: winning silver in 2002 as well as bronze in 2005 and 2006. The Russians were stocked with talent, too, with "superzvezdy" 22-year-old Alex Ovechkin and 38-year-old Sergei Fedorov up front, and Evgeni Nabokov in goal.

Canada made it through its three games in Group B undefeated, its closest match being a 5–4 win over the USA. Canada then won five games in Group F to gain a berth in the medal round. After dispatching Norway 8–2, the Canadians played Sweden in the semi-finals. In a thrilling back-and-forth game, the Canadians were challenged by the Swedes more than any other time so far, but prevailed 5–4.

"When we get pushed," said Canada's coach Ken Hitchcock, "we have this other gear to go to."

Canada had learned—from the days of junior tournaments—that the best way to silence the talented Alexander Ovechkin was with sustained physical punishment. Here, Rick Nash delivers Canada's message to Ovechkin.

After the Russians dispatched Finland 4–0, the two favoured teams would do something they hadn't done since 1993: meet in a gold-medal game.

"It's definitely a dream for both teams," said Russian coach Vyacheslav Bykov. "Canada has a lot of talent, but Russia is ready for them."

The Canadians looked to have found a gear that the Russians couldn't catch, leading 4–2 into the third period to the blood-lusty delight of more than 13,000 at Quebec's Colisée. But then the Russians found a higher gear of their own, coming in waves at the relatively inexperienced Canadian defence corps, scoring the tying goal with just over five minutes left in the game when Ilya Kovalchuk put a shot through a screen that beat Canada's Cam Ward.

And then, in 4-on-4 overtime, Rick Nash accidentally fired the puck over the glass. The Canadians thought it went into the bench, but the Russians protested, and the new rule of "delay of game" for putting the puck out of play, on purpose or not, kicked in.

Rick Nash was in the penalty box when Kovalchuk found a huge hole created when Shane Doan decided to chase Sergei Fedorov, who dished to Kovalchuk who in turn ripped a snap shot to the top corner that won the gold for Russia.

"Probably everybody is drunk right now in Moscow and all of Russia," said an exuberant Kovalchuk after the game. "This is sweet."

For Canada, the loss to Russia, especially on such a fluky call, was bitter. "No one came here to win silver," said goalie Ward. "It's tough right now because you do feel like you let your country down. But there will be other tournaments; there will be more to come."

And the country needed no reminding that the biggest tournament was less than two years away, and on home ice: the 2010 Winter Olympics in Vancouver. The Russians were back at the top of their game, and once again Canada would have to find a way to win at home.

Canada looked good for gold at the IIHF 100th-anniversary tournament, held for the first time in Canada, but an overtime penalty led to a championship-winning goal for Russia.

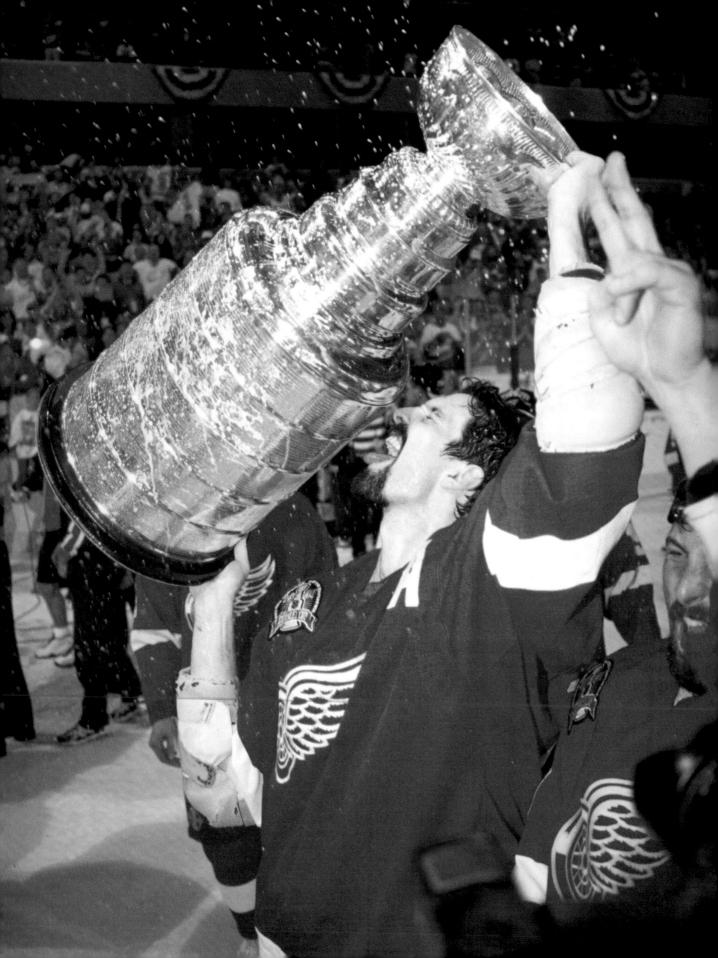

THE MOST EXCLUSIVE HOCKEY CLUB IN THE WORLD

In 2007, the IIHF announced that it would formalize its Triple Gold Club, a pantheon reserved for players and coaches who have won gold medals at the Olympic Games and world championships, as well as the Stanley Cup.

The first presentation was made at the 2008 worlds, and four Canadians made up the inaugural group: Rob Blake, Joe Sakic, Brendan Shanahan, and Scott Niedermayer. The quartet had all won their Olympic gold medals together as members of Team Canada's victorious squad at the 2002 Salt Lake City Olympic Winter Games, with Niedermayer repeating in 2010. Blake, Sakic, and Shanahan had all won world titles as teammates in 1994, with Blake winning another in 1997.

And when it came to the hardest trophy in sports to win, the four of them had ten Stanley Cup victories among them. Joe Sakic had won his first Cup in 1996 with the Colorado Avalanche, and again with the Avs, and with Rob Blake as his teammate, in 2001. Brendan Shanahan had won the Cup three times with Detroit, while Scott Niedermayer had won it three times with New Jersey and once with Anaheim.

Since then, triple-gold champions Chris Pronger, Eric Staal, Jonathan Toews, Patrice Bergeron, and Coach Mike Babcock have all joined the world's most exclusive sporting fraternity.

Brendan Shanahan raises the Stanley Cup in 1998. He would win the Cup three times, as well as winning Olympic gold in 2002, the Canada Cup, and the World Cup.

WOMEN ENTER
THE IIHF
HALL OF FAME

The IIHF also made history on its 100th birthday by inducting women into its Hall of Fame. Women had played the game with international recognition since 1990, and even though the IIHF was founded in 1908, it didn't form its own Hall of Fame until 1997. In 2008, hockey's international governing body honoured its first female players, by adding Canadian stars Geraldine Heaney and Angela James to the august body, along with Team USA's superlative Cammi Granato.

Geraldine Heaney patrolled Canada's blue line with such power and finesse that she was called the "female Bobby Orr." Born in Belfast, Northern Ireland, Heaney moved to Canada as an infant and became a multi-sport athlete, excelling at hockey. She played her first international match for Canada in the first Women's World Championship tournament in 1990, and scored the gold-medal-winning goal. She won gold again in 1992, 1994, 1997, 1999, 2000, and 2001, then added Olympic silver and gold medals at Nagano and Salt Lake City.

Angela James, a pure, powerful goal scorer, has been called the "Wayne Gretzky of women's hockey." She was Geraldine Heaney's teammate at the inaugural championship tourney in 1990, leading Canada to the gold medal with eleven goals in five games. She won international gold medals again in 1992, 1994, and 1997.

The Canadian duo well knew the talents of Cammi Granato, who was a founding member of the United States Women's national team.

Geraldine Heaney played defence for Canada at such a high level she was called "the female Bobby Orr."

She played against Canada in the final of that first-ever women's world tournament in '90, winning silver.

Another pure goal scorer with fine skill and explosive speed, Granato was named the US Women's Player of the Year in 1996. When women's hockey became an official Olympic sport in 1998, Granato captained the US team that pulled off the upset of Canada to win the gold medal at Nagano. She also won the honour of closing the Olympics as the USA's flag-bearer.

In 2010, James and Granato made history again when they became the first women to be inducted into the Hockey Hall of Fame, with Heaney following them into hockey's shrine in 2013.

2013 inductees Brendan Shanahan, Scott Niedermayer, Geraldine Heaney and Chris Chelios (from left to right) showing off their honoured-members rings in the Esso Great Hall at the Hockey Hall of Fame in Toronto.

Angela James, the "Wayne Gretzky of women's hockey," stands with TSN broadcaster James Duthie after her induction into the Hockey Hall of Fame.

THE 2009
WORLD JUNIORS

The 2009 World Junior Championship saw Team Canada trying to equal the astonishing five-straight-gold-medals run that saw them atop the podium from 1993 to '97. Once again, golden glory could be achieved in front of a hometown crowd if they could win the tournament in Ottawa. With John Tavares, Cody Hodgson, P.K. Subban, and Jordan Eberle in the lineup, Canada easily won its first three games of the preliminary round, with a particularly humiliating hammering of Kazakhstan 15–0. The Canadians found their first challenge on New Year's Eve, in their last game of the first round, when Team USA charged out to a 3–0 lead less than thirteen minutes into the first period.

Canada, rudely awakened to the fact that they were playing the USA and not Mexico (who had played their first IIHF game in 2000), roared back with three goals—two from Tavares, and one from Eberle, and the game was tied by the end of the period. Tavares would get a hat trick as the Canadians took their game up a level in the third to win 7–4.

Canada received a bye into the quarter-finals, and then met Russia in a semi-final matchup that was the "unofficial" gold-medal game, as it was whenever these two countries met on the ice in a game that didn't actually result in the winner receiving gold.

It was a classic—a back-and-forth meeting of the titans, with skill and speed and sweat. Every time the Canadians would score, the Russians would answer. And then, with just 2:20 left in the game, the Russians silenced the sold-out crowd in Ottawa's Scotiabank Place by taking the lead, 5–4.

Jordan Eberle scores the tying goal with five seconds left in the third period to keep Canada's 2009 World Junior Championship hopes alive.

367

Canada's coach Pat Quinn pulled goalie Dustin Tokarski, and called a time out. Quinn, a teacher to his core, told right winger Jordan Eberle that if the puck was in play on the right side of the attacking zone, to go to the net. The Russians iced the puck again, and before the faceoff, they were laughing—as if they had already won the game. The Canadians noticed, and with less than ten seconds on the clock, Jordan Eberle saw the puck played on the right-hand side, so he headed toward the slot, and the puck took a bounce right onto his stick. Eberle moved from forehand to backhand, and popped the puck over the Russian goalie. With five seconds left in regulation time, Canada's fifth-straight-gold-medal dream was still alive.

The teams solved nothing in overtime, but Eberle then scored the winning goal in the shootout. It was his "sudden-death" goal in the third period that became the rallying image as Canada went on to beat Sweden 5–1 in the final, to take home the country's fifth straight WJC gold medal, and its tenth gold in seventeen years.

Canada's Patrice Cormier levels a Russian player in the semi-final match.

When Jordan Eberle buried a lucky bounce with seconds left on the clock against the Russians, Canada's hopes of a fifth straight gold were still alive.

WOMEN IN VANCOUVER

The 2010 Winter Olympics were a Canadian affair, from their spectacular venue in Vancouver to the country's stated aim to "own the podium," and nothing was more central to that aim than hockey gold. Canada's women would be trying for their third straight Olympic title, and looked unbeatable as they trampled the opposition 41–2 in the opening round, with breakout stars like goalie Shannon Szabados and 18-year-old scoring wizard Marie-Philip Poulin giving Canadians a taste of just what kind of talent would follow superstar captain Hayley Wickenheiser, playing in her fourth Olympics.

The Canadians continued to roll over the opposition, shutting out Finland 5–0 in the semi-finals to meet the USA in the gold-medal game. Poulin scored two goals less than three minutes apart in the first period, and Szabados shut the door to help the Canadians win gold again with a 2–0 victory.

After the game, when the medals had been awarded, and the anthems sung, the Canadian women let loose with their own private celebration on the ice. Meghan Agosta lit up a cigar where a few hours ago she'd been lighting up faceoffs, and Marie-Philip Poulin went for a skate with a beer in hand. Goalie Kim St-Pierre hauled out a magnum of champagne, with its very own Canadian flag, and the women, for a brief moment, celebrated their victory like schoolgirls.

The IOC was not amused. "It is not what we want to see," said Gilbert Felli, the IOC's executive director of the Olympic Games. "I don't think it's a good promotion of sport values. If they celebrate in the changing room, that's one thing, but not in public."

Captain Hayley Wickenheiser wraps herself in the flag to celebrate her third (of four) Olympic gold medals for Canada.

But the IOC wasn't finished. Jacques Rogge, the IOC president, worried aloud that Canadian and American dominance of the game was in fact endangering it as an Olympic sport. "I would personally give [other countries] more time to grow, but there must be a period of improvement," he said, rattling the sabre at women's hockey. "We cannot continue without improvement."

The players, having heard this kind of threat from the male bastion of sports government before, pointed out that success would breed success. "We're lucky that Canada and the US are hockey countries, but in Russia girls aren't supposed to play hockey," said St-Pierre. "It's the same in China or Slovakia, so hopefully by seeing what we did today will get the other countries going."

Canada's Colleen Sostorics crosschecks USA's Monique Lamoureux during the second period of the gold-medal game.

The question now hanging over the heads of Canadians, however, was would the women's victory inspire the men to bring home gold *at home?* With the memory of the Canadian men's embarrassing failure at Torino in 2006, the stage was set for a massive national celebration— or an Olympic-sized pyre for the gold-medal hope, one that mattered above all else.

Sarah Vaillancourt and Jayna Hefford accounted for twenty of Canada's points during the Olympic tournament. Of the top ten point scorers, six were Canadian.

MEN IN VANCOUVER

Despite the fact that Canadians were expecting the men's hockey team to appear in the gold-medal game, the last three Olympic Winter Games had seen six different teams in the final. Just making it into the final was going to be an accomplishment, given the level of talent now on the international ice. Indeed, the first thing coach Mike Babcock did to prepare for the job of guiding the men's team to gold, at home, was to talk to those who had gone before. It was Pat Quinn who put the f-word into the mix.

"The message I wanted to give to Mike was ... to be aware of the fear," Quinn said, "because it can be overwhelming if you don't deal with it in a proper way. And I'm sure our guys will [deal with it], but they'll feel it, no doubt about it."

Fear was translated into national panic at the end of the preliminary round, with the rumble in danger of triggering that long-overdue major earthquake in Vancouver. Canada began as expected, beating Norway 8–0. It took a shootout to beat the Swiss, and it was Sidney Crosby who scored the lone shootout goal to give Canada a 3–2 win. In the next game, Crosby again tried to save the day for Canada by scoring to bring the team within one goal of the USA, with just over three minutes left. But the US scored an empty netter as goalie Martin Brodeur watched from the bench, and Canada lost 5–3.

At the end of the preliminary round, Canada was ranked sixth in the roster of twelve competing teams with five points—or two more than the eighth-place Swiss. Canada, once admitted to the final game just by virtue of being Canada, would now have to play in the qualifying round.

Sidney Crosby, the next Captain Canada, saves the day for the Canadians with the gold-medal-winning overtime goal in Vancouver.

375

The train wreck of Canada's crushing disappointment in 2006 at Torino was now organically fresh in everyone's memory—especially the six players returning from the 2006 squad, with Canadian goaltenders Martin Brodeur and Roberto Luongo having something to prove.

The country's national newspaper, *The Globe and Mail*, felt compelled to try to calm the national angst. An editorial on the eve of the country's descent into qualifying for the most important round of the Olympic Games that it was hosting, invoked the impassioned spirit of Phil Esposito, who gave disparaging Canadian fans the what-for after a loss in Vancouver during the '72 Summit Series: "Panic is not new among Canadian hockey fans. They panicked in 1972, and in 2002. They panicked in 2006 (justifiably) after a 2–0 loss to Switzerland. And they have their finger edging toward the panic button now. As Mr. Esposito might put it, what the hell. They're getting better. Canadian hockey has risen to the occasion before. Believe they will do it this time."

For the qualifying match against Germany, Canada made a change in goal. Brodeur was out, and Roberto Luongo was in. For Vancouver fans, who saw Luongo forty-one times a year as the number one goalie for their Canucks, it was a moment of both pride and terror. They knew he could make the big game-changing save. They also knew that he could let in the game-losing goal, especially late in the contest. And the bigger the game, the bigger the chance he'd do it. Canada easily beat the Germans 8–2 to move into the quarter-finals. But those Canucks fans couldn't help but notice that the Germans got their second goal with only a minute and two seconds left in the third period.

No one scored late in the game—or even in the third period—in Canada's quarter-final against the Russians. Canada went ahead 4–1 in the first and never looked back, winning 7–3. Suddenly, Canadians who had feared the worst now had that other dangerous thing back: they had hope.

The Slovaks did their best to kill that hope in the semi-final. But they waited until Canada had taken a 3–0 lead, and then struck with two goals, just three and a half minutes apart—with their second goal coming at 55:07. The Slovaks pulled their goalie to ramp up their attack, but Canada scrambled to hold on for a 3–2 win. In the euphoria of now going from goats to golden, those late goals vanished at the prospect of a Canada–USA match for the gold medal. But they would come back with a vengeance.

Canada jumped out to a 2–0 lead against the USA on goals by Jonathan Toews and Corey Perry, but a deflection on a shot by Ryan Kesler, Luongo's Vancouver teammate, sent the puck knuckleballing underneath the goalie's arm. Canada took a 2–1 lead into the third period of the gold-medal game, and so it remained, with Vancouver fans holding their breath especially tighter than Canadian fans, willing the puck not to fluke its way past Luongo. With less than thirty seconds left in the game, the happy ending abruptly became a horror show when Luongo gave up a fat rebound, and Canada couldn't clear the puck. The US, with their goalie pulled and a sixth attacker on the ice, kept it in the Canadian zone. After Luongo made another save, the puck bounced to the stick of Zach Parise. With twenty-five seconds left, the USA had tied the game. Canucks fans had seen this story before and, so far, it had never had a happy ending. Now Canada had one shot to win—or lose.

Team Canada, in sudden-death, four-on-four overtime, put up a defensive wall around Luongo, and the Americans' best scoring chance came on a rare Canadian giveaway, just before the shot heard 'round the world. Sidney Crosby, who had bailed the team out a couple of times already, hollered "Iggy! Iggy!" to Jarome Iginla, who was in the USA corner, protecting the puck.

"There are different pitches to a yell," said Iginla. "Sounded pretty urgent so I figured he was open—I was just hoping I wasn't too late."

He was right on time. Canada had won the game 3–2, and its second Olympic gold medal in men's hockey in three tries. And Sidney Crosby, the hero, was only 22 years old, so fitting that he invoked childhood on the winning goal.

"Every kid dreams of that opportunity," said Crosby, who admitted he had dreamt of it "a thousand times, growing up."

Roberto Luongo, who also had raised his game to a new level, invoked relief for both himself and the nation. "I've got a gold medal around my neck," he said. "Nobody can take it away from me."

UNDER-18 WOMEN ARE GOLDEN IN 2010

Canada's Olympic hockey euphoria continued in spring 2010, when the country's under-18 women made it to the gold-medal round at the world championship in Chicago. Jessica Campbell, the team captain, was a product of Hockey Canada's Pursuit of Excellence hockey academy, which began in 2007 in Kelowna, BC. Featuring an intense hockey development program for players from ages 12 to 17, the private school combines a rigorous academic program with team participation in a Hockey Canada minor hockey league. Led by Campbell, and following in the skate tracks of the elder hockey-playing sisters, the Canadians blew through the preliminary round to meet their nemesis, the USA, in the final.

The USA was leading 4–3 with less than eight minutes left in the game when Canada tied it up. Jessica Campbell, who ranked first in the tournament with six goals and eight assists, scored her biggest goal three minutes into overtime, to win the gold for the first time for Canada's under-18 women. Campbell, who went on to play hockey on scholarship for Cornell University, won the tournament's MVP. And in a nice perk to show how far the women's game had come, Campbell got her own hockey card in the Upper Deck 2010 World of Sports card series.

Jessica Campbell, the next rising star in Canadian women's hockey, scored the goal to win the first under-18 gold for Canada in 2010.

THE WORLD HOCKEY SUMMIT

In late August 2010, the hockey world once again convened in Toronto to take a look at the future of Canada's game. And this time, it really was the world who convened for the Molson Canadian World Hockey Summit: the IIHF, the NHL, the NHLPA, Hockey Canada, USA Hockey, the CHL, and Molson Coors all were there to add their voices to how the winter game beloved by the world could be made even better.

"Think of the story of the truck stuck under the bridge, and the engineers can't figure out what to do until the kid says, 'Why don't you let the air out of the tires?'" said Brendan Shanahan, who had retired as a player in November 2009 after a Hall of Fame career and at the time was the NHL's vice-president of hockey and business development (before becoming president of the Toronto Maple Leafs in 2014). "You never know who you're going to get the best ideas from."

The last summit, in 1999, was a Canadian affair after the tribulations of Nagano, but the idea for this international summit came up when IIHF president René Fasel and other hockey executives started talking, in the run-up to the Vancouver Olympics, about the importance of sharing global hockey knowledge.

And so, over four days, four hundred delegates held formal talks and hot-stove panels and casual chats over some cold Molsons to discuss player safety and skill initiatives, as well as junior development worldwide. The fate of the juniors was especially important to the non–North Americans,

"Women don't expect to make millions of dollars," Canadian hockey legend Hayley Wickenheiser said at a 2010 hockey summit. "They just want a place they can play competitive, elite hockey, and from that, it will build itself into a better product."

as the flood of talented European juniors to North America had created a crisis, though, paradoxically, it had increased the popularity of the world juniors—the Europeans improved because they played in North America.

The women's game was also on the agenda, and the greatest female hockey player that Canada has ever produced gave a visual presentation that included footage of how far the women's game had progressed, and how far it needed to go. Hayley Wickenheiser showed delegates film of women in northern India being scolded by men for trying to play a game that was, in male eyes, simply not intended for women.

At the other end of the spectrum was the need for women to have a hockey league of their own. Wickenheiser saw the existence of a premier league for women's hockey as something that would be good for the game as a whole, from players to fans to investors, just as the NHL had opened up hockey to a wider world.

"Women don't expect to make millions of dollars," she said. "They just want a place they can play competitive, elite hockey, and from that, it will build itself into a better product."

Murray Costello of the IIHF promised $2 million to help women's hockey worldwide, so that one day, world tournaments for women would be about more than just Canada against the USA.

But in the end, the emphasis on hockey's future lay with the state of the game for the next generation. Hockey Canada COO Scott Smith left the gathering with a sobering thought: just 9.1 percent of Canadian kids between the ages of 9 and 15 were playing hockey, a figure that had pretty much stayed flat for a decade. Part of the reason was more foreign-born Canadians with different sporting loyalties, as well as more people living in cities, where ice time was at a premium and expenses had climbed for a game that not so long ago you could play for free on a pond. Once again, Canadian hockey was looking at the future as one of challenge, not golden supremacy.

"I think it's clear that the interest [level] and some of the distractions for 5- to 19-year-old participants have changed," said Smith. "Are we willing to change?"

Murray Costello, the first full-time president of the CAHA, presents the Player of the Game award to Canada's John Tavares at the 2010 IIHF world championship—one bright moment for Canada in their seventh-place finish.

THE 2012
WORLD JUNIORS
GO FOR GOLD
AT HOME

The 2012 World Junior Championship was supposed to be another golden homecoming of redemption for Team Canada, especially after their stunning collapse in the gold-medal game against the Russians before an overwhelmingly pro-Canadian crowd in Buffalo the year before. In that nightmare of a match, Canada was taking a 3–0 lead into the third period, and those eminences who were voting on the tournament's top players had handed in their ballots during that intermission. It was game over, and Canada's Brayden Schenn was the MVP.

Then the Russians woke up, and put five straight pucks past Mark Visentin, three of them in six shots in less than five minutes. And just like that, Russia had won the gold.

"I don't believe we won the silver," said a disconsolate Visentin. "We lost the gold. That's what we came here for."

The 2012 tournament, co-hosted by Edmonton and Calgary, was a record sellout, with more than 475,000 fans showing up in Alberta, ready for a golden party. Canada obliged the national mood by sailing through the opening round with three big wins, and a tight one-goal victory over the USA. But Canada had been leading that game 3–0 until surrendering two goals in the third frame—disturbingly déjà vu.

But worse, Canada once again met the Russians in the semi-final, and this time the Russians were up 4–1 midway through the game. Canadian goalie Scott Wedgewood was pulled, and Mark Visentin found himself back in goal, trying to put a Band-Aid on a bleeding artery. And yet, his teammates clawed back, scoring five goals. But the Russians scored two more on Visentin to win 6–5, and a place in the gold-medal game. The Swedish 1–0 victory was historic: it was the country's first junior title in thirty-one years.

And Canada's loss to the Russians was historic, too, marking the end of Canada's ten straight gold-medal appearances. It was also an omen of sorts. Visentin made a statement by shutting out the Finns 4–0 in the bronze-medal game, and while the Canadians were disappointed with their third-place finish, bronze would be the country's last medal for a while, as the next two tournaments saw Canada finish fourth, after losing the bronze-medal game to the Russians. Once again, Canada will look to step into the golden spotlight on the podium at home, when the world juniors return to Canada in 2015.

Canada's Michael Bournival races away from Russia's Yaroslav Kosov during the 2012 world juniors semi-final game in Calgary.

THE 2012 WOMEN'S WORLD CHAMPIONSHIP

In spring 2012, Canada's hockey women made the country cheer up a bit about its hockey fortunes when they played the world championship in Burlington, Vermont. Despite getting humiliated 9–2 by the USA in the preliminary round, Canada met their archrivals again in the gold-medal game. The pro-American crowd expected another bloodletting by their team, but Canada wasn't going to let that happen again. When Hayley Wickenheiser blocked a shot on a US power play, then skated the puck down the ice to score, notice had been served.

"The losses of the previous years were really weighing on us," captain Wickenheiser said. "None of us wanted to see that happen again."

The score was tied 1–1 after the first period; tied 3–3 after the second; and Canada tied it 4–4 with just two and a half minutes left to play. Caroline Ouellette struck quickly, just 1:50 into overtime, to get her second goal of the game and to win gold for Canada for the first time since 2007.

"Tessa Bonhomme was in front of the goalie and I screamed to Meghan [Agosta] for the puck," said Ouellette. "Yes, I can take credit for scoring, but Tessa made it happen by going to the net and taking everyone with her. I just had to shoot. It was incredible."

Canadian sniper Caroline Ouellette scored in overtime to give Canada their first women's world championship since 2007.

THE ORDER OF HOCKEY CANADA

The Order of Hockey in Canada trophy symbolically elevated the game to its proper place in the cultural landscape. For the inaugural class of recipients, Gordie Howe was a clear choice, seen here representing Canada with distinction in 1974.

On April 2, 2012, hockey took its proper place in Canada's cultural pantheon when the Order of Hockey in Canada was announced. Like the Order of Canada, which honours individuals for outstanding contributions to the nation, the introduction of this honour specific to hockey marked the elevation of the game to a place in the country's culture alongside the arts and sciences. Hockey Canada's initiative would see a maximum of three individuals honoured annually "on the basis of their outstanding contributions or service to the growth and development of the sport of hockey in Canada, which may include players, coaches, officials, administrators, executives, trainers, physicians, inventors or any other person whose role or service in the game is recognized as extraordinary." Those deemed worthy of the honour are chosen by a twelve-member committee, and must receive 75 percent of the vote to have their names inscribed on the trophy. In 2012, the first class of the Order of Hockey in Canada decided to choose five extraordinary individuals for the honour: NHL legends Gordie Howe, Jean Béliveau, and Wayne Gretzky; women's hockey titan Cassie Campbell; and Gordon Renwick, who worked at all levels both nationally and globally for the Canadian Amateur Hockey Association, serving as CAHA president from 1977 to 1979, as well as serving for twenty years on the board of the International Ice Hockey Federation, including eight years as vice-president.

WOMEN
IN SOCHI

For once, Canada went into a Olympic Winter Games with company. In 2014, the Canadian men and women went in quest of Olympic gold in Sochi, Russia, knowing that the home team—as far as the men were concerned—was under so much pressure to win it all they could almost be honorary Canadians.

Indeed, Canada figured large in the Russian hockey imagination. "Russia was humiliated in Vancouver," said Igor Larionov, who had played some of his finest NHL hockey in that city en route to a place in the Hockey Hall of Fame. "And obviously when you have Russian pride, you want to show the world you are still a mighty country, that you can still compete in nuclear weapons with the US and that you can do better than Canada or the US in hockey."

Indeed, the Russian perspective, according to Larionov, was simple. "If Russia wins hockey and no other medals, this Olympics will have been a success."

Canada went to Sochi riding the usual confection of golden expectation and everlasting doom. The national worry in February 2014 was that while the men and women competing for gold had more than a good chance of winning it, the recently completed world junior championship in Sweden saw the Canadians fail to win a medal for the third year in a row. The kids were not all right.

So, more than ever, Olympic hockey gold would be a balm. "Sometimes I think we get a little confused," said Team Canada head coach Mike Babcock. "It's not about who scores the goals or blocks the shots or who plays. It's about winning. It's about Canada. And it's about hockey supremacy. We like to brag it's our game. I think if it's your game, you better show it's your game."

Marie-Philip Poulin scored two thrilling goals against Team USA—one with less than a minute left in the game and then again in overtime—to give Canada the 2014 Olympic gold medal in Sochi. Here, Canada's Catherine Ward shows the grit the team needed to pull off the win.

Canada's women made that attempt first, and as predicted by Canada in response to IOC grumbles in the 2010 Olympics that the women's game had better grow competitive or else disappear from the Olympics, Canada's talented women's team did not steamroll through the first round. After defeating Switzerland 5–0 and Sweden 3–0, the Canadians had to come from behind in their game against the USA. With three goals in the third period—two by Megan Agosta and one by Hayley Wickenheiser—the Canadians defeated their fiercest rivals 3–2.

That come-from-behind strategy would be in play the next time the two teams met, in the gold-medal game at Sochi's Bolshoy Ice Dome. For the first period, neither team could score, as Canada's Shannon Szabados and Team USA's Jessie Vetter put on a display of goaltending that showed one of the reasons why these two teams were so dominant.

The Americans were finally rewarded with a goal midway through the game, and two minutes into the third period, Alex Carpenter made it 2–0 for the USA on a power play. It looked as if dreams of Canada's fourth consecutive Olympic gold medal were quickly turning to silver. As the Canadians pressed harder, without result, the USA circled the team wagon—giving each other pep talks on the bench and huddling up for team rallies, willing themselves up and onto that golden podium.

Even though the Americans had stymied the Canadians with their shot blocking and neutral-zone clogging, and as the game entered its final five minutes seemed to have a lock on the gold, Team Canada played harder. Then, with 3:26 left on the clock, Canada finally got a lucky bounce when Brianne Jenner's shot deflected off a US player and past the Great Wall of Vetter. The most dangerous lead in hockey had just been cut in half.

The Canadians suddenly had a chance, and pulled their goalie. The team pressed in the US zone, and the puck came back to the point toward Canada's Catherine Ward. But disaster seemed imminent when the linesman got in Ward's way, blocking her from the puck, and a US player shot it out of their zone and down the ice toward the empty net, wobbling and skidding 140 feet toward the tally that would put the game out of reach.

"I thought it was going wide but when it hit the post I panicked a little," said Canada's goalie, Shannon Szabados, watching from the bench. "But when it went to the outside, I knew the girls would be okay."

One relieved Canadian fan tweeted, "Nice to see a Canada Post actually deliver when you need it to."

With a minute left, Canada's Rebecca Johnston sent a backhand pass from the corner toward Marie-Philip Poulin. US goalie Jessie Vetter tried to deflect it away from the slot, but accidentally put it on Poulin's deadly stick. And Poulin put the puck in the back of the net to tie the gold-medal game with fifty-five seconds left in regulation time.

Goalie Shannon Szabados (left) and Hayley Wickenheiser take a golden skate on February 20, 2014, at Sochi's Bolshoy Ice Dome.

Now the Canadians had all the momentum, with the Americans stunned by what had just happened. Still, they came out swinging in sudden-death overtime, and Szabados kept her team's golden hope alive with four brilliant saves. Canada, rattled, was stuck in their own end, giving away the puck, and then seemingly the game when Catherine Ward took a cross-checking penalty.

The USA called a time out, detailing strategy to put the Canadians away for good. But six seconds after play resumed, the USA took a penalty for a weak slash to Szabados's pads. Now the teams were playing three on three on the larger international ice surface. Hayley Wickenheiser broke away from Canada's zone with the US's Hilary Knight chasing her. As they crossed the American blue line, Knight caught up to Wickenheiser, and both players fell. Knight would go off for tripping, and Canada would now have a four-on-three advantage.

Canada knew what it had to do: get the puck to Poulin. It took forty seconds of sharp, fast Canadian passing to accomplish the mission. Poulin was in perfect position low in the left faceoff circle, and at 8:10 of sudden-death overtime, she had once again scored the golden goal in one of the most dramatic Olympic hockey finals in memory.

"I think if you wanted, you could probably make a movie about this team, what we've been through this year," said an elated Hayley Wickenheiser. "We believed in each other. Our schedule was incredibly difficult. We barnstormed across Canada. The goal was to physically push this team to the max so that under mental pressure we wouldn't break. And that's exactly what we did tonight—we had the edge in mental toughness."

MEN
IN SOCHI

J amie Benn, a 24-year-old forward for the Dallas Stars, had not been invited to Canada's Olympic orientation camp in August 2013. Benn had been a rookie with Dallas when Canada won Olympic gold at home, and he watched the game on his couch in Victoria, BC, dreaming of playing for his country at the Olympics. He took to heart Canadian head coach Mike Babcock's challenge to players who weren't named to the initial forty-seven-man roster to prove why they should be.

"It gave me a little bit of motivation to come into this year and have a good first half with my team back home," said Benn, who was named captain of the Stars in September 2013. Benn's play in the NHL was good enough, and on January 7, 2014, he was named to the Team Canada Olympic roster.

It was a shrewd bit of casting for Team Canada, who had lost "sure thing" Steven Stamkos when he broke his leg in November. Benn, who would wind up tenth in the NHL points total for the season, immediately made an impact, scoring the winning goal in Canada's first game against Norway, which the Canadians took 3–1.

After defeating Austria 6–0, and squeaking past Finland 2–1 thanks to an overtime goal by Drew Doughty, Canada entered the playoff round in third place with eight points, the same total as the USA, who were in second place thanks to a higher goal differential.

The Canadians defeated Latvia 2–1 in the quarter-final to meet the USA in the semis—winner of which would go on to play for the gold. The USA was still smarting over its overtime loss in Vancouver, and had come

to Sochi looking for revenge. US general manager David Poile stated that his team was "one goal away" from gold in Vancouver, and the team he had built for Sochi was designed to get that goal.

Instead, it was Jamie Benn who scored the only goal of the game less than two minutes into the second period as Team Canada and goalie Carey Price put on the kind of defensive show that only teams who believe in their mission can stage, with superstars and support players alike blocking shots and making selfless choices to keep the USA's scoring chances as low as Canada's goal total throughout the playoff round had been—just three goals in two games.

And the Canadians were relentless, attacking the US rather than sitting on their slender lead. "They came at us with twenty guys tonight," USA head coach Dan Bylsma said. "They came at us with speed for sixty minutes. That was as fast a game as I've ever been a part of. There was lots of speed out there and it was up and down the ice. We weren't able to counter that."

After Canada's women had won their gold medal they sent their male colleagues a letter, one which hung in the men's locker room. "Tonight is yours," it read. "Own the moment. We are proof that every minute matters. The podium is reserved for the brave. Earn every inch, dictate the pace. Go get 'em! From the Girls! :)"

The 33 million assistant coaches for Team Canada—or most of them—were up early to watch Canada meet the top-ranked Swedes for gold. Those on the west coast were up before the sun to see a 4:00 A.M. Pacific time opening faceoff, while even those at the other end of the vast country, in Newfoundland, had to be ready to cheer the team at 8:30 A.M., a time on a Sunday morning when streets are still quiet save for the sound of a church bell or two. And even those who were at Stouffville, Ontario's United Church could see the game, despite the fact the church was hosting its monthly men's breakfast speaker series at 8:00 A.M. on Golden Game Sunday. Participants were able to watch the game on laptops in the church basement.

And what all Canadians saw was a team that dominated the Swedes in a 3–0 victory, a team that had grown better as the Games progressed, with

Canada's triumph at the Winter Olympics in Sochi marked the ninth time the country had won Olympic men's hockey gold since it first competed in the sport's inaugural Olympic tournament in 1920 in Antwerp.

Top:
From left: Duncan Keith, Patrick Sharp, and Jonathan Toews savour their golden moment.

Bottom:
The Canadian coaching staff was an all-star team itself. From left: Andrew Brewer, Ken Hitchcock, Lindy Ruff, Mike Babcock, Claude Julien, and Ralph Krueger.

Carey Price earning his second shutout of the playoffs, and the Olympic Games' best goaltender award.

While it lacked the head-clutching, heart-pounding drama of the women's gold-medal game, it was a welcome relief for Canadians from coast-to-coast-to-coast and in maple-leaf-wearing redoubts around the planet to watch their team so convincingly play the game it had given the world. Canada's gold in men's hockey was our third in four Olympic Games of the twenty-first century, and while the Cassandras might fret over what the future of hockey would bring, the present looked awfully good. Our game had captured the imagination of the world, and was the crowning event of the Olympics. Once more, Canada was the best.

PHOTO CREDITS

ACKNOWLEDGMENTS

Many people have helped me to celebrate Hockey Canada's 100th birthday
with this book, but special thanks go to Nick Garrison, Paul Patskou,
Bruce Newton, Bob Nicholson, Murray Costello, Brent Ladds, Phil Pritchard,
Craig Campbell, Joe Zingrone, and my wife, Nancy, and daughter Rose.
It's a wonderful game, and I'm lucky to play it with such a fine team.

INDEX